Gender and Action Films

Emerald Studies in Popular Culture and Gender

Series Editor: Samantha Holland, Leeds Beckett University, UK

As we re-imagine and re-boot at an ever faster pace, this series explores the different strands of contemporary culture and gender. Looking across cinema, television, graphic novels, fashion studies and reality TV, the series asks: what has changed for gender? And, perhaps more seriously, what has not? Have representations of genders changed? How much does the concept of 'gender' in popular culture define and limit us?

We not only consume cultural texts but share them more than ever before; meanings and messages reach more people and perpetuate more understandings (and misunderstandings) than at any time in history. This new series interrogates whether feminism has challenged or change misogynist attitudes in popular culture.

Emerald Studies in Popular Culture and Gender provides a focus for writers and researchers interested in sociological and cultural research that expands our understanding of the ontological status of gender, popular culture and related discourses, objects and practices.

Available Titles in This Series

Gender and Contemporary Horror in Film – Edited by Samantha Holland, Robert Shail and Steven Gerrard

Gender and Contemporary Horror in Television – Edited by Steven Gerrard, Samantha Holland and Robert Shail

Gender and Contemporary Horror in Comics, Games and Transmedia – Edited by Robert Shail, Steven Gerrard and Samantha Holland

From Blofeld to Moneypenny: Gender in James Bond – Edited by Steven Gerrard

Gendered Domestic Violence and Abuse in Popular Culture – Edited by Shulamit Ramon, Michele Lloyd and Bridget Penhale

Navigating Tattooed Women's Bodies: Intersections of Class and Gender – Authored by Charlotte Dann

Gender and Parenting in the Worlds of Alien and Blade Runner: A Feminist Analysis – Authored by Amanda DiGioia

Gender and Female Villains in 21st Century Fairy Tale Narratives – Edited by Natalie Le Clue and Janelle Vermaak-Griessel

Gender and Action Films 1980–2000: Beauty in Motion – Edited by Steven Gerrard and Renée Middlemost

Gender and Action Films: Road Warriors, Bombshells and Atomic Blondes – Edited by Steven Gerrard and Renée Middlemost

Gender and Action Films 2000 and Beyond: Transformations – Edited by Steven Gerrard and Renée Middlemost

Forthcoming Titles in This Series

Screen Heroines, Superheroines, Feminism and Popular Culture: Forty Years of Wonder Woman – Authored by Samantha Holland

Gender and Action Films: Road Warriors, Bombshells and Atomic Blondes

EDITED BY

STEVEN GERRARD
Leeds Beckett University, UK

And

RENÉE MIDDLEMOST
University of Wollongong, Australia

United Kingdom – North America – Japan – India – Malaysia – China

Emerald Publishing Limited
Howard House, Wagon Lane, Bingley BD16 1WA, UK

First edition 2023

Editorial matter and selection © 2023 Steven Gerrard and Renée Middlemost.
Chapter 2 © 2023 Steven Gerrard.
Chapter 11 © 2023 Renée Middlemost.
Published under exclusive licence by Emerald Publishing Limited.
Individual chapters © 2023 by Emerald Publishing Limited.

Reprints and permissions service
Contact: permissions@emeraldinsight.com

No part of this book may be reproduced, stored in a retrieval system, transmitted in any form or by any means electronic, mechanical, photocopying, recording or otherwise without either the prior written permission of the publisher or a licence permitting restricted copying issued in the UK by The Copyright Licensing Agency and in the USA by The Copyright Clearance Center. Any opinions expressed in the chapters are those of the authors. Whilst Emerald makes every effort to ensure the quality and accuracy of its content, Emerald makes no representation implied or otherwise, as to the chapters' suitability and application and disclaims any warranties, express or implied, to their use.

British Library Cataloguing in Publication Data
A catalogue record for this book is available from the British Library

ISBN: 978-1-80117-515-9 (Print)
ISBN: 978-1-80117-514-2 (Online)
ISBN: 978-1-80117-516-6 (Epub)

ISOQAR certified Management System, awarded to Emerald for adherence to Environmental standard ISO 14001:2004.

Certificate Number 1985
ISO 14001

INVESTOR IN PEOPLE

This second book in our Gender and Action Films collection has been a genuine labour of love for all of us involved in its production. I therefore wish to dedicate this edited collection to each one of our contributors. We are all a part of this crazy world of Action Cinema, and I raise a glass to you all – Cheers!
– Steven Gerrard, 2022

I dedicate my work on this book to Pam, who always supported my academic endeavours, and still reads all my 'Uni work'. Thanks for encouraging my dreams.

And to Aunty Marg, for modelling the path for baby Renée to explore the world of books. Thanks for letting me borrow your Funk & Wagnalls.

My love to you both.
– Renée Middlemost, 2022

Table of Contents

About the Contributors   *xi*

Acknowledgements   *xv*

Introduction   *1*
Steven Gerrard and Renée Middlemost

Part 1 Star Bodies

Chapter 1   Road Warriors, Bombshells and Atomic Blondes: The Action Cinema of Charlize Theron   *7*
Thomas Sweet

Chapter 2   Let Rain Shine: Michelle Rodriguez – Action Star   *21*
Steven Gerrard

Chapter 3   'Musculinity' and the Empowered Female Body in *Haywire* (2011)   *33*
Douglas Rasmussen

Part 2 Transmedia Action

Chapter 4   Gender, Violence and Empowerment: Reworking the Female Action Hero in *Dollhouse*   *47*
Jessica Ford

Chapter 5   All Access Action Heroes – Between Cyberpathy and New Media   *59*
Anne Ganzert

**Chapter 6   Hard Bodies in Virtual Worlds: Assessing the
Reception of Abby's Spectacular Body in** *The Last of Us Part II*
(Naughty Dog, 2020)   73
Dean Bowman

Part 3 Intergenerational Action

**Chapter 7   Dark Fathers and Damaged Sons: The Paternal Betrayal
of** *Jason Bourne*   89
Toby Reynolds

Chapter 8   Beyond Actions: Remodelling Heroine-Hood in *The
Grandmaster*   103
Jasmine Yu-Hsing Chen

Part 4 Politics and Race

Chapter 9   'Always Bet on Black': Wesley Snipes – Action Star   119
Shelley O'Brien

**Chapter 10   Dismal Setbacks and Stunning Breakthroughs: A Look
at Pam Grier's Career and How It Changed Hollywood**   133
Dahlia Schweitzer

**Chapter 11   Playing With Type? Dwayne 'The Rock' Johnson,
Rivalry, and Race in** *Hobbs and Shaw*   143
Renée Middlemost

Conclusion   159
Steven Gerrard and Renée Middlemost

Selected References   161

Index   167

About the Contributors

Dean Bowman has a PhD on the function of narrative in video games within production contexts from the University of East Anglia and for five years has taught game studies and media theory on the TIGA award winning Games Art and Design BA at Norwich University of the Arts. He has published on a variety of topics including providing book chapters on the topic of colonialism and board games in the edited collection *Rerolling Board Games* by McFarland Press; on the gamer person of Jason Statham in the edited volume *Crank it Up – Jason Statham: Star!* for Manchester University Press; and on *GoldenEye 007* in the edited volume *From Blofeld to Moneypenny: Gender in James Bond* also for Emerald Press.

Jasmine Yu-Hsing Chen is an Assistant Professor of Chinese and Asian Studies in the Department of World Languages and Cultures at Utah State University. She specialises in contemporary Chinese and Sinophone theatre, film, media, visual culture and literature. Her first research agenda examines how cross-cultural performance reshapes the performer and the audience's perception of artistry, nation and gender in Martial Law Taiwan. Her second research project explores novel media interventions in traditional performing arts. Currently, she is a member of the board of directors at the North American Taiwan Studies Association.

Jessica Ford is a Lecturer in Screen and Cultural Studies and an early career researcher in the Gender Research Network at the University of Newcastle, Australia. Her research examines women and feminism on TV, and she has published on *Orange is the New Black*, *Girls*, *Crazy Ex-Girlfriend* and *Better Things* in peer-reviewed journals, academic anthologies and journalistic outlets.

Anne Ganzert is a postdoctoral researcher and Media Studies Lecturer at the University of Konstanz, Germany. Her 2020 book on *Serial Pinboarding in Contemporary Television* focuses on contemporary TV series and their pin boards as dispositives of seriality. Other publications include 'In the Footsteps of Smartphone-Users. Traces of a Deferred Community in Ingress and Pokémon Go' (*Digital Culture & Society* 2/2017), 'We welcome you to your Heroes community. A Case Study in Transmedia Storytelling' (*IMAGE 21*, 2015) and *Taking Sides. Theories, Practices, and Cultures of Participation in Dissent* (*Transcript* 2021).

Steven Gerrard is a Reader of Film at Northern Film School, Leeds Beckett University. He has written monographs about *The Carry on Films* (Palgrave-MacMillan) and *The Modern British Horror Film* (Rutgers University Press). He is co-editor for Emerald Publishing's *Gender in Contemporary Horror* series, and sole editor of their *From Blofeld to Moneypenny: Gender in James Bond*. He was instigator and co-editor of *Crank It Up: Jason Statham – Star!* (Manchester University Press). Steve would love to be either *Status Quo*'s rhythm guitarist or the new *Doctor Who*. He'll have a long wait.

Renée Middlemost is a Lecturer in Communication and Media at the University of Wollongong, Australia. Her research focuses on fan participation, celebrity and popular culture, and has been featured in collections *The Routledge Companion to Cult Cinema; Crank It Up: Jason Statham – Star!; Aussie Fans: Uniquely Placed in Global Popular Culture* and *Gender and Australian Celebrity Culture*. Her recent work has been published in journals including *Celebrity Studies, American Behavioral Scientist, M/C Journal* and the *Australasian Journal of Popular Culture*. She is the co-founder of the Fan Studies Network Australasia and a co-editor of *Participations: Journal of Audience and Reception Studies*.

Shelley O'Brien is a Senior Lecturer in Film Studies at Sheffield Hallam University. She completed an MPhil on the emergence and evolution of body horror in 2000 and lectures on horror cinema; music/sound in film; cult/exploitation cinema and supervises MA by Research and PhD students. She has presented papers on Spanish horror; torture porn; cult cinema; sound design in TV and film; horror film scoring; rape/revenge movies. Published work includes chapters on killer priests in horror films; directors Herschell Gordon Lewis and Tobe Hooper; Jason Statham's *Crank* films and title music in James Bond films.

Douglas Rasmussen is a graduate of the University of Saskatchewan where he wrote his Master of Arts thesis of the AMC television series *Breaking Bad*; he is now currently writing on a number of film and television projects. Of particular interest are genre films and television series, especially science fiction, horror and crime. He has written on *Star Trek: Deep Space Nine* and *Picard, Scream, Judge Dredd* and has a couple of music projects under way, with essays on the band Queen and David Bowie.

Toby Reynolds is an independent film scholar specialising in gender, auteurs, film history, and post-Jungian screen perspectives. His first book, *The American Father Onscreen* is now available from Routledge, and his cinema podcast *Dr Kino's Film Emporium* is available from a number of major streaming sites. He also likes good coffee and vintage leather jackets.

Dahlia Schweitzer is an Associate Professor in the Film and Media department at the Fashion Institute of Technology. Her latest book, *Haunted Homes* (Rutgers University Press, 2021), explores the ways haunted homes have become a prime stage for dramatising anxieties about family, gender, race and economic collapse. Her previous books include *L.A. Private Eyes* (2019), *Going Viral: Zombies, Viruses, and the End of the World* (2018), and *Cindy Sherman's Office Killer:*

Another Kind of Monster (2014). In addition to her books, Dahlia has essays in publications including *Cinema Journal, Journal of Popular Film and Television, Jump Cut, Quarterly Review of Film and Video* and *The Journal of Popular Culture*. Regardless of the topic – serial killers, private detectives or even zombies – all of her writing engages directly with questions of self versus other, private versus public space, examining depictions of gender, identity and race and what they mean about our changing world.

Thomas Sweet is an Independent Scholar based in the United Kingdom, who received an MA in Film Studies from the University of Wolverhampton. His research interests include cult film and the post-apocalyptic subgenre.

Acknowledgements

This book would not have been possible without the encouragement, help and patience from the entire team at Emerald Publishing, especially Katy Mathers, Lydia Cutmore, Abinaya Chinnasamy and Helen Beddow who have not only encouraged us but also made our work look like it's part of Action Cinema with this wonderful cover. Both Renée and I want to thank our terrific contributors, some stepping in at the last minute, in the way that they have not only produced excellent, cutting-edge and ground-breaking work in this field, but just as importantly embraced the project.

Introduction

Steven Gerrard and Renée Middlemost

The 2000s was a period of rapid change for the action genre. While the action genre during the 1990s was distinguished by the emergence of new heroes such as Keanu Reeves, it was also a period of experimentation with the boundaries of the genre, as seen in series such as *The Matrix*, which blended action with sci-fi and more cerebral lore. The 2000s saw a blending of these trends – while new action stars such as Angelina Jolie, Vin Diesel, Lucy Liu and Dwayne Johnson, and franchises such as *The Fast and the Furious* and *Jason Bourne* emerged, so too were action fans rewarded with reboots of classic franchises such as *Die Hard*, *Rocky*, *Rambo* and *James Bond*. Franchises based on Young Adult fiction, and capitalising on action sequences (*Harry Potter*), and/or action heavy plots (*The Hunger Games*) also emerged during the 2000s, with enduring popularity. The 2000s also saw remakes of popular action television series into big screen productions, such as *Charlie's Angels* (2000, 2003) and *Miami Vice* (2006). Finally, the now dominant Marvel Cinematic Universe (MCU) made its first entrance onto the big screen with the premiere of *Iron Man* (2008), setting the scene for the franchise dominance that continues with *Thor: Love and Thunder*, and *Black Panther: Wakanda Forever* (amongst others) scheduled for release in 2022.

Despite generic and personnel changes, action film as a genre has yet to contend with (in any meaningful way) issues relating to representations of race, sexuality and gender, such as #Oscarssowhite or #MeToo that have faced Hollywood at large. Writers such as Purse (2011), Dyer (2013) and Roach (2018) have pointed to the potential for queering action cinema, as seen in features such as *Atomic Blonde* (2017).

This volume (the second of three) focuses on the action genre from the 2000s onwards, highlighting specific action stars, prioritising female-led action films. While this is a period that has been less acknowledged, with academic work to date largely focusing on franchises (Hassler-Forest, 2019; Tasker, 2015; York, 2010) and superheroes (Acu, 2016; Flanagan, Livingstone, & McKenny, 2016; Koh, 2014), there has been a move towards analysis of transnational action cinema (Morris, Li, & Ching-kiu, 2005; Provencher & Dillon, 2017), stars (Wing-Fai & Willis, 2014) and the role of female performers (Funnell, 2014).

Since the early 2000s, the emergence of key female action stars has opened up the genre to new possibilities beyond supporting roles. This volume explores several key themes such as embodiment and authenticity, and case studies of action stars such as Michelle Rodriguez, Zhang Ziyi and Pam Grier that demonstrate how female action stars have grappled with, and moved beyond Mulvey's (1975) 'male gaze'. This volume is divided into four parts. The first, 'Star Bodies' uses case studies of Charlize Theron (Sweet), Michelle Rodriguez (Gerrard) and Gina Carano (Rasmussen). While Gerrard argues that Rodriguez has been underacknowledged for her contribution to the genre, Charlize Theron has been widely recognised for her physicality and diverse roles across genres, while Carano's career can be viewed as disruptive not only for her atypical physicality but her problematic personal views which have led to the loss of roles which would have further solidified her star persona. The connection between action film and other media is explored in part 2 of this volume, 'Transmedia Action'. In a case study of Joss Whedon's television series *Dollhouse*, Jessica Ford rearticulates the mechanics of filmic action hero creation; concluding that the series' poor reception was linked to the delayed empowerment of the heroine in contrast to filmic tropes. The transmedia elements of *Alpha* and *Heroes* are discussed by Ganzert to illustrate how the use of media technologies can be considered an extension of the heroic abilities of key characters. Finally, Bowman's chapter utilises key theory from action cinema (Brown, 2011; Purse, 2011; Tasker, 1993) to unpack the audience reception to the Abby character's body in *The Last of Us Part II* (2020), and ask what happens when the 'spectacular' and 'hard' bodies of the action heroine enter the soft virtual world of the video game.

Part 3 of the volume contends with 'Intergenerational Action'. While Reynolds focuses on the *Jason Bourne* franchise in terms of narratives about fatherhood and paternal betrayal; Chen demonstrates how female stars in action films also transform long held tropes and stereotypes, highlighting Zhang Ziyi's impact on Chinese action cinema and her portrayal of remodeled daughterhood. The fourth and final section of this volume closes with a focus on 'Politics and Race'. O'Brien's chapter highlights the career of Wesley Snipes, arguing that he is deserving of late career success, and reminding the reader of his contribution to the action canon. In her chapter on Pam Grier, Schweiter highlights the significance of her breakthrough performances in Blaxploitation roles, and the shifting portrayal of her star image in her comeback role in *Jackie Brown* (1997). The volume concludes with Middlemost's case study of Dwayne Johnson's performance in *Hobbs and Shaw* (2019), which highlights how his growing success as a transnational action star has influenced his ability to portray characters based on his Sāmoan identity.

References

Acu, A. (2016). Time to work for a living: The Marvel Cinematic Universe and the organised superhero. *Journal of Popular Film and Television*, *44*(4), 195–205.

Brown, J. A. (2011). *Dangerous curves: Action heroines, gender, fetishism, and popular culture*. Jackson, MS: University Press of Mississippi.

Dyer, R. (2013). *Heavenly bodies: Film stars and society* (2nd ed.). London: Routledge.

Flanagan, M., Livingstone, A., & McKenny, M. (2016). *The Marvel Studios phenomenon: Inside a transmedia universe.* New York, NY: Bloomsbury.
Funnell, L. (2014). *Warrior women: Gender, race, and the transnational action star.* New York, NY: SUNY Press.
Hassler-Forest, D. (2019). Setting fire to wet blankets: Radical politics and Hollywood franchises. *Mediations, 33*(1–2), 181–188. (Fall 2019–Spring 2020). Retrieved from www.mediationsjournal.org/articles/setting-fire
Koh, W. (2014). 'I am Iron Man': The Marvel Cinematic Universe and celeactor labour. *Celebrity Studies, 5*(4), 484–500.
Morris, M., Liu, S. L., & Ching-kiu, S. C. (Eds.). (2005). *Hong Kong connections: Transnational imagination in action cinema.* Hong Kong: Hong Kong University Press.
Mulvey, L. (1975). Visual pleasure and narrative cinema. *Screen, 16*(3), 6–18. doi: 10.1093/screen/16.3.6
Provencher, K., & Dillon, M. (2017). *Exploiting East Asian cinemas: Genre, circulation, reception.* London: Bloomsbury Academic.
Purse, L. (2011). *Contemporary action cinema.* Edinburgh: Edinburgh University Press.
Roach, S. (2018). Black pussy power: Performing acts of black eroticism in Pam Grier's Blaxploitation films. *Feminist Theory, 19*(1), 17–22.
Tasker, Y. (1993). *Spectacular bodies: Gender, genre and the action cinema.* London: Routledge.
Tasker, Y. (2015). *The Hollywood action and adventure film.* Hoboken, NJ: John Wiley & Sons.
Wing-Fai, L., & Willis, A. (Eds.). (2014). *East Asian film stars.* London: Palgrave Macmillan.
York, A. E. (2010). From Chick Flicks to Millenial blockbusters: Spinning female-driven narratives into franchises. *Journal of Popular Culture, 43*(1), 3–25.

Part 1
Star Bodies

Chapter 1

Road Warriors, Bombshells and Atomic Blondes: The Action Cinema of Charlize Theron

Thomas Sweet

Abstract

Since the 1990s, Charlize Theron has appeared in films from a wide range of genres but has seen significant financial success from starring in action films, such as *Mad Max: Fury Road* (2015) and *Atomic Blonde* (2017). However, unlike some female action leads, she has not solely been defined or pigeonholed by these roles but has been able to transition between action roles and more 'respectable' dramatic roles, as well as the other conventions of female celebrity, such as being the face of advertising campaigns for perfume brands.

Theron has notably received several physical injuries during filming, such as breaking her teeth practising fight choreography during the production of *Atomic Blonde*. These injuries have frequently been added as part of the publicity campaign for the films and Theron's star image overall as signs of 'authenticity', leading these action films a sense of increased legitimacy. Tasker states that a female action star's '[public] formulation is indicative of the uncertainties generated by her image' (1993, p. 14). Media attention is divided between focusing on Theron's physicality, both in the sense of the traditional Hollywood gaze and in terms of Theron's molding of her marketable image. Theron has managed to succeed as both a mainstream star and an action heroine. This has enabled Theron to transition between genres and franchises such as *The Fate of The Furious* (2017), and an Oscar-nominated dramatic role in the biopic *Bombshell* (2019).

This chapter will unpack the public persona of Charlize Theron as an action film star, exploring both the filmic texts and the presentation of Theron's often complicated and contradictory image in the media.

Keywords: Charlize Theron; action; *Mad Max: Fury Road*; authenticity; physicality; *Atomic Blonde*

Since the 1990s, Charlize Theron has appeared in films from a wide range of genres but has seen significant financial and critical success from starring in action films, such as *Mad Max: Fury Road* (2015) and *Atomic Blonde* (2017). However, unlike some female action leads, she has not been solely defined or pigeonholed by these roles but has been able to transition between action roles and more 'respectable' dramatic roles, as well as the other conventions of female celebrity, such as being the face of advertising campaigns for Dior's J'Adore perfume. After starring in the violent action film *Atomic Blonde*, which uses female violence and aggression in a transgressive subversion of genre norms, Theron then starred in the political biopic *Bombshell* (2019), for which she was nominated for the Best Actress Oscar at the Academy Awards, demonstrating a versatility that few other female action stars have been able to achieve. Although being a female film star inevitably means being subjected to the male gaze, Theron has managed to largely avoid being submissive to it, by taking dominant roles in action films, and promoting that sense of dominance through the media. For example, Theron has received several physical injuries during filming, and these injuries then become part of the publicity campaign for the film and Theron's star image.

Image, Persona and Embodiment

Star image is based on audiences receiving a stable, fixed marketable persona of an actor. Yvonne Tasker states that a female action star's '[public] formulation is indicative of the uncertainties generated by her image' (1993, p. 14). It is this notion of image uncertainty that has unpinned the fluidity of Charlize Theron's media persona: despite being born in South Africa and speaking English as a second language, she physically fits the model of the blonde American movie star and has no noticeable Afrikaans accent. This extra-textual knowledge beyond Theron's image as a conventionally attractive film star and model shapes the audience's perception of her performances. As Richard Dyer (1979) explains, star persona is just as much a performance as the performer's acting roles – it is carefully created and honed in the media, through selected information that is revealed in interviews and the choice of film roles. Star personas are crafted to be larger than life, and Theron's is based on a mix of glamour and an authentic sense of physicality through stunt work and having creative input in these projects (1979, p. 20). However, a star persona is based on 'unstable authenticity' and must be 'buoyed' up (Dyer, 1991, p. 142), not only by the content of the films themselves but also by the star's media image, especially during promotional work for the films. Theron does not use the 'method' technique of acting (Lindsay, 2020) – a style of acting associated with the search for onscreen 'authenticity', but instead creates a sense of authenticity through linking physicality with character and star persona.

Since the release of *Mad Max: Fury Road*, Theron has often been classed as an 'action star' despite action films taking up only a portion of her filmography, and only some of those being a critical or financial success. However, such a shift in perception is notable as classically the action genre is 'an almost exclusively male space, in which issues to do with sexuality and gendered identity can be worked out over the male body' (Tasker, 1993, p. 17). Although action films featuring female main characters are more common than in the past, the genre still tends to lean on overwhelming male. Laura Mulvey's theory of the gaze states that women in film are there to be passive and submissive for the 'male gaze' (1975, p. 21), but Theron's relationship with the gaze has been far more complex. In traditional action films, according to this theory, male characters are the ones who drive the narrative, and the female characters are mainly there for the visual pleasure of the audience, to be looked at for their beauty. Although Theron's role as a model and actress puts her under the gaze, her onscreen physicality – such as performing her own stunts, her choice of roles where she plays active main characters and her assertive behaviour in interviews – challenges this. As gender roles in society have changed, the concept of the gaze is more open to interpretation and challenge by actresses.

Æon Flux

After a series of roles in smaller films, such as *The Yards* (2000), *Reindeer Games* (2000), Theron first received major attention for her portrayal of serial killer Aileen Wuornos in the biopic *Monster* (2003), for which she won the Best Actress Academy Award. Despite receiving critical acclaim for her performance, contemporary media coverage focused heavily on Theron's physical appearance, as she radically transformed her onscreen image to resemble Wuornos more closely. According to Wise, this level of method acting from someone previously primarily known for their appearance suggests that 'American culture's obsession with female bodies and feminine appearance overshadowed Theron's talent, as well as the underlying message of the film' (2019, p. 70). Rather than focusing on Theron's mimicry of Wuornos, media coverage focused on how Theron removed herself from the gaze in the film, by removing herself from conventions of beauty. Following the success of *Monster*, and after a supporting role in the remake of *The Italian Job* (2003), Theron starred in *Æon Flux* (2005), a science fiction action film. *Æon Flux* is vastly different from *Monster* in terms of genre and tone. Adapted loosely from an MTV animated series, *Æon Flux* stars Theron as the titular Æon, an assassin living in a futuristic, dystopian walled city ruled by a totalitarian government that clones and oppresses its citizens. In promoting the film, Theron stated that 'You cannot compare a film like *Aeon Flux* to *North Country* or *Monster*...they are different genres and you have to celebrate them for that and it does not make one easier than the other' (Manco, 2005), acknowledging the abrupt shift in genre and tone from her other films, from drama to action.

Æon Flux received a negative critical response, and failed to make a profit on release, despite an attempt to tap into the contemporary action film tropes popularised by *The Matrix* (1999) and similar films. Jeffrey A. Brown described *Æon Flux* as part of a cycle of action films that feature the 'cliche' of heavily armed, leather wearing heroines fighting corrupt establishments that focus more on providing a fetishised spectacle of a 'beautiful woman doing backflips, throwing punches and firing weapons', rather than creating an engaging protagonist or narrative (Brown, 2011, p. 224). The film removes the philosophical subtext of the original cartoon, instead placing Theron's character in a generic 'chosen one' narrative; the film ends with Æon destroying the oppressive government and tearing down the wall, revealing a renewed Earth, ready for recolonisation. The film reveals that the city's inhabitants have been repeatedly cloned in secret for centuries, and that Æon, who has only been cloned once, is giving back the citizens the ability to reproduce naturally and have control over their own bodies. Despite removing much of the original cartoon's subtext, the theme of the body persists through the film, not only in the cloning ethics of the plot but also the gaze the film makes Theron's body a major focus.

Although Æon is a revolutionary who threatens the social order, the film only allows her to do so in a safe, non-threatening way, without any sense of physical danger or injury to the body, keeping with expectations of feminine action stars. As Purse notes, the film goes out of its way to keep Æon's face, and by extension, body, unmarked (2011, p. 185) – one shot that was heavily used in promotion was Æon sneaking through a security system, ending with her face balancing perilously close to razor blades hidden within blades of grass. The threat is to her face – the possibility of damage to her physical appearance, more than serious injury. With the plot justification of 'genetic engineering', Æon is able to complete impossible, gravity defying stunts during fight scenes. This is part of a wider trend identified by Tasker, who stated that the cultural tension between having female characters in an action-heavy role is often explained away by making the female lead 'defined as exceptional' to 'explain her actions' (1998, p. 69). Rather than placing the character in a more grounded setting, genetic engineering is used to rationalise why Æon can perform such acts, reassuring the audience that the character exists in a fantasy space, removing her from anxieties about the traditional male and female divide in action films. In contrast to later female-focused action films with a revolutionary theme (Brown, 2015, p. 172), Æon Flux presents a female character who provides surface level visual gratification, while not examining the corrupt political structures that she questions and dismantles in relation, or comparing them to any real-world political parallels.

Æon Flux was the first film shoot in which Theron received a major injury during production. An unsuccessful attempt at performing a backflip led to Theron herniating a disk in her spine, almost resulting in paralysis. This accident resulted from Theron trying to perform the stunt in platform shoes as part of her character's costume, despite platform shoes being impractical for Æon to wear for a lifestyle of impossibly athletic violence, this is but one example among many female action costumes that have prioritised fetishism of the female body, over plausible character development. This issue is further compounded by the fact that in contrast, during the filming of *Atomic Blonde*, Theron performed stunt work, including fight choreography, while wearing high heels, without any widely publicised accidents. In contrast to *Æon Flux*, the choice to wear heels for *Atomic Blonde* was framed as Theron's, in line with her role as producer. In consultation with the creative team, they were keen to emphasise that Theron's physical ability was not only on par with male performers, but above and beyond many. As *Atomic Blonde* Costume Designer Cindy Evans stated: 'Bond could never do it – so you have to' (Branch, 2017).

Following the negative reception of *Æon Flux*, Theron moved away from the action genre for several years. In an interview 15 years later, she reflected that the production of *Æon Flux* had been difficult due to 'pre-conceived notions' of her acting image, and that the poor reception was blamed on an action film having a female lead, rather than the quality of the film.

> There was this moment in my career where I realised very clearly that because that movie didn't perform...I wasn't going to be given another opportunity [to star in an action film]....it was like, 'No, women can't make these movies successful'.
> (Theron in Schwartz, 2020)

Despite the film's lacklustre box office performance being blamed on the female protagonist, the cycle of films that Brown identifies as being aesthetically similar to *Æon Flux*, such as the *Underworld* and *Resident Evil* franchises, were financially, if not critically, successful. These franchises rely heavily on marketing their female leads performing impossible feats of athleticism while wearing leather outfits and fighting corrupt authorities. Therefore, the poor box office results cannot be blamed on the female star, but rather marketing and poor word of mouth from audiences (Vary, 2016).

Dramatic Roles, and *Mad Max: Fury Road*

In the following years, Theron's filmic output instead leaned towards drama, with some more action themed outliers, such as supporting roles in *Hancock* (2008), where she played Mary, a suburban middle-class woman who is revealed to be a superpowered immortal. Despite Theron taking part in several action scenes, she remains largely side-lined in the marketing. The film serves as a vehicle for Will Smith, who was a much more bankable film star than Theron at the time, so his image dominates the film's marketing, focusing on his character carrying out acts of super heroism. For much of the film, the character sticks to the classic Mulvey (1975) coding of the active/passive male/female binary narrative structure. Mary remains a supporting character, to provide a domestic grounding to Jason Bateman's character, and plays a passive role in the narrative. It is only when her powers are revealed that she becomes an active part of the story. Despite the film being financially successful, the focus on Smith over Theron in the marketing and the necessity of keeping Theron's role in the third act's action scenes secret meant that it did little to change Theron's public image at the time.

One notable outlier from this time period is not a film, but rather a music video. In the video for the Brandon Flowers single *Crossfire* (2010), the plot features three action sequences showing Flowers being tortured by ninjas, and rescued by Theron's character. Due to the short run time and lack of dialogue, the narrative gives the audience little context as to why these events are occurring. However, despite being the featured singer, and the intended main appeal for the audience, Flowers spends the video in a passive state, restrained and bruised by his captors repeatedly. It is Theron, showing injuries reflecting her active role, who commits acts of violence to save Flowers, and at the end, drives the pair off towards freedom.

It was Theron's subsequent performance as Imperator Furiosa in *Mad Max: Fury Road* that acted as a turning point in her (action) career. The fourth film in George Miller's post-apocalyptic franchise sees Max (Tom Hardy) continue to roam a world that has descended into violent anarchy after a nuclear war triggered by the depletion of natural resources, with different groups fighting each other in elaborate vehicle-based combat. Furiosa serves as a lieutenant for the Warlord Immortan Joe (Hugh Keays-Byrne), before revolting against him and attempting to liberate his concubines – referred to as 'the Five Wives' from slavery and escape to her matriarchal homeland, the 'Green Place'. Although Theron was not entirely absent from the action genre after the release of *Æon Flux*, *Mad Max: Fury Road* marked her return to lead billing in an action film. Theron reflected upon her comeback, and the significance of her role as Furiosa in a 2020 interview, stating: 'A lot of women don't get a second chance, but when men make these movies and fail miserably, they get chance after chance after chance to go and explore that again. That doesn't necessarily happen for women' (Davids, 2020). This reflects a long-standing issue with studio system's perception of action films starring women, where successful female lead films are treated as outliers, and unsuccessful female action films are used as reason not to invest in future projects, a standard male action stars aren't held to as strictly. *Atomic Blonde* was produced by Theron's own production Denver and Delilah Productions, further removing it from the gender restrictions of the studio system and allowing for more creative freedom.

Unlike *Æon Flux*, *Mad Max: Fury Road* was well received by critics and audiences, with many highlighting Theron's performance as a standout for defying her previously defined onscreen persona. Tasker states that roles for female fighters are often coded through two stereotypes: the 'butch tomboy' and the 'feisty heroine' (1998, p. 68), allowing the audience to quickly contextualise the role that the female character will play, based on their understanding of how generic tropes, and the visual communication of gender roles. Furiosa's costume design, much like *Monster*, is another rejection of mainstream Hollywood beauty standards: while Æon wore impractical, almost fetishically stylised outfits, Furiosa wears practical apparel for desert survival. The alteration in Theron's appearance is striking; her blonde hair removed, cut down to a buzz cut, covered in motor grease – and her missing arm, created through digital effects. The buzz cut was not initially a part of the character's costume, but was suggested by Theron during production: she explained that since Furiosa had been 'discarded' from Joe's society due to her infertility, and sent to live among the male soldier underclass, she shaved her head to make them 'forget' that she was a woman, and that she poses 'no threat' to their lifestyle of male violence (Sperling, 2015). It also communicates to the audience that Furiosa has had to sacrifice outward signifiers of her femininity in favour of survival: long hair being a hindrance for a combat-heavy lifestyle based around maintaining and operating machines in a desert. Du Plooy (2019) states that previous entries in the *Mad Max* series presented their female characters as victims; with minimal roles in the story, or tyrants, whereas in *Fury Road*, the female characters are 'recognised', which '…breaks away from the conventional male narrative action formula, as well as the perennial feminized fairy-tale formulas' (2019, p. 419), providing a different interpretation of the female role in action films, beyond the simple 'girl with a gun' trope common to the genre. In contrast, the last major female character in the series played by a well-known star – Auntie Entity, as portrayed by Tina Turner in *Mad Max: Beyond Thunderdome* (1985) – was closely based on Turner's pre-existing public persona. If Auntie Entity was an exaggeration of Turner's celebrity persona, then Furiosa is a complete rejection of Theron's.

Aside from her missing arm, Furiosa's body has been marked by male violence: she has Immortan Joe's insignia branded on the back of her neck – implying that she has been branded as property, and at the end of the film, she is stabbed in the torso by one of Immortan Joe's henchmen, requiring a blood transfusion from Max to save her life. The issue of gender representation in the film is complex – Max acts passively throughout most of the film, preferring to be alone, whereas Furiosa is the active force which drives much of the plot, in an inversion of Mulvey's gaze theory. It is instead vital to look beyond this binary division to understand the character of Furiosa. Elizabeth Hills argues that some films present audiences with the image of the 'female character who is both victim and her own rescuer' (1999, p. 43), defined by her actions within the plot. Although Furiosa's trauma at the hands of men is a primary motive for the character, it is conversely the active, more 'male' role she assumes that helps to overcome it, creating a character that transgresses the gender roles of the genre.

Atomic Blonde

It is Theron's next major starring role in an action film that further cemented her in the public consciousness as an action star, if an unconventional one. After *Fury Road*, the next major action film that Theron appeared in was *Atomic Blonde*, a spy film set in Berlin in 1989, as the Berlin Wall falls, and the Cold War ends. Unlike *Max Mad: Fury Road*, *Atomic Blonde* was produced by Theron's production company Denver and Delilah Productions, giving her far more creative control than her previous action roles – with Theron's company optioning the film rights to Antony Johnston's graphic novel *The Coldest City* even before the book's publication.

Theron's Lorraine Broughton – a spy for MI6 – is introduced to the audience, emerging naked from a bathtub full of ice, drinking whiskey under a harsh neon blue light. Rather than subjecting her to the gaze for the titillation of the audience, the camera instead focuses on the injuries and bruises on her body – the ice and whiskey being makeshift methods of pain relief. The opening scene is a framing device, and the film, told in flashback, focuses on how Lorraine obtained these injuries. The focus on Lorraine's injuries is unusual in action films: although is common for the male body to suffer injury (for example, the protagonist of the *Mad Max* series limps and wears a leg brace from injuries sustained in the first film), these images of realistic violence against a female character are unusual. Theron explained the choice to focus on the physical punishment endured by the character: 'A lot of times studios or producers are not comfortable with seeing a woman with bruises….[but] We really wanted to pay attention to that authenticity' (Setoodah, 2017). This is a notable contrast to the sanitised depiction of violence in *Æon Flux*, where injuries have no lasting impact, except for the unfulfilled threat of damage to her physical appearance in the grass scene. As she prepares to go outside, the song 'Cat People (Putting Out Fire)' by David Bowie plays – a song with lyrics referring to revenge and violence. Without any context, the audience might assume that this character fits into the stereotypical role of women in action films – to be the victim of violence to motivate male characters to action (Tasker, 1993, p. 16). However, as Lorraine leaves her apartment, walking to her mission debrief in a montage set to a cover of 'Blue Monday' by New Order, she puts on a white coat and sunglasses, covering up the evidence of this violence, blending both of the 'glamourous' and 'action star' aspects of Theron's star persona. Another unusual aspect of the film is Lorraine's motivation for both committing and being on the receiving end of these acts of violence. *Atomic Blonde* is unique for subverting the clichéd motivations of many action heroines: that is, the need to protect a child, or avenge a murdered love (reflecting the film's somewhat cynical outlook on the Cold War era). Throughout the film, Lorraine is involved in multiple acts of extreme violence – killing 18 other characters during the film – but notably firearms are rarely used in the action scenes, instead the focus is on hand-to-hand combat. In the film's first major fight scene, Lorraine escapes an ambush in a car by stabbing an assailant with a stiletto heel, an improvised weapon that a male action hero would traditionally have no reason to access, reflecting the gendered lens applied to the representation of violence in the film.

Towards the climax of the film, there is a ten-minute-long sequence where Lorraine fights her way through an apartment complex, edited in a way in which it appears to be one long unbroken take. In this scene, the cinematography shifts to a shaky, handheld style, with no non-diegetic music. This emphasises the sense of realism, as the camera follows Lorraine's battle up flights of stairs and through different rooms – where notably, she shows signs of fatigue and exhaustion. As the sequence continues, Lorraine is hit multiple times, and misses several of her own strikes, becoming more and more beaten and bloodied. There is a moment where one of the men refers to her as a 'bitch' in their fight, she responds by dealing him a fatal blow, answering 'Am I your bitch now?' as he dies

(Sperling, 2017). This inversion of gendered insults shows a reclaiming of an exclusively male space – although set in the 1980s, and taking inspiration from the films of that decade, *Atomic Blonde* is not limited to the gender politics of that era. In action films of that decade, in the rare occurrence female protagonists are featured their femininity is either emphasised to put them in passive roles or suppressed in service of the plot. Jeanine Basinger criticised this trend, stating that 'putting women in traditional male action roles, without changing their psychology, is just cinematic cross-dressing' (Brown, 1996, p. 53). In *Atomic Blonde*, Lorraine is a character who transgresses traditional gendered roles, as typically 'active and aggressive women in the cinema can only be seen as phallic, unnatural or "figuratively male"' (Hills, 1999, p. 39). Although Lorraine is a violent and active character, her femininity is highlighted throughout the film, primarily through costume, as Theron wears period appropriate designer clothes throughout the film, even during stunt sequences. Although she switches to more masculine leaning office wear in the debriefing scenes that frame the narrative, her femininity is still highlighted and signified through the focus on her hair, which is lit to stand out against the almost monochrome design of the MI6 interrogation room.

Tasker states that 'female action heroes are constructed in narrative terms as macho/masculine, as mothers or as Others: sometimes even as all three at different points in the narrative' (1998, p. 69) – however, Lorraine does not fit into any of those categories neatly. Although she has an affair with female spy Delphine Lasalle (Sofia Boutella), her bisexuality is not treated as being 'other', nor is it exploited for the voyeuristic gaze of the audience. The film places Lorraine into two protective roles: first, to escort defecting Statsi officer Spyglass (Eddie Marsen) across to the West, in addition to her relationship with Lasalle. Unlike the other male characters in the film, Spyglass is visually coded as being unsuited for dangerous and stressful field work: with his glasses, moustache, ill-fitting raincoat and awkward body language contrasting with Lorraine's confident and purpose. Despite the film's focus on Lorraine, the audience is encouraged to empathise with Spyglass during a scene where he prepares his wife and daughter to cross over the Berlin Wall. Unusually for an action protagonist, Lorraine fails to protect him as he is shot and drowns in a sinking car – whereas in a standard action narrative, this lowest part of the character's arc would generally take place earlier in the film. The other protective role Lorraine fulfils is her relationship with Lasalle. Much like contrast between Furiosa and the Wives, Lasalle is a naïve and inexperienced figure, out of their depth in the dangerous world that Theron's character is adept at surviving in. At the film's climax, Lasalle is ambushed in her hotel room after trying to blackmail another spy, oblivious to danger as she listens to music through headphones. Lorraine is unable to prevent Lasalle's murder and finds her strangled with her own headphone cords, a victim of male violence. It is these two acts of violence which drive Lorraine to take revenge on her traitorous ally Percival (James McAvoy), killing him and framing him as a mole. Normally, when female action stars are given another character to look after, it is a child, providing a sympathetic maternal aspect that the audience can relate with (Tasker, 1993, p. 15), but this is subverted in Theron's action films. The action heroine acting as a surrogate mother to a child figure has been a trope engrained in the genre since Ripley in *Aliens* (1986), so the shift is particularly notable. By removing the notion of motherhood, Lorraine moves even further past stereotypical aspects of the gender divide – Hills argues that to see action heroines as masculine or 'figuratively male' is limiting, and therefore action heroines should instead be regarded as 'transformative, transgressive and alternative women' (1999, p. 49) – a category befitting Lorraine's agency.

As well as the fictional construct of Lorraine's body and the insistence on showing more realistic injuries than are common for action heroines, Theron's real body also became a source of media interest. Theron trained and sparred with Keanu Reeves during pre-production, while he was preparing to film *John Wick: Chapter 2* (2017) and this information was used to promote the film, further emphasising Theron's action credentials to be on par with her male counterparts. Despite the differences in tone between *Atomic Blonde* and the chronological gap between the settings of the two films, reporters began to speculate on the possibility of a crossover between the narrative worlds of *John Wick* and *Atomic Blonde*. In addition, it was widely reported that Theron had cracked several of her teeth during training and required surgery (Setoodah, 2017a, 2017b): what would have been a piece of trivia about the production for most films instead became a part of the marketing – providing more of the sense of authenticity that Dyer suggested (1979, p. 21), where the divide between the actor and the roles they play is minimised by the media. This theme of creating a sense of authenticity (Dyer, 1991, p. 142) to Theron's public persona only increases as the number of action films increases.

The Physicality of Theron: *Tully* (2018) and Beyond

Recent years have emphasised more facets of Theron's onscreen persona while still retaining the media and audience interest in her physicality. Following *Atomic Blonde*, the adaptable approach to Theron's onscreen persona could be seen in *Tully* (2018), where she plays Marlo, a woman suffering from postpartum depression after the birth of her third child. Released a few months after *Atomic Blonde*, the film retains its focus on Theron's embodiment of the role; but rather than glamour or athleticism, this role focuses on Marlo/Theron's body as a source of trauma from childbirth – Theron gained 50 pounds for the role and spends most of her screen time without make-up, in casual clothes, as she deals with the emotional strain of childbirth. In one scene, Marlo becomes jealous of a younger female jogger, and then tries and fails to outrun her, collapsing from the effort. In *Atomic Blonde*, a nightclub toilet is a space of espionage and intrigue, as Lorraine meets with Delphine and initiates a sexual encounter. In *Tully*, a nightclub toilet leads to Marlo vomiting and expressing breast milk due to the changes in her body. Although actors transforming their bodies for roles often attracts media attention, with both men and women, this tends to be for weight loss or muscle gain, rather than weight gain.

Although Theron's addition to the stunt heavy *Fast and Furious* franchise as an antagonist didn't create as much media interest with this sense of authenticity, it did continue in the promotion of *Long Shot* (2019). This was not an action film, but instead a straightforward comedy, with more mainstream appeal than the dark comedy drama seen in *Tully*. Despite not being an action film, *Long Shot* was also promoted through the injuries suffered by Theron: during filming, she fell over while putting on a pair of knee pads needed for a shot and was taken to hospital with a suspected concussion. This story was widely repeated in the media, reframed as a humourous anecdote rather than a medical emergency, as part of the film's promotional cycle (Evans, 2019). As with the media coverage of Theron's dental surgery during *Atomic Blonde*, the injuries suffered accidently have their context changed to focus on Theron's perceived work ethic, and the notion of 'suffering for art' and authenticity, similar to how performers like Jackie Chan are promoted based on their ability to risk bodily harm.

Theron's star persona, coupled with her ability to successfully navigate multiple genres has resulted in greater freedom to choose her next project. Netflix agreed to co-fund and distribute the action blockbuster *The Old Guard* (2020) for an estimated $70 million budget, with Theron receiving creative control through her production company. This was despite the fact that the film was going straight to online streaming, and therefore would not be potential as profitable as a full theatrical release. In *The Old Guard*, Theron plays Andy, the leader of a group of immortal mercenaries, who use their mysterious and unexplained regenerative abilities to take part in conflicts throughout human history. The character of Andy bears some superficial similarities to characters Theron has played before: like Mary in *Hancock*, she is an immortal woman who has lived for thousands of years and has superhuman abilities, her hairstyle resembles the one that Theron had as Æon, and like Lorraine, much focus is given to her hand-to-hand fighting. Unlike the previous films discussed in this chapter, *The Old Guard* was co-funded and distributed by Netflix and premiered on this platform. This has interesting implications for star image – since the film is not reliant on sales via box office, the streaming company must be convinced that the film will attract new subscribers – since Theron is able to exist in the space of being both a movie star and an action star, there is wider crossover appeal for audiences. As an immortal character, Theron's body becomes the focus of the film once again. Andy's body is shot, stabbed and damaged repeatedly in hand-to-hand combat, only to simply heal instantly from injuries. Andy serves another example of an 'exceptional' female action protagonist (Tasker, 1998, p. 69) that therefore justifies their presence in a traditionally male dominated genre. Andy can simply heal from any wound, even fatal ones; the audience is encouraged to suspend their disbelief, unlike the more visceral approach to injury seen in *Atomic Blonde*. As has happened with her previous films, the injuries that Theron received on set were worked into the film's promotional cycle: Theron tore a tendon in her thumb filming a fight scene, which required surgery after filming (Coggan, 2020). This was highlighted during promotional interviews, such as Theron's appearance on the talk show *Jimmy Kimmel Live!* where she wore a noticeable brace on her hand, tying discussion of her injuries directly into the promotion of the film. Again this recontextualises a potentially dangerous on-set injury into an amusing anecdote, emphasising Theron's dedication to a sense of physical realism in action scenes and a sense of authenticity in filming these scenes. Theron's physical endurance has arguably become as much a part of the promotional campaign for the film, alongside materials such as posters, trailers and behind the scenes videos – something normally reserved for male action stars such as Jackie Chan and Tom Cruise.

In analysing the development of the 'violent female action character', Katy Gilpatric (2010, p. 743) observes that there had been a significant increase in the depiction of female characters using violence onscreen over several decades with studios attempting to appeal to a wide demographic as possible. However, despite the rise in active female characters onscreen, Gilpatric suggests that these characters are still subject to gender stereotyping, noting that the majority of 'violent female action characters' end up being submissive to the male protagonist, normally ending the film by being romantically involved with him. Again, Theron's action films tend to subvert this trend: of the action films discussed here, only *Atomic Blonde* explicitly features a romantic subplot. However, this subplot subverts the heteronormative couplings of action films, as Theron's character involved with a supporting female character, who does not survive until the end of the story. Rather than being submissive to men, Lorraine ends up killing or outsmarting the other male characters. In multiple interviews, Theron mentions that female stars struggle to get action films made, stating in one that 'We've had moments like this, where women really showcase themselves and kind of break glass ceilings. And then we don't sustain it. Or there's one movie that doesn't do well, and all of a sudden, no one wants to make a female-driven film' (Setoodah, 2017a, 2017b). Theron's output in recent years shows an increasing acceptance by audiences not only of female action stars committing violence onscreen, but a comfort with this violence being carried out by mainstream film stars, rather than being regulated to a few cult actresses.

Conclusion

In general, female action stars tend to be cult figures, who rarely transition to mainstream success, or actresses who have mainstream appeal and star in a handful of action films, before returning to more 'respectable' dramatic roles. However, Charlize Theron's filmic output, especially post *Mad Max: Fury Road* has shown a willingness to transgress cinema's traditional boundaries between 'action stars' and mainstream actors, further pushing the notion of genre and cultural fluidity as a key aspect of her appeal as an actress and a movie star.

Central to this notion has been the use of her injuries during production as part of the promotional cycle of these films. Media coverage of these incidents tends to frame them as either light-hearted anecdotes to provide background trivia for potential audiences, or as evidence of Theron's authenticity as an action star. The contrast between the two extremes of Theron's star persona – the authentic action heroine willing to suffer physically for the sake of onscreen realism, and the Hollywood actresses – has become increased blurred through the action genre. Traditionally star image is based on a largely static public image, where a performer is tied to one genre predominantly. However, Theron's movement between genres, from action films to drama and then back again, shows how audiences are more willing to accept genre fluidity from stars, especially in the mainstream.

References

Branch, K. (2017). Charlize Theron on fighting men twice her size in a blonde bob and 6-inch heels. *Vogue*. Retrieved from https://www.vogue.com/article/charlize-theron-blonde-bob-atomic-blonde-movie-spy. Accessed on November 5, 2021.

Brown, J. (1996). Gender and the action heroine: Hardbodies and the "point of no return". *Cinema Journal, 35*(3), 52–71. University of Texas Press, Austin.

Brown, J. (2011). *Dangerous curves: Action heroines, gender, fetishism, and popular culture*. Jackson, MS: University Press of Mississippi.

Brown, J. (2015). *Beyond bombshells: The new action heroine in popular culture*. Jackson, MS: University Press of Mississippi.

Coggan, D. (2020). The old guard: Inside Charlize Theron's transformation into an ax-wielding, millennia-old warrior. *Entertainment Weekly*. Retrieved from https://ew.com/movies/the-old-guard-charlize-theron/. Accessed on February 10, 2021.

Davids, B. (2020). Charlize Theron on 'the old guard' and her heartbreak over the Furiosa Prequel. *The Hollywood Reporter*. Retrieved from https://www.hollywoodreporter.com/heat-vision/charlize-theron-old-guard-heartbreak-furiosa-prequel-1301957. Accessed on February 3, 2021.

Du Plooy, B. (2019). 'Hope is a mistake, if you can't fix what's broken you go insane': A reading of gender, (s)heroism and redemption in Mad Max: Fury Road. *Journal of Gender Studies, 28*(4), 414–434. Routledge, London.

Dyer, R. (1979). *Stars*. London: BFI Publishing.

Dyer, R. (1991). A star is born and the construction of authenticity. In C. Gledhill (Ed.), *Stardom – Industry of desire* (pp. 136–144). London: Routledge.

Evans, N. (2019). That time Charlize Theron ended up in the hospital filming long shot. *Cinemablend*. Retrieved from https://www.cinemablend.com/news/2471257/that-time-charlize-theron-ended-up-in-the-hospital-filming-long-shot. Accessed on November 30, 2021.

Gilpatric, K. (2010). Violent female action characters in contemporary American cinema. *Sex Roles, 62*(11), 734–746. Springer, Berlin.

Hills, E. (1999). From 'figurative males' to action heroines: Further thoughts on active women in the cinema. *Screen, 40*(1), 38–50. Oxford University Press, London.

Lindsay, B. (2020). Charlize Theron lets us inside her head + her acting process. *Back Stage*. Retrieved from https://www.backstage.com/magazine/article/charlize-theron-bombshell-acting-career-advice-69448/. Accessed on January 3, 2022.

Manco, M. (2005). Sci-fi femme: Charlize Theron talks about 'Aeon Flux'. *The GW Hatchet*. Retrieved from https://www.gwhatchet.com/2005/12/01/sci-fi-femme-charlize-theron-talks-about-aeon-flux/. Accessed on February 2, 2021.

Mulvey, L. (1975). Visual pleasure and narrative cinema. *Screen, 16*(3), 6–18. Oxford University Press, Oxford.

Purse, L. (2011). "Return of the angry woman": Authenticating female physical action in contemporary cinema. In M. Waters (Ed.), *Women on screen: Feminism and femininity in visual culture* (pp. 185–198). London: Palgrave Macmillan.

Schwartz, T. (2020). Charlize Theron: Evolution of a Badass – An action hero career retrospective. *Comic-Con International*. Retrieved from https://www.youtube.com/watch?v=MeeH5s3U-bA&feature=youtu.be. Accessed on February 3rd, 2021.

Setoodah, R. (2017a). Charlize Theron cracked two teeth while filming 'Atomic Blonde'. *Variety*. Retrieved from https://variety.com/2017/film/news/charlize-theron-atomic-blonde-training-cracked-teeth-1202007730/. Accessed on February 3, 2021.

Setoodah, R. (2017b). How Charlize Theron got ripped, bruised (and naked!) for 'Atomic Blonde'. *Variety*. Retrieved from https://variety.com/2017/film/features/charlize-theron-atomic-blonde-female-action-stars-1202489664/. Accessed on February 3, 2021.

Sperling, N. (2015). Charlize Theron on 'Mad Max: Fury Road', being part of a feminist action movie. *Entertainment Weekly*. Retrieved from https://ew.com/article/2015/05/14/mad-max-fury-road-charlize-theron-shaving-her-head-eating-dirt-and-being-part/. Accessed on February 3, 2021.

Sperling, N. (2017). How Atomic blonde got its most insane action sequence. *GQ*. Retrieved from https://www.gq.com/story/atomic-blonde-david-leitch. Accessed on November 30, 2021.

Tasker, Y. (1993). *Spectacular bodies: Gender, genre and the action cinema*. London: Routledge.

Tasker, Y. (1998). *Working girls: Gender and sexuality in popular cinema*. London: Taylor & Francis.

Vary, A. (2016). How Hollywood turned its back on one of its most exciting filmmakers. Buzzfeed. Retrieved from https://www.buzzfeed.com/adambvary/karyn-kusama-the-invitation-girlfight#.awjwLNeRB. Accessed on November 6, 2021.

Wise, M. (2019). "You'll never meet someone like me again": Patty Jenkins's Monster as Rogue Cinema. *Text Matters*, 9(9), 66–80. University of Łódź Press, Łódź.

Chapter 2

Let Rain Shine: Michelle Rodriguez – Action Star

Steven Gerrard

Abstract

An amateur boxer; A professional soldier turned indestructible zombie; A fast-driving heister; A combat pilot on another world; A taco truck driver with a heart of gold; A Smurf; Michelle Rodriguez, American actress, has played them all. As Leticia 'Letty' Ortiz, Rodriguez' most famous role offers both a sensitive portrayal of a tenacious woman living out a tough existence who exhibits as much courage, strength, moral standing and fibre as her male counterparts, whilst also revealing a softer, emotional side and one that focuses on family and ideals of accepting Motherhood. This is what makes Rodriguez such a fascinating contradiction. Whilst much praise is heaped on other actresses for their roles in action films, this chapter will offer, through both an overview of her action-hero career and in-depth look at Rodriguez's work in the *Fast and Furious* films, an insight into the importance of this actress to the growing canon of action hero(ine) characters and film stars.

Keywords: Michelle Rodriguez; female action stars; star types; *The Fast and The Furious*; Latin American actresses; gender; action; femininity; Latina; actress

> People don't like talking about it, but if you're Spanish, you feel a weight. I don't have much history – I've got Rosie Perez, Jennifer Lopez, Rita Moreno. That's it. That's the history of Latin women in Hollywood, really. I'm like, 'Well, damn, that means that I have to carry a flag'. I don't have the freedom to just do anything, because I have the political weight of having this last name and my heritage. It's not like I've transcended, Will Smith-style. It takes a lot to pull that off, to cross over, and transcend.
> –(Michelle Rodriguez, *Interview* 12 January 2015).

Introduction

According to Mary Beltrán (2004), developments in the Hollywood action film in the post-millennial era has seen the rise of a Latina protagonist. In her article, she notes that the Nuyorican actress and singer, Jennifer Lopez had – as of 1997s *Anaconda* and 1998s *Out of Sight* – alongside Salma Hayek (*From Dusk Til Dawn*), and Alexa Vega's character Carmen Cortez in the *Spy Kids* films, brought into Action Cinema strong, independent, tough female characters with Latin American heritage. Beltrán argues that these performers, in addition to the earlier work of Elpidia Carrillo in *Predator* (1986), and Maria Conchita Alonso in *Predator 2* (1990), form a small but important role within Action Cinema. She writes that:

> Latinas have become prominently visible icons within the action genre. While verbally assertive Hispanic female characters have appeared throughout the history of US film [...] Latina protagonists with a sense of physical purpose that puts them among the ranks of the action hero embody a new trend on the rise since the late 1990s (p. 187).

As we have seen in other chapters in this volume and throughout the overall collection, the work of Tasker, Jeffords and others is important in chronicling Action Cinema's origins and the way that the genre focuses on issues of gender. Even though there were exceptions, it was obvious from their (and others) investigations that the genre was fundamentally focused on white, male action heroes. Of course, times change, and rightly so. Action Cinema is now more reflective of both the characters/types and the actors who portray them. One of those actors is American born, but with Dominican Republic and Puerto Rican heritage, Michelle Rodriguez.

Before this chapter turns towards analysing Rodriguez' body of work, it is worthwhile to discuss – albeit briefly – the way that female action heroes and Latin America/Hispanic characters are usually depicted onscreen. For the traditional action hero, there is emphasis on the physical rather than their mental agility. Toned physiques, muscular frames and bulging biceps are always displayed. These heroes fight against the forces of villainy, either through an individual or a corrupt system that needs dismantling. As Tasker says, 'the body of the hero, or heroine, is their ultimate, and often their only, weapon' (quoted in Beltrán, p. 188). With this in mind, and especially with the action film being so Hollywood dominated, the Latina is normally seen as flamboyant, assertive and arguably excessive (Beltrán, 2002; Holmlund, 2002) and usually placed within the background to the narrative and the main characters. Such earlier performers include Lupe Velez, Dolores del Rio, Carmen Miranda and Maria Félix. Lupez was essentially a fine comic actress; del Rio and Miranda were polished singers and dancers who demonstrated strong acting talent; Félix carved a niche image of herself as a tough, no-nonsense one-liner who broke free from the traditional

Mexican female stereotype. As Fregoso's work attests (1995), these actresses' roles could clearly be categorised as *Pachuca-chola*: fiery, feisty, independent and strong. Many of the Latina performers/performances seem to be found in the heyday of the studio Western, where there are often assertive characters seen in *My Darling Clementine* (1946: Linda Darnell as Chihuahua – even though she was an Anglo actress), *High Noon* (Helen Ramirez, played by Katy Jurado) and more. However, these characters were often used as social representations that form a distancing from the usual tropes of the white female character's virtues of being homely, wifely and therefore 'safe'. For the Latina, they were usually given the role of prostitute or socially transgressive woman within the narrative, clearly positioned to upset the 'accepted' ideas of the patriarchal homestead.

By the 1960s, such terrific actresses as Rita Moreno and her role as Juanita in *West Side Story* (1961) had enabled Latina characters to branch away from those earlier roles, and especially those seen in teen delinquency movies of the 1950s. Whilst they were usually on the periphery of the action, their screen presence was undeniable. Arguably one of the most important female roles of this period was not found in the more mainstream catalogue. Rather, it was in the delirious Russ Meyer movie, *Faster Pussycat, Kill! Kill* (1966), in which the wonderfully ripe performance from Tura Sutana as the skin-tight black denim wearing Varla destroyed both men and women in her path with no discrimination against either. Whilst this may readily conform in some ways to the stereotyping that Holmlund and Beltrán discuss (both 2002) and bearing in mind Satana was of Japanese American heritage, a role like Vala is a strong, powerful one that clearly showed the importance of promoting these rebellious types of characters into the cinematic arena. Whilst conservative and mainstream Hollywood may have steered clear of Satana and others, low-budget filmmakers clearly saw that money was to be had in the sensationalising of both the subject matter and the figures seen onscreen.

Moving towards the new millennium, it was clear that the action genre was mutating. Female action stars such as Sigourney Weaver in *Alien* and its numerous sequels sat comfortably alongside Arnold Schwarzenegger and his action exploits. For the Latina, there were the occasional powerful characters moving towards the centre of the narrative: the aforementioned heroes of the first two *Predator* films are evidence of this. Likewise, the roles of Rachel Ticotin are interesting and may be set for further study. As the rebel freedom fighter Melina in *Total Recall* (1990), Detective Sandra Torres in *Falling Down* (1990) and Guard Sally Bishop in *Con Air* (1997), all the narratives place her in a curious position. On the one hand, Melina is a freedom fighting rebel, but she is a prostitute. At the end of the narrative, despite her shooting the villain (Cohagen) in the shoulder before his eventual demise on the Martian surface, she falls into the arms of her lover, Quaid (Arnold Schwarzenegger) only for her to question if their entire adventure is all a dream. As Torres she plays second fiddle to her colleague, Prendergast. In *Con Air*, she is bound and gagged by a homicidal prisoner.

For (non-Latina) Jenette Goldstein as Private Vasquez in *Aliens* (1986), it clearly shows that there was room for these Hispanic characters to inhabit the same cinematic plain as their white male and female counterparts. When asked by the white, male Corporal Hicks if she had ever been mistaken for a man due to her muscles, her reply of 'No. Have you?' makes the assembled team of soldiers laugh at *his* inferiority. At the end of the film, she sacrifices her life by helping to blow up a pack of chasing predators: she places her hand on her commanding officer's – who is holding the grenade – and says, 'You always were an asshole, Gorman!' seconds before the explosion kills them all. Again, this clearly defines Vasquez as a strong character who is prepared to make sacrifices for the greater good. In relation to Rodriguez, and the characters she has portrayed, it is perhaps now evident to see that she is part of a growing body of actors that can 'play' Latina stereotypes whilst subverting them, and just as importantly being able to demonstrate that they are creating 'types' that their work can begin to reflect, whilst simultaneously opening up questions about gender portrayals.

Types and Michelle Rodriguez

Following on from Orrin E. Klapp's 1971 work in *Heroes, Villains and Fools*, in which he sees the role of the film star as performing the function of 'a collective norm of role behaviour formed and used by the group: an idealized concept of how people are expected to be or to act' (p. 11), Richard Dyer's work on *Stars* (2002) signposts and discusses areas of film stardom that provide a strong reading of how film stars 'work'. He puts forward three main areas of investigation when analysing film stars. The first sees the star as a form of social phenomenon, in which stars are both a production and creation of a 'system' (in this case, Hollywood) that includes the films in which they appear and other sources such as celebrity magazines, talk shows etc., which is then consumed by the public. This also sees the star becoming replete with ideological implications, which are read through the roles they play (which are coded with usually capitalist and conservative ideologies), or other sources, in which perhaps their political views may become apparent (pp. 1–32). The second level of 'reading' stardom is to see the film star as a set of images (pp. 33–86). These images become a paradox: on the one hand they are deemed as 'ordinary' in that an audience can somehow relate to them through their film roles or their behaviour and lifestyles away from the silver screen (stars are seen shopping or taking their children to school etc.). Dyer argues that stars become a form of social 'type' and following and expanding on Klapp's ideas about *The Tough Guy*, *The Good Joe* and *The Pin Up* argues that whilst these types affirm the status quo, there are 'alternatives' as discussed through such anomic creations such as *The Rebel* and *The Independent Woman* (pp. 52–59). The final aspects of Dyer's work (pp. 87–159) are twofold: one element focuses on the characters that the star has created, and just as importantly, the stars that have been created *through* their characters, whereby one becomes the same as the other at least in terms of audience recognition. His closing arguments discuss work as performance, and how actors use different methods to create, shape and finally deliver their role. Of course, these 'types' are now open to negotiation. What was once seen as a 'tough guy' persona can now easily transfer to 'tough woman'.

So how does Klapp and Dyer's work have any bearing on Rodriguez? When Klapp discusses stars and star-reception (p. 11), he argues that 'the type may describe the way people should be, should not be, or simply are predicted to be. And, though it is found in various media, often as the creation of artists, it is really made by the people who use it'. If this is the case, then it is not just the individual themselves that creates the 'star'. It is the triumvirate of actor/star/audience that formulates the final creation of such a phenomenon. Therefore, when analysing the Michelle Rodriguez canon, one must first take into account her personal backstory, and whilst this chapter primarily focuses on her film persona, it is interesting to see that out of all the Klapp and Dyer 'types', it becomes clear that despite her ability to move from one to another (as will be seen in the case studies that follow), it is with the 'rebel' to which she could arguably be most easily situated in the roles afforded her, and that is possibly due to events offscreen where her rebellion appears to offer a base from which her persona stands.

Prison

In March 2002, Rodriguez was arrested for assault after becoming involved in an altercation with her then-roommate. The charges were dropped by the roommate and no further legal action was taken (Grossberg, 2002). In November 2003, she faced eight misdemeanour charges in which she was accused of hit and run and driving under the influence (DUI). She pleaded 'guilty' to three of the charges (hit and run, DUI and driving with a suspended licence), went to jail for 48 hours, worked in the morgues of two New York hospitals, was given a probationary period of three years and completed a three-month alcohol programme (Hall, 2005). In 2005, Rodriguez was arrested by Honolulu police numerous times for speeding violations. On 1st December 2005, she was arrested for another DUI incident. At the trial in April 2006, Rodriguez cited allergy-relieving medication as one reason as to why she behaved erratically. She pleaded guilty to one charge of driving under the influence, paid $500 (US) and spent five days in jail. However, as this broke her 2003 probationary period of three years, the actress was given a 60-day jail sentence, had to attend a mandatory 30-day rehabilitation programme, and undergo 30 days of community service (Finn, 2006). In September 2007, Rodriguez apparently violated both the community and alcohol educational programme she had been told to complete (Lee & Silverman, 2006). On 10th October 2007, she was sentenced to 180 days in prison, but served only 18 days due to overcrowding (author n/k, Today.com). It was reported that in January 2009, she had completed her community service (author n/k, *Latina, 2009*).

Acting Career

Rodriguez was born in Texas, United States, in 1978 to a Dominican mother and Puerto Rican father. Her father served in the US army and the family moved to

Nicaragua when she was eight years old. Following some years of moving around, she settled in Jersey City, New Jersey, United States. Over her formative years, she was expelled from five schools before eventually settling on pursuing an acting career.

Her first audition was for the film *Girlfight* (2000). Beating over 350 other applicants to win the role of Diana Guzman, a troubled teenager who channels her aggression through amateur boxing, the film garnered notable acclaim for Rodriguez: she won Best Actress awards at the National Board of Review, Independent Spirit Awards, Deauville Film Festival, and at the Cannes Film Festival she was the recipient of Award of the Youth. The film sees her play Diana Guzman, a young woman who enters the world of boxing. The narrative focuses on her training and then her eventual entry into the world of competitive boxing. What makes the film interesting is that the outer elements of the film – Guzman's home life, family tensions, love life – come to the fore. As Cauldwell argues, the film is not necessarily about boxing per se. Rather, it provides an insight into gender constructions as implicating sexuality and race (2008).

Moving on from this, Rodriguez' following film work included such supporting role fare as the New York thriller, *3AM* (2001), which follows her character, taxi driver Salgado, who was forced into prostitution at the age of 12 and is convinced her fare has a devil on his shoulder. Other supporting work includes *Blue Crush* (2002) as the expert surfer; Eden who wants to live out her dream of surfing in Hawaii; Officer Sanchez in *S.W.A.T* (2003); the period horror video game adaptation of *Bloodrayne* (2004) where Rodriguez plays the rebellious Katarin; Captain Trudy Chacon in *Avatar* (2009); Technical Sergeant Elana Santo in *Battle Los Angeles* (2011), who despite being billed as second-lead (clearly indicating her rising stardom) has very limited screen time and dialogue; the aptly titled *iNAPPROPRIATE COMEDY* (2013) in the segment entitled 'The Porno Review'; lent her gravel-voice to *Smurfs: The Lost Village* in which she voiced the character of Smurf Storm; the BBC-based film version of *Widows* (2018) in which she co-starred alongside Bafta-nominee Viola Davis, and which afforded her an opportunity to flex her acting talent as Linda, a clothing store owner; *She Dies Tomorrow* (2020) sees Rodriguez in the role of Sky, a woman who is dying, and may already be dead; and *Crisis* (2021), where her role of DEA Supervisor Garrett has her, despite equal size billing on the poster, in a minor role.

As a performer, Rodriguez also lent her talent to music videos, video games and television. Clearly showing that as a new type of star which could move across media boundaries, much like Jason Statham has in his career (see Gerrard & Shail, 2019 – numerous chapters), she appeared in 'I Can Do Too' featuring Cole and Queen Latifah (2000), 'If I Could Fall in Love' by Lenny Kravitz (2002) and 'Nice for What' by Drake (2018) amongst others. In the gaming world, she helped vocalise *Driver 3 (2004)* and *Halo 2 (2004)*, whilst reprising her roles in both *James Cameron's Avatar: The Game (2009)* and Fast and Furious Crossroads (2020). Rodriguez' television work is primarily notable for her role as Ana Lucia Cortez (like many of her roles, the name emphasises an Hispanic background) in *Lost* (2005–) in which she was both a guest star in seasons one, five and six, whilst being part of the main cast in season 2. What all these works clearly display is that, in the main, Rodriguez is almost always seen as a second lead or lower in the cast. That is not denigrating her work at all. Rather, it demonstrates that – arguably – her Hispanic looks (and therefore the cliched Hispanic temperament) comes to the fore. In a genre (and especially a franchise) that most often focuses on male characters, she has found room for negotiation. It is in two franchises that perhaps Rodriguez is best known: *Resident Evil* (2002–2016) and *The Fast and the Furious* (2001–2023).

Resident Evil

J.D. Salinas: I shot her five times. How was she still standing?

Rain Ocampo: Bitch ain't standing now.

(Resident Evil, 2002)

The *Resident Evil* franchise of six movies is based on the Capcom game series (1996–2022). Rodriguez appeared in two of the films: *Resident Evil* (2002) and *Resident Evil: Retribution* (2012). The first instalment (2002) sees her portray the tough, no-nonsense, sarcastic Umbrella Corporation soldier, Rain Ocampo. The film sees a devastating poison being released which turns almost everyone into rabid zombies. Project Alice (see Gerrard, 2019, pp. 205–218) wakes in a mansion that sits above The Hive, Umbrella's underground headquarters. As Alice wakes, a tactical team break in. Over the course of the next hour and a half, they take her into the Hive to find out what has happened there. In this first movie, Rodriguez plays Rain Ocampo, a tough, no-nonsense soldier. She is a member of the Umbrella Corporation's elite special operations team. She isn't physically weak, yet over the course of the narrative, her emotional defences are steadily broken down. Ocampo gets bitten by a zombie and begins to turn into one. Yet, despite this, she tries to help Project Alice escape the bunker. In her penultimate scene, she turns on Alice and is shot in the head.

In *Resident Evil: Retribution*, Ocampo appears in a dual role. First, as chaos erupts in an idyllic suburban town, Alice is fleeing from hundreds of zombies. A car pulls up and Ocampo, dressed in jeans, t-shirt and jacket, screams at her to get in. Alice looks confused, not realising that Ocampo is part of Umbrella's cloning experiments. As they drive away, a truck smashes into the car. Alice escapes. Rain does not and sees zombies approaching her. However, the zombies move past, and she flees. Later in the narrative Rain meets Alice and at this point she is terrified. Alice trains her briefly to hold and shoot a gun, then leaves her 'daughter' Becky with Rain. Later in the film, Ocampo is killed by a giant mutated human-hybrid. However, towards the end of the narrative, *another* Ocampo appears: this time she is a member of a squad of Umbrella commandos. As The Hive is flooded, Ocampo injects herself with a parasite that transforms her into a superhuman killing machine. She attacks Alice's male friends, killing one of them with a punch to the chest. When Alice collapses to the ground dying,

Ocampo moves in to kill her. Alice shoots the ice underneath Ocampo's feet and she falls into the iced water. When she attempts to crawl out, zombies emerge and drag her back into the depths to be consumed.

Whilst only appearing in two movies in the franchise, Rodriguez plays three versions of Ocampo – each one different from the previous version. There is strength on display in the first and third incarnations: she wears combats, she can handle a gun, she beats up zombies. She is the Tough Woman. In her 'middle Ocampo' phase, she is fragile, her curly black hair, makeup, clothing all accentuating her femininity and she has 'typical' female emotional traits: she cries, she gets upset. But coupled with this is that Alice leaves her 'daughter' in her hands. Here, Ocampo become the nurturing 'mother' or in the case of Klapp's 'types' becomes the Good Jane.

The Fast and the Furious

> If you can't really push the envelope on the female action, then you're not making action movies, because that's where it's at, declares the actress, who got her start in the boxing indie Girlfight. I think most women are more concerned with how good they look than how badass they can really come across on the screen and what crazy or chaotic action they could pull off. And for me, that's more important than looking good. I could give two rats' asses what I look like. I want to kick some serious ass – or at least get my ass kicked really seriously!
> (Michelle Rodriguez, *Entertainment*, 11th June 2021)

The Fast and the Furious franchise has become one of Hollywood's biggest box office blockbuster franchises, with a combined gross box office figure of over $6billion (US). Since its first outing in 2002, which basically saw a gang of streetcar thieves hoodwinking both rival gangs and the police, the franchise has turned into a global cinematic phenomenon which now has the gang (led by Dominic Toretto – played by Vin Diesel) not only averting nuclear Armageddon but also having the ability to drive their cars through and from one skyscraper to another. Rodriguez plays Letitia 'Letty' Ortiz, Toretto's girlfriend-cum-wife. In this first outing, despite her limited screen time, Rodriguez' character is strong, with a solid screen presence, and her position within the franchise is assured. When she is involved in a predominantly male arena (car racing), the emphasis on her gender is a key focus in one particular racing sequence. As Letty drives her car up to a starting grid, a young man looks surprised at his having a female rival opposite him. He constantly refers to her as 'baby' and says, 'How about I raise you for that sweet little ass?' which stresses that the female has nothing but sexual or monetary value. The man then asks, 'Shouldn't you be watching this from the sidelines?' again emphasising that she is an outsider to this male-dominated arena. Ortiz ignores him and wins the race. This seems to provoke numerous readings that she (as a female) can be bought and sold, and that her ignoring him demonstrates that this type of language and occurrence remains part-and-parcel of the masculinised place/space (the racing circuit), where she *as a female* is seen as Other. If one takes into consideration de Certeau's (1980) arguments that institutions of power (in this case the world of male-dominated racing) become 'producers', and individuals ('consumers' – in this case, Letty) become those who act within an institution's walls, then Ortiz (as a 'consumer') is accepting and acknowledging that this world is replete with gender barriers that she is breaking down. If one takes this further, where 'space' and 'place' are taken into consideration (de Certeau argues that individuals move within a 'place' and they learn within a 'space' [ibid.]) it becomes evident that the racing circuit becomes the 'place' in which Letty's car – that which she knows, trusts and through which she can question ideas about masculinity and femininity – becomes her 'space'. As the build-up to the race commences, there are cross shots of cars' engines revving, cheering crowds, individuals chanting, the two drivers anxiously waiting for the green light to begin the contest. Whilst the gendered aspect of the situation is predominantly *male* (as seen through the masculinized cars), Ortiz's position within the idea of 'place' is defined: she is a female in a male arena, and as such whilst she may not readily question the male driver over the way he verbally assaults her, the idea that she can beat him from the comforting surroundings of her car ('space') demonstrates that her self-control over her own temper and the way she drives her vehicle shows that her strength in overturning gender norms in this area are defined. *She* has beaten *him*.

Even though Ortiz was not in the following films in the franchise, she returned in *Fast and Furious 6*, in which she has become a lethally skilled mercenary. Despite leaving Dom temporarily to sort through her amnesia issues in *Furious 7* (2015), she regains her memory to find she has married him in an offscreen ceremony before *Fast & Furious* (2009). In the ninth outing, *The Fate of the Furious* (2017), she becomes the group's moral compass when she defends Dom, who has seemingly switched allegiance to the villain Mr Nobody. Interestingly, the last sequence in this sees her meeting Dom's infant son, Brian for the first time. As the group sit together emphasising the 'family' ethos promoted through the entire franchise, the camera rests on Letty, Dom and the child. She is accepting of Brian, despite him not being of familial blood. In some ways this could significantly damage the character – but, it only adds another dimension to it. On the one hand, she remains the defiant, strong, rebellious Letty who can drive cars, jump off bonnets, beat up men; But on the other, she then falls back into the domestic sphere, becoming both wife and surrogate mother. Yet, the way that she is positioned at the end of the film clearly signifies that she is strong in both areas. Rather being constrained, she *grows*. Whilst the 10th outing saw her return to her action status, it is *The Fast and the Furious* that sets the groundwork for Ortiz, and then *The Fate and the Furious* that sees her character trajectory complete.

Recognising Rodriguez

Despite Rodriguez' large body of work, she is somewhat neglected in the pantheon of contemporary female action stars. Whilst actors such as Charlize Theron may have garnered plaudits for the performances they give, and despite her breakthrough role in *Girlfight*, Rodriguez' canon remains both tantalisingly intriguing and slightly underwhelming. On the one hand, she is primarily known as Letty Ortiz, an incredibly tough character that remains just as strong as her male counterparts. The role of Rain Ocampo sees her move from tough soldier to scared suburban housewife (albeit a doppelganger as part of the Umbrella Corporation's cloning programme) and then to genetically advanced super soldier who kills men with a single punch. Other roles such as Captain Trudy Chacon in *Avatar* and Technical Sargent Elana Santos in *Battle: Los Angeles* repeat this tough woman type, so that Rodriguez's career borders on her being pigeonholed and typecast as a tough, no-nonsense, straight-talking badass. Whilst her role as Luz/She in *Machete* and *Machete Kills Again* (2010 and 2014) sees her change from a gently spoken Hispanic taco-seller to a sexualised, one-eyed, gun-toting leader of an underground organisation that helps illegal Mexican immigrants set up lives in America, it is clearly done with a tongue firmly in cheek. There is a further sequel, at least in trailer terms, called *Machete Kills Again – In Space*, which has Rodriguez reprising her role as Luz/She. She is first seen talking to Machete: 'This is a new future. It's all galactic and shit'. Then, as she turns towards the camera, with her jet-pack engines on and her laser gun blasting, she shouts, 'Eat photons, bitches!' The *faux* trailer is playful in its homage to both itself and other material, notably *Star Wars* (1977) and *Buck Rogers in the 25th Century* (1979–), though it appears to be arguably more in line with 1979s *Starcrash* in terms of actual quality. However, the film *Trópico de Sangre* (2010) has her taking on a complex role as the real-life Dominican freedom fighter, Minerva Mirabel, that positions her both through the structures of 'type' as a rebel but also as a tough woman, and a Latina. In arguably the most interesting role of her career, the film *Tomboy* (aka *The Assignment*) can only remain a disappointment. The initial premise is suitably odd: Frank Kitchen (Rodriguez) is a male hitman. After being kidnapped, he finds that he has been transformed into a female by The Doctor aka Dr Rachel Jane (Sigourney Weaver) a plastic surgeon bent on revenge for Kitchen killing her brother. Once recovered, Kitchen tries – and succeeds – to hunt down The Doctor, who she sets up as the perpetrator of a mass killing. The final scenes see Kitchen accepting her new gender, whilst Jane is revealed to have had her fingers (and therefore the tools of her trade) amputated.

The opening sequences see Rodriguez dressed in a black jacket, combat trousers and bulletproof vest, topped off with a black baseball cap. Kitchen's hair is tied back, and 'his' beard is unkempt. 'He' is shown to be an expert assassin, dispatching various men as part of his contracted killings. Later, he has sex with a blonde woman. When Kitchen wakes up, 'he' screams in agony at the emotional and physical loss of 'his' manhood, his virility and his masculinity. But this is short lived. Within a few minutes of screen time 'he' has somehow overcome this trauma to become a hitwoman. 'She' finds and dispatches her victims as she tries to track down The Doctor. Eventually 'she' finds the blonde and they begin a relationship. When they finally move to have sex, Frankie says, 'I'll try my best'. This is the most interesting line in the film: it offers a teasingly tantalising insight into the issues that befall action heroes from a transgendered viewpoint – something that will, hopefully, be addressed with much more validity in other films than afforded in this movie. Whilst the film could have become risible in its treatment of sex at this point, it does move quietly away to a fade out. This issue is never mentioned again, which is a genuine shame, because here was a point where investigations into how one aspect of gender *could* be explored further is left in need of wanting.

Conclusion

If we return to the notion of 'types' discussed earlier in this chapter, it becomes apparent that an analysis of Rodriguez's work is clearly worthy of investigation. Her earlier roles such as *Blue Crush* and *The Creed* not only gave her action sequences (the latter sees her climbing and zip-wiring from zombie dogs), but they also blatantly accentuated her near-naked figure making her the 'pin up' type. Later roles saw her become a bona fide action star, in which she becomes the 'tough woman'. There are also those films such as *Trópico de Sangre* and the family drama *Milton's Secret* (2016) that clearly demonstrate her ability to produce interesting performances that either celebrate her Hispanic origins or are ignored altogether and that any stereotyped traits are removed. What remains at the cornerstone of all her film roles is that she is clearly an actress that can negotiate these various 'types', and that she often overturns the male-dominated ones into female-oriented. It is this that makes Michelle Rodriguez such a fascinating, though unfortunately often unsung action hero in Action Cinema's pantheon.

References

Beltrán, M. (2002). The Hollywood Latina body as site of social struggle: Media constructions of stardom and Jennifer Lopez's "cross-over butt". *Quarterly Review of Film and Video*, *19*(1013), 71–86.
Beltrán, M. (2004). MÁS MACHA: The new Latina action hero. In Y. Tasker (Ed.), *Action and adventure cinema* (pp. 186–200). London: Routledge.
Cauldwell, J. (2008). *Girlfight*: Boxing women. *Sport in Society*, *11*(203), 227–239.
de Certeau, M. (1980). *L'Invention du Quotidien. Vol. 1, Arts de Faire/the practice of everyday life*. France: Editions Gallimard.
Finn, N. (2006, May 22). More jail time for Michelle Rodriguez. *E! magazine*.
Fregoso, R. (1995). Homegirls, cholas, and pachucas in Cinema: Taking over the public sphere. *California History*, 317–327. Fall 1995.
Gerrard, S. (2019). *"My name is Alice. And I remember everything." Project Alice and Milla Jovovich in the resident evil films*. Bingley: Emerald Publishing Limited.
Gerrard, S., & Shail, R. (2019). *Crank it up: Jason Statham – Star!* Manchester: Manchester University Press.

Grossberg, J. (2002, April 8). "Girlfight" star off the hook. *E!* Retrieved from https://www.eonline.com/news-fullhttpnotknown. Accessed on April 25, 2022.

Hall, S. (2005, December 14). Rodriguez: Fast and furious driver. *E!* Retrieved from https://www.eonline.com/news-fullhttpnotknown. Accessed on April 25, 2022.

Holmlund, C. (2002). *Impossible bodies: Femininity and masculinity at the movies.* London: Routledge.

(Author not known) Latina. (2009, January 6). Michelle Rodriguez finishers her community service in stride. *Latina.* Retrieved from https://latina.comhttps://www.eonline.com/news-fullhttpnotknown. Accessed on April 25, 2022.

Lee, K., & Silverman, S. M. (2006, May 22). 'Michelle Rodriguez gets 60 Days in jail'. *People.* Archived from the original source on 12th Feb 2007. Retrieved from https://people.com/celebrity/michelle-rodriguez-gets-60-days-in-jail/. Accessed on April 25, 2022.

Rodriguez, M. (2015, January 12). 'Michelle Rodriguez' by Jovovich, M. Interview. Retrieved from https://www.interviewmagazine.com/film/michelle-rodriguez#_. Accessed on April 25, 2022.

Rodriguez, M. (2021, June 11). 'Michelle Rodriguez on her long fight to bring 'dimension' to Letty, F9 doing 'justice for all the girls'' by Lawrence, D. Entertainment. Retrieved from https://ew.com/ew-binge-podcast/fast-saga-michelle-rodriguez-furious-7/. Accessed on April 25, 2022.

(Author not known) Today.com. (2008, January 10). Michelle Rodriguez out of jail after 18 days. Retrieved from https://www.today.com/popculture/michelle-rodriguez-out-jail-after-18-days-1C9417269. Accessed on April 25, 2022.

Discography

Cole and Queen Latifah. (2000). I can due to. Capitol Records.
Drake (2018). Nice for what. Young Money, Cash Money, Republic.
Kravitz, L. (2002). If I could fall in love. Virgin America.

Gameography

Driver 3. (2004). Reflections Interactive and Atari, Inc. Dir: MartinEdmondson; Writer: Maurice Suckling.

Fast and Furious Crossroads. (2020). Slightly Mad Studios and Bandai Namco Entertainment. Dir: Andy Tudor. Writer: n/k.

Halo 2. (2004). Bungie and Microsoft Game Studios. Dir: Jason Jones; writer: Joseph Staten.

James Cameron's Avatar: The Game. (2009). Ubisoft Montreal and Ubisoft Gameloft. Dir/writer: n/k.

Chapter 3

'Musculinity' and the Empowered Female Body in *Haywire* (2011)

Douglas Rasmussen

Abstract

For much of its peak popularity in the 1970s and 1980s, women in action films were relegated to the damsel in distress and/or the romantic interest for the male lead. This was particularly evident in action films where women were depicted as being petite and submissive, especially towards the heroic male. Rarely did women occupy the primary focus in action films. Nowadays women are more frequently occupying positions of creative power as producers and actors, and there are some notable examples of progressive female roles in modern film. Female action stars tended to occupy one of two roles, that of what Marc O'Day (2004) labelled 'action babe' cinema, using the colloquial and dismissive term 'babe' as an indication of the derogatory nature of the female action hero who was often just a supermodel with a gun. However, there has emerged another type of female action star, the tough, aggressive and physically capable female action star, such as Sarah Connor in *Terminator 2: Judgement Day (1992)*.

Yvonne Tasker coined the term 'musculinity' to define this new model of tough women; female action stars who appropriate what are considered traditionally masculine traits (developed muscles, aggression, confidence, leadership skills, bravery). The presence of athletic women in action films, especially when compared to their male counterparts, defies expectations for women, and as such provides a unique example to analyse in terms of gender dynamics. This is especially true of combat sports, where aggression is a feature of the sport and still considered a testosterone-oriented attribute. Indeed, in the 1970s and 1980s, the peak of the male action star, martial arts and associated combat sports provided opportunities for many former athletes to transition into action films. Using Tasker's framework of musculinity, I will examine *Haywire (2011)* as a notable progression in the representation of female action stars and musculinity. Focusing on a case study of Gina Carano's role in *Haywire*, and her subsequent career narrative, this chapter highlights how perceptions of masculinity and femininity in both combat sports and action films have previously limited roles for women and how much that has shifted in contemporary filmmaking.

Keywords: Gina Carano; *Haywire* (2011); action film; gender dynamics; female muscularity; masculinity

The presence of professional female athletes who have successfully transitioned into action films is a rarity, even though action films demand intense physical activity, and regularly features impressively muscled male athletes who have transitioned into successful film careers (Arnold Schwarzenegger, Chuck Norris, Jean Claude Van Damme, Dwayne 'The Rock' Johnson). Historically in action films, women have been frequently confined to roles of the damsel in distress and/ or the romantic interest for the male lead and depicted as being petite and submissive. In terms of contemporary popular culture, the presence of athletic or non-sexualised and physically tough representations of women seem to be on the increase, however gradually and incrementally. Celebrity is a type of capital, with high-profile actors and musicians being able to effect significant changes in culture. This influence of celebrity culture produces changes to the virtual embodiment of society and how individuals see themselves, how they interact and contributing to their mannerisms, gestures and physicality, and reflecting societal standards. The presence of physically strong female fighters in action films goes a long way in de-stigmatising these types of athletic and physical roles for women, with mixed martial arts being a popular media space for audiences. Modern examples include Imperator Furiosa (Charlise Theron) from *Mad Max: Fury Road* (2015), Beatrix Kiddo (Uma Thurman) from *Kill Bill: Volume One* and *Two (2003/2004)* and Korra from the animated series *The Last Airbender: The Legend of Korra* (2005–2008). *The Last Airbender: The Legend of Korra* notably features a female protagonist with a mixed martial arts build and thicker muscles than typically seen in a children's cartoon. So, the idea that tough women can participate in successful action franchises, whether animated or live action, is gaining traction.

Following the popularity of characters like Sarah Connor (Linda Hamilton) in *Terminator 2: Judgment Day* which featured an actress undergoing an intense physical regime in order to play a tough and hardened warrior, Yvonne Tasker (1993, p. 3) coined the term musculinity to define this new archetype: 'Musculinity indicates the extent to which a physical definition of muscularity in terms of developed musculature is not limited to the male body within representation'. Action films, much like sports, are very gendered spaces with rigid gender hierarchies regarding attributes considered masculine (strength, power, confidence, aggression, bravery) and attributes that are considered feminine (biologically weaker, nurturing, submissive). Musculinity, then, describes how this new model of the female action hero has shifted the genre beyond its traditional modes of representation, which is that of the submissive female and the heroic, muscled male lead.

Empowered Female Body in Haywire (2011) 35

In this chapter, I will examine Gina Carano's transition from professional athlete to action film star and how she has altered traditional perceptions of hypermasculinity present in popular 1970s and 1980s action films, with the goal of determining how modern society has shifted its perception of gender norms. The athletic female body represented by Carano is an empowered body that challenges the perceptions of masculinity and femininity. The athletic female body is significant when discussing the question of shifting gender norms given the challenge and disruption that athleticism presents to the conventional narrative of the female body. The athletic body subverts the idealised vision of femininity typical of action films, where women are often presented purely as objects of heterosexual desire for the male leads. These stereotypes also persist in combat sports, which tend to adhere to the female form as a fantasy figure, not as an empowered body, as evidenced by how the UFC treated its female competitors and how they marketed female fighters with swimsuit calendars or discussed their physical attractiveness as a part of the on air sports commentary. In this chapter, I will examine Carano's breakthrough role in *Haywire*, in addition to her career progression to illustrate the demands placed on women in professions coded as masculine.

Women and Sport

Before examining the muscular female body in action cinema, this section examines how athletic women are regarded by mainstream culture through the lens of sport. For women to pursue athletics, especially those associated with aggression and combat, there is the extra burden of struggling against deeply entrenched gender norms. In fact, the mixed martial arts league UFC was initially reluctant to allow a women's division, with its female competition only beginning in 2012. However, as Allyson Quinney (2016, p. 46) argues, the UFC is still not entirely receptive to female fighters, despite promoting themselves as being inclusive: 'The efforts to sexualise female fighters in the UFC brings women into the league under the guise of women's rights, but in reality female fighters are not on equal ground with male fighters'. The narrative of female empowerment, then, is superficial at best and serves as a marketing brand to sell calendars and posters of female MMA fighters.

The athletic female body poses a significant challenge to prominently masculine-oriented endeavours, such as sports and action films and their respective marketability. In her article on challenging hegemonic femininity, Vicki Krane (2001, p. 116) notes that 'sportswomen tread a fine line of acceptable femininity'. 'Acceptable' femininity is reinforced by popular media and follows a traditional conception of femininity that, as Anne Bolin (1992, p. 81) echoes, frames women as the weaker sex whose form must conform to a softer, rounder, more curvaceous physique that appeals to heterosexual desire. Mass media, such as advertising, magazines, music videos, television and films – in this specific case, action films – have contributed to this image of 'acceptable femininity' and the perpetuation of the idea of the softer, more curvaceous female form that appeals to heterosexual desire.

The athletic female body, then, whether it is on the small screen in sports or the silver screen as a character in an action film, disrupts this media reinforcement of acceptable femininity. As a consequence, female athletes, and by extension female action stars, face repercussions for their transgressive bodies and behaviours. Women in the UFC often deal with misogynistic language, lesser payouts in comparison to their male counterparts, less coverage on sports channels, online abuse from social media platforms, a sexual objectification by the UFC itself in order to promote female fighters, and even incidents of domestic abuse from relationships with male athletes as a result (Navejar, 2017, p. 45). Darvin and Sagas (2017) also point to a number of factors that impact representation of female athletes, observing women's divisions in various sports have fewer diverse camera angles, fewer special effects, less coverage than their male counterparts and sports commentators 'often explicitly refer to a female athlete's attractiveness' as examples of how women are not given equal treatment to men in sports (180–182). A number of these conditions exist in equal measure for women attempting to participate in action films, drawing less of a salary for their roles, online social media abuse from irate viewers and an overly sexualised focus on their bodies. Sports and action films co-exist as very gendered spaces that are only now incrementally changing the rigid binary representations where submissive femininity and masculinity as strength and power exist as opposites.

Muscularity as a physical feature of sports also has a more significant impact on women. Krane, Choi, Baird, Aimor, and Kauer (2004, p. 316) summarise the essential paradox of female muscularity in sport, that 'negotiating the performance of hegemonic femininity while avoiding masculine behaviours becomes problematic for these physically active women'. In sport, this paradox results in a series of contradictions where the female athlete must negotiate how to achieve athletic excellence without compromising traditional conceptions of femininity. These contradictions often have a negative effect on career or how they are received by sports writers as an athlete. Charlene Weaving (2014) contends that it is necessary for female athletes, particularly mixed martial artists, to emphasise their femininity in order to be accepted by media and society (Weaving, p. 136). In terms of marketing, this means that female fighters outside of the ring have to establish a hyper-feminine persona as a counterbalance to their career as a fighter.

The stigmatisation of women in combat sports has a parallel in action films, which is a genre that has a tendency to conform to mainstream socio-cultural attitudes, if not outright traditional and conservative values. There is a potential for a greater range in writing active women in action films that is not being utilised because of the restrictive demands of the typical male-oriented action film. Both sports and action films are marketed to a similar male demographic which tends to emphasise traditional conceptions of femininity and muscularity, with the latter being almost solely associated with masculinity. Muscularity in both sport and action films is considered acceptable for men, but aberrant and unnatural for women.

Defining 'Musculinity'

While the presence of women as action heroes, not just as love interests to the male lead, is not a new phenomenon, the female action hero and musculinity as a new archetype is a more recent phenomenon. In his essay 'Beauty in Motion: Gender, Spectacle and Action Babe Cinema', Marc O'Day (2004) uses the term 'action babe' cinema, deliberately invoking the dismissive term 'babe' as a reflection of cultural attitudes to images of women in power. O'Day identifies this model of the female action hero whereby a studio casts a shapely, slim, young, typically Caucasian and heterosexual (or at least marketed as such) actress as the action film protagonist (O'Day, 2004, p. 206). In this way studios preserve traditional codes of femininity to appeal to the male gaze, while simultaneously attempting to signify 'empowerment' to a growing female audience wanting more positive representations of women on the screen. This 'action babe', according to O'Day (2004, p. 203), can be seen simultaneously as the action subject of the narrative and as an erotic object designed as part of the visual spectacle. The patriarchal gaze is thus reinforced while also being able to market these action stars to a growing demographic of empowered female audiences.

Musculinity provides a new model of female action heroes where traits perceived as 'masculine' are ascribed to female action stars in radically different ways. As significant as Linda Hamilton's role as Sarah Connor was in terms of normalising, to a certain extent, the image of the muscular female hero, she was not previously an athlete or a fighter. The casting of professional mixed martial artists has the effect of de-stigmatising the iconography of the aggressive female as something less than feminine and therefore unnatural.

In the action films of the 1970s and 1980s, women rarely occupied central roles as protagonists or exhibit proactive behaviours, especially ones gender coded as 'masculine' (physical toughness, aggression, combat, tactical mentality). Aggression was, and for the most part still is, viewed as a masculine trait. In her book on boxing, Joyce Carol Oates (2006) discusses how aggression is perceived when it comes to women: 'Raw aggression is thought to be the peculiar province of man, as nurturing is the peculiar province of women. The female boxer violates this stereotype and cannot be taken seriously – she is a parody, she is a cartoon, she is monstrous' (Oates, 2006, p. 78). The coding of women as the biologically weaker sex in need of masculine protection is still prevalent in modern action films, despite the shifts in demographics as the genres of action and science fiction have begun to recede from being almost exclusively masculine and oriented towards a male viewer. While Lisa Purse (2011, p. 91) suggests that the 'action babe' genre has been quite homogeneous in its containing strategies, recent developments in action films have begun to break down barriers to representations of female physicality. Mixed martial artist Gina Carano is an example of this shift, however gradual and incremental it might be.

'Musculinity' and *Haywire (2011)*

A UFC fighter with an impressive 7-1-0 fight record, Carano was spotted by happenstance as a result of late-night channel flipping by the director Steven Soderbergh, who was sufficiently awed by her 'warrior look' and her fighting abilities, deciding to build a 1960s-style spy film around her (Q&A with Steven Soderbergh, Gina Carano, *Haywire*, 1:34–3:29). Steven Soderbergh's film *Haywire* (2011) breaks from the traditional Hollywood formula; rather than casting a thin and blonde 'action babe' for the role, the more than physically capable Gina Carano was cast to fight on equal grounds with her male co-stars. *Haywire* subverts the traditional emphasis of action films on the muscled male body as their heroic centre, associating muscularity with masculinity. Tasker notes that the presence of female bodybuilders – although the same principle can be applied to other variations of the tough female, such as mixed martial arts – disrupts the social perceptions of muscularity, manual labour and strength being so closely connected with masculinity in that the muscled male action star exists as an exaggeration of what is conveniently thought to be masculine, while women who take on this muscularity are considered to be taking identifiably masculine traits (Tasker, p. 142). The physically capable female protagonist, whether it is a bodybuilder or a martial artist, calls attention to this symbolic transgression and destabilised restrictive gender norms that are used to identify masculinity and femininity.

In *Haywire*, these attributes, typically connected with male leads, such as combat skills, exceptional command of guns and other weaponry, technological proficiency, defensive driving skills, confidence, are transposed onto a female protagonist. In doing so, *Haywire* visually challenges the idea that women in action films are required to be frail and vulnerable, in constant need of protection from their tougher male co-stars. The idea of women as biologically weaker is absent in *Haywire* as the female protagonist takes on the archetypal action star role of the tough spy/agent embroiled in espionage and conspiracy.

Haywire is unique in its determination to situate the female body as an active agent in the narrative and to cultivate musculinity (as opposed to the 'action babe' approach) as a viable ethos for the action film genre. The 'action babe' cinema still eroticises the female body, centering the male gaze in action film even while paying lip-service to narratives of empowerment. Whereas representations of musculinity, as we see in *Haywire*, regard the muscular or toughened female body as being constructed as a countermeasure against a hypermasculine world, where it seems like every single person (with the notable exception of her father John Kane, played by Bill Paxton) either dismisses Mallory (Gina Carano) or is actively conspiring against her.

Musculinity and Combat Against Men: Eliminating the 'Action Babe' Trope

In *Haywire*, Carano plays a former black ops agent Mallory Kane, now working in the private sector, going toe to toe against male co-stars in brutal and unsparing fight scenes. In numerous action films such as there is an unfortunate gender segregation in action scenes that limits and restricts what female action stars are capable of. Films such as *Charlie's Angels: Full Throttle* (2003), *Die Another Day* (2002), *Fast and Furious 6* (2013) and *7* (2015) largely consign women to fighting their female co-stars. By having Carano's character Mallory Kane fight men, and more importantly, win those fights, *Haywire* subverts the Hollywood formula of woman-on-woman only combat. *Haywire* revisits the traits identified by Lisa Purse in early female action stars that embodied musculinity, notably Brigitte Nelson in *Red Sonja* (1985), Cynthia Rothrock in *China O'Brien* (1988) and the aforementioned Sarah Connor. For Purse, musculinity destabilised the binary logic of dominant, normative notions of masculinity as natural and that the traits typically attributed to it (physical toughness, aggression, tactical mindset) are not the exclusive domain of men (Purse, p. 77). In *Haywire*, we have a female protagonist with a developed musculature, notable combat skills, who often physically dominates her male combatants in the film. Carano is far from a glamorous celebrity entering the genre in an 'action babe' mode.

Mallory Kane works in the hypermasculine environment of private security and espionage, not unlike the UFC or Hollywood, where men either conspire against her, dismiss her or attempt to manipulate her. Her colleague Aaron (Channing Tatum) is largely clueless about his environment, not investigating too closely who he works for or even his mission parameters, yet continually disregards Mallory. In the mission in Barcelona which involved the rescue of a hostage, Aaron attempts to dictate terms to Mallory, who has been assigned as the team leader, in effect 'mansplaining', to use a modern colloquialism, the mission to her. Aaron's male ego will not accept orders and commands from a more capable female, even though Alex Coblenz (Michael Douglas), a top-level governmental official has contracted Kenneth's (Ewan McGregor) private security firm with the expressed wish that Mallory be installed as team leader. Kenneth is fully aware that Mallory intends to leave his company, taking all her contacts and business with her. Kenneth later sends Aaron to retrieve Mallory after a failed assassination attempt in Dublin by a mercenary named Paul (Michael Fassbinder) without informing him of the reasons why he sent him in to retrieve her, leaving Aaron ignorant as to how Kenneth tried to set-up her and had failed.

In *Haywire*, gender dynamics are subverted through a reversal of stereotypes, largely in its action scenes where Mallory is placed on equal footing with male combatants. One of these strategies is that the men in the cast either resort to deceptive and sneaky tactics as a first measure of attack to catch Mallory off guard and level the playing field. The viewer sees this in the film's first fight when former co-worker Aaron is sent to bring Mallory back to Kenneth. Aaron's first move is to throw hot coffee in her face to catch her off guard. Aaron and Mallory then proceed to fight, with the two combatants brutally kicking and punching each other without regard to gender sensitivities. The implication that women are biologically inferior to men is disregarded in this fight scene, as two equal combatants square off against each other. Indeed, for much of the fight, it appears as if Mallory has the upper hand, inflicting more damage upon Aaron than she receives.

Mallory's fight with Aaron reinforces the image of the tough female fighter in an action film as an archetype of masculinity. Purse comments on the visual impact of seeing muscular, tough or athletic women in the action film genre, observing that the image of straining muscles, sweat and physical exertion acts as a visual reminder of the hard work that goes into building such a powerful body, and if that body is female it counteracts the association of muscularity as the exclusive domain of masculinity (Purse, p. 77). Seeing Carano as Mallory perform arm bars, grappling with physically capable men like Aaron, outrunning the police and exchanging blows with men in a believable manner exposes the false equation of men with muscularity, particularly in the action film genre. The spectacle of the female body in *Haywire* is not in its eroticism, but simply a feature of the genre, in the same way as muscled male leads feature as a spectacle of the action genre. Having women occupy the role of action star in the mode of muscularity de-stigmatises gender norms and the binary logic of masculine and feminine.

Mallory and Paul: Asserting Dominance

Midway through the film, there is a hotel fight scene between Mallory and Paul, a former MI-6 agent, now a mercenary, which provides a similar inversion of gender dynamics. Even the beginning of the fight plays with a subversion of gender dynamics, as Paul initiates the fight by hitting Mallory from behind, using deliberately sneaky and deceptive tactics to gain an immediate advantage over a female opponent. During the fight, Paul is consistently on the back foot, using objects from the hotel, pulling out a knife, and eventually resorting to pulling out a gun he had hidden earlier. Although Paul uses a variety of weapons against Mallory's punches and kicks, he still finds himself outmatched by her physical prowess.

The hotel fight scene between Mallory and Paul also inverts the sexualised symbolism of most action films. After Paul is thrown through a door, Mallory calmly saunters in, establishing dominance. Paul begs for his life, taking on a distinctly 'feminine' characteristic – feminine in terms of stereotypical gender norms often found in action films – and reversing the image of the tough male and passive female. Mallory then proceeds to throw Paul onto a bed whereby she engages in a thigh choke hold, with Paul's head squeezed firmly between her legs as she holds onto his head, choking the life out of him. The visual effect is to symbolically infer cunnilingus, except that in this instance it is the woman acting as a 'sexual aggressor'. When Paul is almost dead, Mallory throws him off the bed, being 'done' with him, thereby asserting her sexual and physical dominance.

In *Haywire*, it is the woman in this instance who succeeds and dominates by using raw physicality against the deceptive tactics of an outmatched male fighter. Amy Taubin (2012) comments on this scene, noting that '*Haywire* is more interested in confronting us with the actuality of an adult woman who can use her body in her defence better than any man (or at least any man in this movie)' (Taub, p. 26). While the superior physical display of a female protagonist is a central facet of *Haywire*, it is one that is infrequently explored in other action films, making it an outlier in the action film genre.

Complicating Carano: Later Career and Controversy

Haywire had the potential to propel Carano to greater success, and in some ways her follow-up roles in *Fast and Furious 6*, *Deadpool* (2016) and as Cara Dune in the commercially successful Disney+ series *The Mandalorian* (2019–present) would seem to have cemented her position as a champion of tough female fighters seeking success as an action star. Unfortunately Carano's career in recent years has been defined not by her physical prowess, but by her racist and transphobic views, leading to her being fired from Disney. Carano was warned multiple times to cease and desist from posting incendiary, offensive and indefensible tweets, but refused to acquiesce to Disney. It is an unfortunate incident that damaged the career of one of the few notable female action stars in the genre who had the potential to reverse gender stereotypes about female toughness.

Complicating matters further is that Carano has also now firmly aligned herself with the anti-vaxxer movement in the wake of COVID-19 (among other questionable political views, such as supporting unfounded voter fraud conspiracies which resulted in the violent insurrection on 6 January 2021) through a series of tweets, further limiting her ability to find work as most studios, including her former employer Disney, have vaccine mandates on their productions. Despite this recent sequence of events, nevertheless I would argue that *Haywire* does progress the image of the female fighter on screen and is still important for representation of female action heroes in the mode of Tasker's musculinity, even if Carano's disturbing political views and repeated social media offences have negatively impacted her career.

Carano's recent controversies bring into view the difficulty in considering problematic celebrities, and how to separate the artist from the art. In the specific case of *Haywire* and its relationship to gender dynamics and the concept of musculinity, we can still focus on the onscreen performance and focus on the creative vision of writer/director Steven Soderbergh. Carano was a notable element in the film, but at the time her connection with extremist and transphobic views were unknown and not publicly expressed by the actress at the time, which needs to be taken into context. I would argue that Soderbergh accomplished a significant feat in the portrayal of female musculinity in film with *Haywire*, even if from this point forward Carano can no longer be said to be an avatar for this cinematic progression in gender dynamics.

Conclusion

Haywire is a unique action film for attempting to establish Carano, best known as a professional athlete, as a legitimate action film star. In both the UFC and Hollywood industries, there is a gender imbalance which has presented less-than ideal images of women on screen, even after they have allowed them to participate. For the UFC, this meant that after finally (and reluctantly) allowing a woman's division, female competitors were also presented in a highly sexualised manner as a marketing tool. For Hollywood this has meant that studios tended to promote the 'action babe' approach whereby a supermodel, beauty pageant contestant, or some other professional from the beauty industry, was propped up with a gun and a vague empowerment message as some conciliatory appeal to an increasing female demographic. Neither of these approaches do strong women justice in terms of normalising and de-stigmatising athletic and muscular women.

In contrast to the 'action babe' trope, Tasker identified musculinity as an alternative, which transposed these male-identified attributes onto a tough female action hero who does not necessarily conform to the beauty standards demanded by the 'action babe' trope. The term is a neologism that combines the words masculinity and muscularity, two common features of the heroic male lead in an action film and ascribes them to a powerful female action star who embodies the rugged and aggressive characteristics that are usually connected with masculinity. Musculinity, then, is a symbolic transgression of hardness not usually seen in female protagonists in their typical iconography (which is usually stereotypically feminine, i.e. nurturing, soft, attractive, passive).

Using the espionage thriller *Haywire* with Gina Carano as a case study, the key features that define the concept of musculinity can be more clearly outlined. Reservations about Carano's personal politics aside, this film does accomplish an inversion of gender stereotypes by having the female protagonist be the most physically capable and dominant force in the film against her physically capable male co-stars. As such the film embodies the concept of musculinity and can be considered as an innovator for normalising the idea of strong female warriors. While Carano's career is at a crossroads given her offensive social media posts and damage to Disney, in addition to her anti vaccination rhetoric, the film should not be disregarded because of these recent revelations. At the time of filming *Haywire*, Carano's toxic views were not a factor, and the film should be judged on its own merits. As such I would contend that *Haywire* can be considered as a distinctive example within the action canon for its positive representation of female musculinity.

References

Bolin, A. (1992). Vandalised vanity: Feminnine physiques betrayed and portrayed. In F. E. Mascia-Lees (Ed.), *Tattoo, torture, mutilation and adornment: The denaturalization of the body*. New York, NY: Suny Press.

Darvin, L., & Sagas, M. (2017). Objectification in sport media: Influences on a future woman's sporting event. *International Journal of Sport Communication, 10*, 178–195.
Film at Lincoln Centre. (2012, March 9). Q&A with Steven Soderbergh, Gina Carano, *Haywire*. *YouTube*. Retrieved from https://www.youtube.com/watch?v=yPpgtiDcGaQ&t=258s&ab_channel
Krane, V. (2001). We can be athletic and feminine, but do we want to? Challenging hegemonic masculinity in women's sport. *Quest, 53*(1), 115–138.
Krane, V., Choi, P. Y. L., Baird, S. M., Aimor, C. M., & Kauer, K. J. (2004). Living the paradox: Female athletes negotiate femininity and muscularity. *Sex Roles, 50*($^5/_6$), 315–329.
Navejar, N. (2017). The fight beyond the octagon: Women in the ultimate fighting championship. *Women Leading Change: Case Studies on Women, Gender and Feminism, 2*(1), 45–71.
Oates, J. C. (2006). *On boxing*. New York, NY: Harper Perennial Modern Classics.
O'Day, M. (2004). Beauty in motion: Gender, spectacle and action babe cinema. In Y. Tasker (Ed.), *Action adventure cinema* (pp. 201–218). London: Routledge.
Purse, L. (2011). *Contemporary action cinema*. Edinburgh: Edinburgh UP.
Quinney, A. (2016). The UFC and third wave feminism? Gender, fighters, and framing on Twitter. *Martial Arts Studies, 2*, 34–58.
Tasker, Y. (1993). *Spectacular bodies: Gender, genre and the action cinema*. London: Routledge.
Taubin, A. (2012). The defiant ones: The dauntless women of *Haywire* and *the girl with a dragon tattoo*. *Film Comment, 48*(1), 24–27.
Weaving, C. (2014). Cage fighting like a girl: Exploring gender constructions in the ultimate fighting championship. *Journal of the Philosophy of Sport, 41*(1), 129–142.

Part 2
Transmedia Action

Chapter 4

Gender, Violence and Empowerment: Reworking the Female Action Hero in *Dollhouse*

Jessica Ford

Abstract

Unlike Joss Whedon's cult series *Buffy the Vampire Slayer* (1997–2003), *Angel* (1999–2004) and *Firefly* (2002–2003), *Dollhouse* (2009–2010) is largely considered to be both a critical and commercial failure. *Dollhouse* is often dismissed as Whedon's worst television series, with critics citing their discomfort and disgust in watching hero Echo's (Eliza Dushku) repeated exploitation. Unlike other popular acclaimed TV series featuring a female action hero like *Xena: Warrior Princess* (1995–2001), *Alias* (2002–2006) and *Nikita* (2010–2013), the hero of *Dollhouse* is not empowered from the series' outset, but rather she slowly comes to her power and agency due to various traumatic and violent experiences. This chapter argues that *Dollhouse* stages a reworking of the cinematic female action hero figure by delaying empowerment and forcing the audience to linger in the hero's lack of agency. *Dollhouse* enables an unpacking of the female action hero popularised in films like *Terminator 2: Judgement Day* (1991), *Long Kiss Goodnight* (1996), *The Fifth Element* (1997) and the *Alien* franchise (1979, 1986, 1992, 1997). By exposing the mechanics of hero-creation, *Dollhouse* forces viewers to consider how heroes are made and who is exploited in the process. As such, this chapter considers *Dollhouse* as an intervention into the female action hero film and television cycle through an analysis of how the series adheres to and subverts the tropes of the cycle.

Keywords: Empowerment; women; violence; trauma; genre; agency

Unlike Joss Whedon's cult TV series *Buffy the Vampire Slayer* (1997–2003), *Angel* (1999–2004) and *Firefly* (2002–2003), *Dollhouse* (2009–2010) is largely considered to be both a critical and commercial failure. Despite its relatively short run, two seasons of 13 episodes each, *Dollhouse* has received considerable scholarly attention and critical engagement (Espenson, 2010; Ginn, Buckman, & Porter, 2014; Porter & Starr, 2021). At the same time, *Dollhouse* is often dismissed as Whedon's worst television series, with critics citing their discomfort and disgust in watching the 'hero' Echo's (Eliza Dushku) repeated exploitation (Bernardin, 2009; Nguyen, 2009; Press, 2009). This makes *Dollhouse* a particularly rich text for exploring the norms and structures of the action genre and how it constructs heroes through violence and trauma. As Catherine Coker writes, '*Dollhouse* is very different from Whedon's prior works: it's darker, more serious, less fantastical...the only superpowers the Dolls have, are quite literally, their brains. When Echo is struck and bloodied, she is not going to heal rapidly, and she may or may not be programmed with fighting skills' (2010, p. 227). This distinction frames my analysis of the *Dollhouse* and how I situate its 'hero' Echo in relation to her filmic and televisual predecessors.

Dollhouse centres on the titular fictional shady organisation that uses 'mind wiping' technology to imprint 'dolls' with complete personalities and skillsets. The Dollhouse serves an exclusive clientele who, for a large sum of money, hire 'dolls' who have been imprinted with their desired personality, skills and temperament. The Dollhouse trades in a kind of science-fiction inflected sex work, whereby the workers are 'erased' at the end of each engagement and return to a child-like 'doll-state' to await their next outing. Owing to its high-concept premise, *Dollhouse* is inherently about bodily constructions of gender, violence and empowerment. As Kate Rennebohm highlights, '[b]y addressing the body in ways that have been largely untouched in Whedon's previous shows, *Dollhouse* alters and expands the conception of identity found in the Whedonverse' (2010, p. 6). While I am less concerned about the place of *Dollhouse* in the Whedonverse than Rennebohm, I am interested in how Whedon has been central to the construction of the female action hero on contemporary TV. As Holly Randell-Moon asserts, 'Whedon's work is characterised by an engagement with the links between representation, identity, and embodiment' (2012, p. 265).

Dollhouse focuses on Echo, who unbeknownst to the Dollhouse can retain imprint information after she has been 'wiped'. Throughout the series' two seasons, Echo repeatedly goes beyond the parameters of her imprints, slowly transforming into an action hero, because with each imprint and engagement she gains more skills, power and capacity. Unlike other popular acclaimed series like *Xena: Warrior Princess* (1995–2001), *Buffy* and *Alias* (2001–2006), the 'hero' of *Dollhouse* is not empowered from the series' outset, but rather the series depicts the slow process of her becoming a hero. For the majority of *Dollhouse*'s first season, Echo is weak and vulnerable with no stable identity, cause or mission. As such, *Dollhouse* is very different from most female-centric action films and TV shows like *Terminator 2: Judgement Day* (1991), *Long Kiss Goodnight* (1996), *Alias, Nikita* (2010–2013) and *Terminator: The Sarah Conner Chronicles* (2008–2009), which depict their hero as physically empowered and dedicated to her mission from early on. In most action films and TV series, the audience is positioned to identify with a hero who is capable, self-sufficient, strong and devoted to seeing through her mission. However, *Dollhouse* forgoes this structure; instead Echo's journey of empowerment is prolonged because for most of the first season she is powerless with no stable personality. While Echo has some identifiable moments of heroism in the first season, she does not consistently perform the role of the female action hero until halfway through the second season.

This chapter argues that by delaying empowerment and forcing the audience to linger in the hero's lack of agency, *Dollhouse* offers a reworking of the female action hero figure and questions the trauma and violence required to create a female action hero. By exposing the structures of hero creation, *Dollhouse* examines how heroes are made and who is exploited in the process. This chapter suggests *Dollhouse* is an intervention into the forms of empowerment that dominate female action hero films *Terminator 2: Judgement Day, Long Kiss Goodnight, The Fifth Element* (1997) and the *Alien* franchise (1979, 1986, 1992, 1997) and similar TV series like *Xena, Buffy Alias, Nikita* and *Terminator: The Sarah Conner Chronicles* (henceforth *Terminator: TSCC*). Through a close analysis of *Dollhouse*, I will unpack how the series adheres to and subverts the tropes of the female action cycle, but first I will outline how the female action hero has been theorised and conceptualised in screen studies scholarship.

Making a Hero: Final Girls, Warrior Women and Avenging Angels

Dollhouse centres on female action hero Echo, who begins the series relatively helpless, but obtains power and agency through violence and trauma. Echo's characterisation is informed by and indebted to a long history of action, horror and science-fiction films and TV shows which centre on kick-ass female heroes who protect others and save the day. Like other action films and TV with a female-lead, *Dollhouse* employs sleek, modern sci-fi costuming and sets alongside futuristic technology and familiar contemporary weaponry and fighting styles. The female action hero is a popular figure who moves across film and TV genres, appearing in horror, action, spy thrillers, superhero blockbusters and science-fiction. She is defined by her take-charge attitude, physical strength, capacity for violence and employment of bodily forms of empowerment. She is most often thin, white, heterosexual, and conventionally attractive, but with a masculine energy that Yvonne Tasker calls 'butch femme' (1998, p. 68). She is dedicated to her mission, which often takes the form of revenge, rescue or protecting her loved ones and/or the world.

Broadly speaking, the female action hero participates in activities and performs roles that have been typically reserved for men. Many different types of characters come under the umbrella of 'female action hero', including the final girl (Clover, 1992), warrior woman (Early & Kennedy, 2003; Heinecken, 2003), working girls (Tasker, 1998) and tough women (Inness, 2004). As Laleen Jayamanne writes: 'I prefer to use the phrase *female hero* because the structural connotations of the term *heroine* make the woman named by it a figure in need of rescue, while agency is synonymous with the hero function' (2001, p. 281, emphasis in original). Although the female action hero takes different forms depending on genre conventions, they are united in how they conflate physical strength, violence and power with empowerment and agency. The female action hero relies on a bodily construction of power and agency often born out of violence and trauma. She must be victimised, exploited and/or traumatised to occupy the position of 'hero'. *Dollhouse* highlights the extent to which contemporary filmic and televisual constructions of heroism rely on victimisation. To 'become' the hero, the character must first endure hardship or 'baptism by fire'; while this is similar for some male action heroes, many are just powerful without the need for victimisation or trauma. Ellen Ripley (Sigourney Weaver) of the *Alien* franchise is arguably the first mainstream female action hero in Hollywood cinema (Brown, 1996; Hills, 1999). Over the course of the *Alien* films, Ripley is transformed from an innocent victim forced by circumstance to fight the monster in *Alien* to the reluctant hero who chooses to fight for herself and her surrogate child in *Aliens*. Then in *Alien 3*, she is literally and metaphorically stripped of her womanhood before she sacrifices herself to stop the monster. Finally in *Alien Resurrection*, her transformation is completed when she is resurrected as a clone and the monster's mother, further linking her journey to empowerment and sense of agency to the existence of the monster.

Ripley has also been characterised as what Carol J. Clover (1992) famously called the 'final girl'. Clover coined 'final girl' to describe a common character type 'who encounters the mutilated bodies of her friends and perceives the full extent of the preceding horror and of her own peril; who is chased, cornered, wounded; whom we see scream, stagger, fall, rise and scream again' (1992, p. 40). The final girl is masculine in appearance, can castrate the monster and has an acute awareness of the impending horror about to befall her. She is a solitary figure who is 'different' from those around her. The final girl is important for both the female action hero and Whedon's film and TV work, as *Buffy the Vampire Slayer* has been widely read as a subversion of the final girl (Battis, 2005, p. 69; McCracken, 2007; Middleton, 2007, p. 161; Ono, 2000, pp. 19, 177). Clover's analysis of the final girl's experience is similar to that of the female action hero: she is hunted, pursued and forced to fight back. Many female characters on contemporary US TV are highly indebted to the final girl, including Starbuck (Katee Sackhoff) in *Battlestar Galactica* (2004–2009), Sookie Stackhouse (Anna Paquin) in *True Blood* (2008–2014), Sarah Connor (Lena Headey) in *Terminator: TSCC*, Daenerys Targaryen (Emilia Clarke) in *Game of Thrones* (2011–2019) and, of course, Buffy.

Buffy (Sarah Michelle Gellar), Xena (Lucy Lawless) and the other TV female action heroes of the 1990s are a pivotal intervention into depictions of female heroes on television. These characters signify a shift away from the 'soft' heroes of *Wonder Woman* (1975–1979) and *Charlie's Angels* (1976–1981) towards a contemporary understanding of female power that focuses on physical and mental strength being asserted in traditionally male public spaces (Heinecken, 2003, pp. 1–2). According to Sherrie A. Inness, 'toughness' is communicated through the body in two primary ways: a fit, athletic body which is raised to a mythic level and costuming and style that suggests masculinity (2004, p. 25) and a tough attitude that can be seen in how the character displays little to no fear and is in control even under the most threatening circumstances (Inness, 2004, p. 25). Action can be recognised in how the tough woman acts in ways that few (if any) real women could and in doing so she creates a 'power fantasy' that does not reflect reality, which is identical to how the male action hero performs his power (Inness, 2004, p. 26). However, this toughness is often predicated on, or a response to violence, abuse or trauma. In both *T2: Judgement Day* and *Long Kiss Goodnight*, heroes Sarah Conner (Linda Hamilton) and Charly (Geena Davis), respectively, transform themselves into tough action heroes when their children's lives are threatened.

The relationship between masculine power structures and women's empowerment in the action genre is well theorised by feminist film and television scholars. As Sue Thornham writes: '[t]he female action hero in film has been viewed with ambivalence at best' (2012, p. 12). Furthermore, for Lisa Coulthard, 'the violent woman of contemporary popular action cinema does not upset but endorses the status quo' (2007, p. 173). As feminist film and television scholars argue, female action heroes are continually contained by the infrastructure of male power. Mary Magoulick highlights how female heroes are 'conceived of and written mostly by men in a still male-dominated world', and as such, they 'present male fantasies and project the status quo more than they fulfill feminist hopes' (2006, p. 729). Magoulick contends that female action hero-centric TV shows like *Xena*, *Buffy*, *La Femme Nikita* (1997–2001) and *Alias* 'did not make the women any less sexualised, nor did they conceive freshly of the very notion of heroes drawn as women' (2006, p. 731). The contours of masculine power – violence, trauma, toughness – are embedded in the female action hero character because 'the valorisation of masculinity' underpins current constructions and depictions of female heroism in action films (Constable, 2005, p. 190).

The umbrella term 'female action hero' describes the role and function of Echo and other characters like her. She is almost always a white, physically fit and attractive female in her late-teens or early twenties with long hair who is deceptively strong. Tasker's masculinity is not prominent in television heroes; however, Inness's attributes of 'toughness' are present, especially in her intelligence, attitude and emotional strength. Like Clover's 'final girl', she is a lone figure, who is hyperaware of the horror that is to come, even when those around her remain ignorant and thus she bears the burden of that knowledge. She has been forced or coerced by an omnipresent institution to fight for them or against them and therefore she is a hero of circumstance, rarely of personal choice. In the next section, I will examine *Dollhouse* in terms of how it locates itself in relation to other female action hero–centric films and TV shows and how it operates as intervention into the norms and values of the popular figure.

Dollhouse: Building a Hero, One Imprint at a Time

By 2009, there was a robust tradition of female action heroes on TV and in film. The territory that *Dollhouse* operates in is no longer male dominated, as it was for

Ellen Ripley, Sarah Connor or Nikita (Peta Wilson). Bronwen Calvert argues that in *Dollhouse*, 'the notion of the "natural" body is complicated and becomes overlaid with the concept of performance or masquerade' (Calvert, 2010, para. 17). I argue that *Dollhouse* is best understood as a deconstruction of the kinds of violent, bodily empowerment that films and TV shows that feature female action heroes rely on. As a straightforward female action hero narrative, *Dollhouse* fails because it extends and protracts the 'becoming' phase, delaying the cathartic experience of seeing the hero 'kick ass'. Yet the series is still very much in conversation with other female action hero films and TV shows, as I will outline, because *Dollhouse* offers a meditation on the role and repercussions of violent bodily empowerment through intermittent glimpses of action, intertextual references and the prolonged period of hero-construction.

Echo is positioned in relation to the history of female action heroes on screen in both the marketing materials and the text itself. For example, in season two when Echo is prepped for the spinal fluid extraction that will be used to form an antidote to the memory wipes, she is naked except for white bandages wrapped around her body like a bikini. The costuming is reminiscent of *The Fifth Element*, as she is restrained and subjected to needles in her spine. Furthermore, the marketing and promotion of *Dollhouse* foregrounds the idea of Echo as an action hero, as Catherine Coker highlights, '[g]iven the early critiques of *Dollhouse* by both critiques and viewers, most of which concentrated on the repugnance they felt for human trafficking and body exploitation on the show, the FOX network's advertisements were bewildering' (2010, p. 235). The season one FOX trailer features Echo bursting through doors, wielding guns, engaging in hand-to-hand combat and riding motorcycles with her hair blowing in the wind. FOX's promotional images feature Dushku in black leather pants and a tank top looking directly at the camera. Dushku is positioned at the centre of the frame in an assertive stance, at times pointing a gun, mirroring the promotional imagery for *La Femme Nikita, Alias, Terminator: TSCC* and *Nikita*, which employed similar costuming, stance and weaponry. Costuming also foregrounds the connection between *Dollhouse* and *Buffy*, as Dushku's *Buffy* character vampire slayer Faith was similarly dressed in black figure-hugging outfits.

Throughout the early episodes of *Dollhouse*, we get glimpses Echo's capacity to be the kind of female action hero promised in the promotional materials. In the second episode, Echo is imprinted as Jenny, an outdoor adventurer and romantic partner who is hunted by her date and Dollhouse client Richard (Matt Keeslar). Echo articulates the paradox that violence is required to depict the action genre, saying, 'You know what gives someone the right to live? Not hunting them' ('The Target' 1.02). In other words, violence begets violence. Echo's body language and costuming transforms her from victim to action hero. Earlier in the episode, she is hunched over and scuttling about the cabin desperately seeking help. She seems fragile and exhausted. In contrast, when Echo confronts Richard at the end of the episode, she is standing tall, having removed the white long-sleeve top, now wearing a red tank top drenched with sweat. Echo conforms to the 'butch-femme' aesthetic that Tasker identifies as typical of the female action hero figure. The primary factor that instigates this change is that she is given a gun by her

Gender, Violence and Empowerment 53

Dollhouse 'handler' Boyd (Harry Lennix). It is her newfound ability to inflict violence, to fight back, that propels the character from victim to hero. She is 'given' the gun, and with it the power to fight back, from Boyd, a representative of the institution responsible for her oppression. This is a similar image to that of the female action heroes of *Long Kiss Goodnight* or *Terminator 2*, who were each empowered by their victimisation and access to weapons. It is the gifting of the gun and the assertion that she is and will be perpetually hunted which forms the foundations for Echo to exceed the parameters of her imprint and assume the position of hero.

In *Dollhouse*, hero creation is made explicit and integrated into the narrative. The series is premised on using technology to imprint and wipe dolls; however, this is subverted by Echo's ability to exceed the parameters of her imprints and hold multiple imprints at a time. As Holly Randall-Moon writes, '*Dollhouse* complicates both the notion of the body as a "blank slate" onto which identity is written as well as the idea that identity creation is limitless' (2012, p. 270). It is the science-fiction conceit that the dolls can be rendered 'blank slates' and subsequently programmed to fulfill the client's desires that highlight the cycle of victimisation required to create a female action hero. Both in *Dollhouse* and other series that deploy a female action hero like *Buffy, Alias, La Femme Nikita* and remake *Nikita*, victimisation and heroism have a causal cyclical relationship whereby they inform and compound one another. What differentiates *Dollhouse* from these other series is how both Echo's victimisation and empowerment are prolonged. While the other female action heroes like Buffy, Xena and Nikita (Maggie Q) begin their respected series with enhanced physical skills, Echo begins as a vulnerable 'blank slate' ripe for victimisation and empowerment. Echo becomes a female action hero out of necessity. As Sherry Ginn writes, '[o]ne could argue that the entire series is predicated upon the abuse of women' (2012, p. 58). Without being hunted, there is no need to fight back and within the action genre, power is the ability to fight back; therefore, it is the repeated act of being victimised that creates the impetus and capacity for the character's heroism.

There are various glimpses at Echo's potential heroism in season one, such as in the sixth episode, when she confronts FBI Agent Paul Ballard (Tahmoh Penikett), who is investigating the existence of the Dollhouse. The first time Agent Ballard sees Echo is in the reflection of a glass panel on a swinging door, the image is there for a moment and then gone, much like the imprints. Ballard goes into the kitchen looking for her and what proceeds is the first real action-hero sequence of the series that is stylised, filmed and choreographed for maximum spectacle. At the end of season one, Echo is kidnapped by rogue doll Alpha (Alan Tudyk) and is victimised into empowerment. Alpha himself is a victim of a 'composite event' and as such is determined to imprint all of Echo's previous personalities onto her at the same time, to create himself a friend, an equal. It is in this act that Echo, the female action hero of *Dollhouse*, is created. After Echo is imprinted with all her earlier personas, she bounds out of the chair and stands tall, powerfully glaring down at Alpha. The low camera angle enhances her aura of power as she says, 'I get, yep…now I get it' ('Omega' 1.12). She takes a large metal pipe and hits Alpha across the head and says, 'I understand everything'

('Omega' 1.12). Echo is what the Dollhouse made her; she is all of them and none of them at the same time. While the imprints and their personalities are supposed to die at the end of the engagement, within Echo they continue to live on. Echo's capacity to hold the various fractured personalities allows her to become an action hero. While Echo's biological ability to retain imprint information and exceed the parameters of her imprints sets the conditions for her hero-status, it is Alpha's violation that expedites her so-called empowerment.

When Echo returns to the Dollhouse in the second season, she is processing her trauma, as well as the Dollhouse and Alpha's violation of her mind and body. As she takes ownership of the many identities imprinted onto her, she now has a mission: destroy the Dollhouse. The revenge narrative is a staple in series that feature a female action hero. In *Alias*, Sydney Bristow (Jennifer Garner) makes it her mission to take down SD-6 after she learns they are not part of the CIA. In the rebooted *Nikita*, Nikita escapes the rogue government organisation Division and then plots her revenge against them for enslaving her. This popular trope can also be seen to a lesser extent in *Buffy*, in Buffy's rejection of the Watchers' Council and the Shadow Men who created the first slayer by infusing the soul of a demon into a captive young girl. Like her predecessors, Echo returns to the Dollhouse with the intention of breaking it from the inside. *Dollhouse* goes further than these other series, as it not only dismantles the 'evil institutions' that create female action heroes, but also the genre conventions that perpetuate the cycle of violence that enables empowerment. Towards the end of season two is the pre-destined showdown between the heroic figure and the woman who claims to have 'created her'. The spectacular image of two women acting violently towards one another is sanctioned by the genre conventions and the assumption that violence is inevitable. Directly challenging this narrative, speaking to her former captor and head of the Dollhouse Adelle DeWitt (Olivia Williams), Echo says: 'So now you're trying to take credit for making me. You didn't make me. I made me. You may think all these people knocking around in my head are useless, but that's 40 more brains than you have. So, I think we can agree that I'm smarter, tougher and a whole lot scarier than you could ever hope to be' ('Stop-Loss' 2.09).

Echo begins to resemble the female action hero promised by the series' promotional material and genre by the middle of the second season. By the seventh episode of season two, Echo has left the Dollhouse and has learnt to access her various imprints, using her skills to rescue a falsely imprisoned young immigrant. Not only has Echo been developing her access to the different imprints but she is also training her body to be a fighter, a warrior woman. She trains, sparring with Ballard. This is shot in close-up, with an aural emphasis on their heavy breathing and the intensity of their movements. Echo is not one or the other but an amalgam of the imprints and the layers of illusion and experience that has been constructed around her. As Echo gets mental control of the imprints and the subsequent physical powers, she is again reduced to her bodily existence. While Ballard wants to 'save' Caroline (Echo's original personality), she wants to save herself, Echo. Yet, as Ginn writes, 'Even Ballard abuses Echo when it suits his agenda, thereby suggesting that violence against women is sometimes necessary, especially when it serves the perceived greater good' (2012, p. 59). Once she assumes the role of female action hero consistently, the trauma and violence of her creation is foregrounded and not erased.

Despite evolving mentally beyond the confines of doll-state, Echo's power is linked to her physical body, multiple imprints and the physical, mental and emotional trauma she has endured. While the other dolls are attached to their original identities, Echo becomes their saviour because she is not limited by the idea of Caroline, despite it being Caroline's particular biological makeup that allows her to retain multiple imprints. Both seasons of *Dollhouse* finish with an episode set in 2019 (10 years ahead of the present timeline) in an apocalyptic future where the imprinting technology has been used on much of the human population. The Dollhouse has been transformed from a prison to sanctuary for those hoping to evade the mind wiping technology that has been weaponised globally. Due to her ability to resist wipes and hold multiple imprints, Echo is an anomaly and folk-hero. In the 2019 world, most of the world's population has been 'wiped' due to a mass phone call that erased everyone who answered it. Echo, along with former Dollhouse dolls, employees and Ballard, work to reverse the damage that 'the tech' has done to the population. It is in this future world that Echo is the most evolved version of the female action hero, who asserts her agency and determines her own path. Yet, the Echo presented in this future timeline is the product of the near-constant trauma and violation of being printed with personalities, wiped and re-printed. Ultimately to protect who she has become, Echo must isolate from the rest of the world. *Dollhouse* ends with Echo alone in her sleeping pod with her many imprints and a new one – Ballard.

Conclusion

Throughout the series, *Dollhouse* both offers commentary on the process of hero creation and highlights the violence and trauma it requires. Perhaps *Dollhouse* is best understood as what Jason Jacobs calls 'body trauma TV', which refers to medical dramas which specularise and fetishise the violent acts leading towards physical injury or death (2003, pp. 1–2). From the earliest episodes when Echo is hunted by a Dollhouse client for sport, she offers a seething critique on the violence-empowerment cycle of saying: 'You know what gives someone the right to live? Not hunting them' ('The Target' 1.02). When she is imprinted with various personalities by Alpha, Echo proclaims: 'Don't hand me any more of your crap about you being some superior ascended being. To ascend to anything, at minimum, you don't cut up women'. ('Omega' 1.12). Ultimately Echo's journey to become a hero, to save the world, is in service of the people around her and not a quest for agency. Even though she evolves beyond the doll-state intended to confine her, Echo is a female action hero of necessity. She fulfills the role of hero within the series because the world and narrative demands it.

Dollhouse raises questions about the nature of empowerment offered by the female action hero and genres that rely on bodily physical constructions of power. Like Echo, *Dollhouse* is an anomaly and an outlier. There have been female action heroes in film and TV before and after the series, but there have been few as complex, difficult and deconstructed as Echo. While *Dollhouse* did not resonate with audiences, it continues to intrigue critics, because of how it recalibrates female action hero norms and unpacks structures of empowerment. The tropes of the female action hero are evident in Echo, she is victimised and forced to fight for her existence, she is 'created' by forces and people beyond her control, she is 'tough' in both physicality and attitude. Yet she must, not only metaphorically, but also literally, leave behind her original self and subject herself to repeated trauma as to access the position of female action hero.

References

Battis, J. (2005). *Blood relations: Chosen families in Buffy the vampire slayer and Angel.* Jefferson, NC: McFarland.
Bernardin, M. (2009, November 11). 'Dollhouse' canceled: Are we peeved or pleased by this development? *Entertainment Weekly.* Retrieved from http://popwatch.ew.com/2009/11/11/dollhouse-canceled-are-we-peeved-or-pleased-by-this-development/
Brown, J. A. (1996). Gender and the action heroine: Hardbodies and the "point of no return". *Cinema Journal, 35*(3), 52–71.
Calvert, B. (2010). Mind, body, imprint: Cyberpunk echoes in the dollhouse. *Slayage: The Journal of Whedon Studies, 8*(2–3).
Clover, C. J. (1992). *Men, women, and chain saws: Gender in the modern horror film.* Princeton, NJ: Princeton University Press.
Coker, C. (2010). Exploitation of bodies and minds in season one of Dollhouse. In E. B. Waggoner (Ed.), *Sexual rhetoric in the works of Joss Whedon: New essays* (pp. 226–238). Jefferson, NC: McFarland.
Constable, C. (2005). *Thinking in images: Film theory, feminist philosophy and Marlene Dietrich.* London: Bloomsbury Publishing.
Coulthard, L. (2007). Killing bill: Rethinking feminism and film violence. In Y. Tasker & D. Negra (Eds.), *Interrogating postfeminism: Gender and the politics of popular culture* (pp. 153–175). Durham, NC: Duke University Press.
Early, F., & Kennedy, K. (Eds.). (2003). *Athena's daughters: Television's new women warriors.* Syracuse, NY: Syracuse University Press.
Espenson, J. (Ed.). (2010). *Inside Joss' Dollhouse.* Dallas, TX: BenBella Books.
Ginn, S. (2012). *Power and control in the television worlds of Joss Whedon.* Jefferson, NC: McFarland.
Ginn, S., Buckman, A. R., & Porter, H. M. (Eds.). (2014). *Joss Whedon's Dollhouse: Confounding purpose, confusing identity.* Lanham, MD: Rowman & Littlefield.
Heinecken, D. M. (2003). *The women warriors of television: A feminist cultural analysis of the new female body in popular media.* New York, NY: Peter Lang.
Hills, E. (1999). From 'figurative males' to action heroines: Further thoughts on active women in the cinema. *Screen, 40*(1), 38–50.
Inness, S. (2004). *Action chicks: New images of tough women in popular culture.* London: Springer.
Jacobs, J. (2003). *Body trauma TV: The new hospital dramas.* London: British Film Institute.
Jayamanne, L. (2001). *Toward cinema and its double: Cross-cultural mimesis.* Bloomington, IN: Indiana University Press.

Magoulick, M. (2006). Frustrating female heroism: Mixed messages in Xena, Nikita, and Buffy. *Journal of Popular Culture*, *39*(5), 729–755.

McCracken, A. (2007). At stake: Angel's body, fantasy masculinity, and queer desire in teen television. In E. Levine & L. Parks (Eds.), *Undead TV: Essays on Buffy the vampire slayer* (pp. 116–144). Durham, NC: Duke University Press.

Middleton, J. (2007). Buffy as femme fatale: The cult heroine and the male spectator. In E. Levine & L. Parks (Eds.), *Undead TV: Essays on Buffy the vampire slayer* (pp. 145–167). Durham, NC: Duke University Press.

Nguyen, H. (2009, November 11). 'Dollhouse': Why we're happy it got canceled (other than the obvious). *Zap2It*. Retrieved from http://blog.zap2it.com/frominsidethebox/2009/11/dollhouse-why-were-happy-it-got-canceled-other-than-the-obvious.html

Ono, K. A. (2000). To Be a vampire on bufiy the vampire slayer. In E. R. Helford (Ed.), *Fantasy girls: Gender in the new universe of science fiction and fantasy television* (pp. 163–186). Lanham, MD: Rowman & Littlefield.

Porter, H. M., & Starr, M. (Eds.). (2021). *Re-entering the Dollhouse: Essays on the Joss Whedon series*. Jefferson, NC: McFarland.

Press, J. (2009, October 26). Dollhouse: Many unhappy returns. *Vulture*. Retrieved from https://www.vulture.com/2009/10/dollhouse_many_unhappy_returns.html

Randell-Moon, H. (2012). "I'm Nobody" the somatechnical construction of bodies and identity in Joss Whedon's Dollhouse. *Feminist Media Studies*, *12*(2), 265–280.

Rennebohm, K. (2010). The mind doesn't matter, it's the body we want. In J. Espenson (Ed.), *Inside Joss' Dollhouse: From Alpha to Rossum* (pp. 5–20). Dallas, TX: BenBella Books.

Tasker, Y. (1998). *Working girls: Gender and sexuality in popular cinema*. London: Routledge.

Thornham, S. (2012). *What if I had been the hero?: Investigating women's cinema*. London: Bloomsbury Publishing.

Chapter 5

All Access Action Heroes – Between Cyberpathy and New Media

Anne Ganzert

Abstract

A young man plucks information from digital data streams; a woman leaves digital clues about herself online – no screen, keyboard, or cable in sight. Characters found in TV series like *Alphas* and *Heroes* offer only two examples for a (fairly) new superpower that has been added to the catalogue of abilities for action heroes: that is, they have the power to manipulate digital information, and hacking into systems without using any kind of device.

This chapter analyses which visual mechanisms are used to convey these 'new (media) superpowers' by focusing primarily on *Alphas* and *Heroes* and considers them important predecessors for filmic examples. Such analysis will examine ideas about their transmedia extension as well as real-life developments in the field, such as specific hand movements that remind the viewer of the 'Apple Swipe' or social media trends. Combining theoretic approaches of cultural, television and media studies, this chapter discusses the 'wireless' connection between the new (super)heroes, their televised abilities, and the (online) audience, which also allows for a projection of (possible) future developments.

Keywords: Heroes/heroines; new media; technology; internet/wireless; aesthetics; media studies

Our heroine makes her way through a maze of CCTV cameras, traffic lights and locked doors while her colleague is in a nearby inconspicuous van feeding her the necessary information and keycodes she needs to open doors or manipulates a surveillance feed for her safe passage through the villain's lair. Scenes like this, even if entirely hypothetical are familiar, and can be found in almost any show or movie that includes a team of investigators, criminals, activists, spies or agents.

Yet in recent years there have also been moments in the movie and television landscape that are different, or at least moving away from that often overused corps of some characters being 'in action' (for example, Tom Cruise's Ethan Hunt in the *Mission: Impossible M:I* films) and others being the infrastructural, tech-savvy, supportive sidekick (like Ving Rhames' Luther Stickell in the *M:I* franchise). For example, rather than seeing an agent tapping into some online data plans for a hidden laboratory in Eastern Europe, an alternative has appeared. This usually occurs like this: when we see a young man almost plucking information from digital data streams seemingly out of thin air, or when a woman leaves digital clues about herself online – but there is no screen, keyboard, or cable connection in sight. This ability to influence wireless data and access invisible networks is called 'cyberpathy'. It is a contemporary addition to action and superhero movie character traits that warrants academic attention as it is both a reflection of current media developments as well as a stylistic expansion in the movie industry's repertoire. 'Cyber' here stands for anything that involves computers and networks, and cyberpathy is described as the ability to manipulate them without physical touch or interaction. Sometimes the term 'technokinesis' is synonymously used, which is a variant of technopathy, both describing the more general power to control machines that has been a longer standing trope in comic books, games, films and TV shows. Recent publications about the superhero genre tend to focus on aspects of representation, genre developments and social implications (Brown, 2017; Hatfield, Heer, & Worcester, 2013; Rosenberg & Coogan, 2013) – with cyberpathy only being a small part of the discourse even though variants of it appear in almost all current films and shows in the genre.

Interestingly, psychology uses technopathy to describe a condition of distancing from human affect as technopathy that only retains the passion for technology and aims to eliminate all other aspects (Masullo, 2019). It is understood as an effect of technological progress and focuses on the consequences for/of the human condition – a reflection carried out in many films, too. Any cyborg storyline carries this aspect, and many a movie villain was created by an unfortunate accident with technology: for example, Psi in *Doctor Who* (also see further). Sometimes this is how a heroic character gains their superpowers, too: here one thinks of Tom (Bill Milner), the protagonist in the movie *iBoy* (2017) who becomes a cyberpath after shrapnel from an iPhone is lodged into his brain. First, he can see and hear signals and telecommunications but later he learns how to telepathically hack into networks, in order to operate cars or make them explode. Throughout the movie familiar filmic devices overlay with his ability: anytime Tom texts someone the message shows up like a pop-up text for the viewers – but as he indeed has the ability to see electrical signals this can be considered a Point-Of-View (POV) effect. This cyberpathic POV increases throughout the film. With Tom's increased control over his power, his view becomes a data-informed overlay over the film's images. For *iBoy*, the aesthetics that already have the characteristic for cyberpathy in film and TV are specifically present and observable.

The TV series *Alphas* and *Heroes* with their characters Gary Bell (Ryan Cartright) and Hana Gitleman (Stana Katic) were produced before *iBoy* and offer valuable insights into the development of this (fairly) new superpower of cyberpathy. Because of their formative status for the trope, they are the focus of this chapter. Both *Heroes* (Kring, 2006–2010) and *Alphas* (Prenn & Kranow, 2011–2012) told the interwoven stories of people who received special, superhuman abilities either from a brain anomaly or genetic mutations. While the team of *Heroes* slowly came together to avoid different catastrophic scenarios, the protagonists on *Alphas* are a team that fights other 'Alphas' who have become criminal superhumans. While the former is an expansive transmedia construction with cross overs to games, graphic novels, mini-series etc. (Ganzert, 2015), the latter show is part of the same fictional universe as the (more successful) Sci-fi series *Eureka* (2006–2012) and *Warehouse 13* (2009–2014).

Because cyberpathy is a mix between hacking and technopathy, and because it is less hardware-based – in fact both main examples of this chapter don't need any hardware to access data – and it is inherently globalised, fictional characters such as Tom, Gary and Hana can virtually 'travel' anywhere, to any folder, information, or local network – provided it has a technological framework at its core. That framework does not have to be a supercomputer, but something that has technology 'behind' it. And this works best in a narrative situated in times of the World Wide Web and even the so-called Internet of Things, a fact very comprehensively reflected in the 2005 Disney production, *Sky High*. In this instance, student Gwen Grayson (Mary Elizabeth Winstead) has the ability to control technology with her mind. Gwen was born as Sue Tenny – two decades earlier – but with the same skill set. The film shows through a series of flashbacks that she was called 'weird', 'mad scientist' and 'geek' by other students in the 1980s, with her power being both misunderstood and considered useless at the time. So much so, that the high school, which is only for superhumanly gifted students, gives her the official classification as a 'sidekick'. Fuelled by her fury about this, Sue becomes a villain, but at 17 the infantilising weapon she has developed accidently turns herself into a baby. She is then adopted, renamed as Gwen, and years later returns to Sky High and enrols as a student. While somewhat chaotic, it is most important to notice, that after the turn of the millennium, in a more computer-driven society, her power is considered extremely valuable and makes her the 'popular girl' in school. Gwen's storyline emphasises part of this article's argument: that this branch of superpowers is something distinctly contemporary and tied to media developments of the last two decades.

The central hypothesis of this chapter is that what used to be merely a technological infrastructure is now a source of action, a weapon, a battlefield, both an ally and enemy all rolled into one. The all-encompassing access to data streams is weaponised and, as seen during *iBoy, Alphas* and *Heroes* has transfused with the heroes' bodies, becoming part of their superpower, identity, DNA, and their skills. Their strength lies within the bandwidth and the data available to them, as these media conditions are their weapons and ammunition, as well as their protection. But these scenes of action are virtual and/or digital – and therefore must be made visible to the audience. Like a well-choreographed fight scene, a cyberpathic attack needs an aesthetic, a look, and a sound. In television shows, movies and games, as in our everyday experience, the invisible infrastructures that surround us become most obvious in glitches or disruptions, yet for cyberpathy not only do the disruptive effects need to be visualised but the skill needs to be seen when it is working as intended, too. The visibility of the cyberpaths' actions is essential, whereby the aesthetisation of the invisible becomes a feat of computer-generated special effects illustrating the powers at work. The interest of this chapter is thus twofold: to explore the televised modes of presentation for these (action) heroes' skills and to reflect upon their significance in the ever-evolving landscape of popular narratives.

Cyberpathy in Action

Depending on their realisation and specific setting, Cyberpaths could also be called 'new media superheroes', 'streaming superheroes' or 'all access action heroes'. But the term 'new media' is both blurry and outdated at the time of this chapter being written. Nonetheless it is important to write it at precisely this moment. This is because the cyberpathic aesthetics and skill sets found in existing examples have already undergone one major development – from touch-based technopathy to wireless cyberpathy – and it is only a matter of time until future characters appear with skills that are updated to then-contemporary technologies and beyond.

Without delving into historic specifics of the trope, variations of this have been around for decades. Cyborg heroes, heroines and villains are often technologically enhanced humans with implanted technology that makes them faster, smarter, or more lethal. Such examples include the original Cybermen in *Doctor Who* (BBC, 1963), whilst the hive-mind collective Borg in *Star Trek: The Next Generation* became the cinematic villains of *Star Trek: First Contact* (1996). Even characters such as Marvel's Iron Man, Nova and the cybernetically enhanced human/mutant Cable have some elements of these traits, even though here it is usually part of other powers such as general telekenisis that is paired with more 'actionable' character traits as being able to use martial arts or fire rockets in their general arsenal of talents. Nonetheless, all of these characters communicate with technology, and '[t]his is usually accomplished by psionically "reading" the computer's electronic impulses or converting their own thoughts into electronic signals which they mentally transmit into the computer'. According to Marvel's Fandom database (marvel.fandom.com), Technokinetics can also fight with the advantage of enhanced or even 'smart' armoury or weaponry. Here one thinks of *Iron Man*'s suit, as well as the fact that Tony Stark became a technopath in 'the Extremis process' that merged him with the Iron Man armour, which in turn became a much lighter design with more range (Ellis/Granov 2013). They can also have night vision or superhuman sensory skills and lend them to their collaborators as Chris Bradley in *X-Men Origins: Wolverine* does to fight the evil Deadpool. They can be the antagonist or antithesis to nature-based characters, who draw their strength from the elements and conjure nature's physical forces. In this case, cyberpaths represent technological progress (for better or worse). This may be one of the reasons why they are sometimes displayed as having a lack of emotional or social capability (see further) – due to their partial machine-like status.

In his book *The Contemporary Superhero*, Terence McSweeney (2020) elaborated on the relations between media representation regarding ethnicity, gender, sexuality and cultural and global contexts in superhero films of the recent years (namely *Superman, Batman, Wonder Women, The Incredibles, Hancock* and *Black Panther*). And while there has been progress in the genre in general, there is still ways to go. Yet, it is noteworthy that the 'new media superpowers' this chapter discusses seem to be less gender-biased than other powers or action skills in past iterations. They are also furthering the ongoing emancipation of the classic hacker trope, where recent years have brought more female characters to the screens (from film characters like the *Matrix*'s Trinity, to Kate in *Hackers*, Lisbeth the *Girl with the Dragon Tattoo*, to TV series' roles such as Penelope in *Criminal Minds*, Felicity in *Arrow* or *NICS*'s resident 'super nerd', Abby). In the action film *Furious 7* a WoC hacker's identity was revealed to the protagonist team and caused some confusion with one character asking Ramsey (Nathalie Emmanuel): 'You're the hacker? That's not what a hacker is supposed to look like.' This is followed by the more poignant question of: 'Well then what is a hacker supposed to look like?'

Cyberpaths elevate these issues around representation and technical skills to a superhuman level. As the ability to access data streams is not tied to preconceived ideas of physical strength and thus does not play into misogynist concepts of masculinity or femininity, cyberpathy is attributed to characters of any gender. Both Western comic giants like DC or Marvel as well as the vast world of Anime have also increasingly diversified their casts. Nonetheless, Superheroines rarely can evade male commentary about their unexpected toughness, or destruction (Maslon & Kantor, 2013, p. 258). Sage/Tessa, who is a 'living computer' in Marvel's *X-Men* comics, and *The Gifted* TV series is a strong example for this, being very much a male-gaze comic book fantasy figure in black latex. The younger iteration is a lot less sexualised – but noticeably less powerful. Nonetheless, technology-savvy characters are still often seen as distinctly non-athletic, and most significantly, socially awkward. Whether 'super' or human, they often fulfil clichés such as the pale night owl, nerds with glasses and hoodies, or introverted tinkerers who are 'famous for denying their bodies sleep, at least for short periods' (Coleman, 2013, p. 13). The cyberpaths also tend to be portrayed as somehow impaired or at least overwhelmed by the data they can access – and it comes as no surprise there are articles that discuss Gary Bell's *Alphas* representation as being on the autistic spectrum (Deamer, Lieu & Lonsdale, 2014; Walker, 2017). The show directly links the superhuman skill to brain anomalies, which in Gary's case might also link to his autism. It might also be that he would have been on the autism spectrum without his abilities, but it will become clear why it makes sense from a narrative standpoint that they are connected. In the *Heroes* graphic novel Hana Gitleman says: 'All the emails, text messages, and satellite transmissions float invisibly around the world. I don't know how it was possible, but I could see, read, sense every one of them. Every FYI memo. Every sappy, "I love you." text. Cans and cans of email spam.' (Hana, *Heroes*, Wireless,

Part 2) She herself quite fittingly calls it spam – and has a strong physical reaction towards it. Both Gary and Hana learn to deal with their powers eventually, and even though Hana received this skill as an adult and did not grow up to learn how to use the power or navigate and structure data, she seems to have fewer problems with it. As a parallel to our everyday world, 'Digital Natives' navigate the information technologies and 'new media' more effortlessly – and fittingly, the *TV tropes* database states that in fictional worlds with a large variety of superpowers such as *Heroes*, technopathy is often ascribed to children or youth, 'as a magical metaphor for the way that people who grew up around technology are generally more comfortable with it.' It is usually either that or the debilitating amount of information has a direct effect on the person's wellbeing. Sometimes this means that the cyberpathic character needs a sidekick themselves to manage their live or assignments – just like the non-tech hero often needs their hacker support as mentioned previously. For example, in *Scorpion* (Santora, 2014–2018) we find many instances where the genius protagonist is basically a savant who needs a 'world manager' to interact with clients and others. In *Alphas*, Gary has both his mother's active support and Dr Rosen who leads the team but who himself is not a superhuman, just like Nick Fury is not technically an *Avenger* in the Marvel Universe. The 'handler' figures for the enhanced-yet-helpless cyberpath often navigate their efforts or give them tasks. Gary is quite comfortable with this role as the team's oddball character, whilst in *Heroes* Hana actively runs from malignant powers who want to control and (ab)use her and her power, leaving her handler behind and feeling betrayed and hunted. Being highly sought after seems to be the logical consequence of the cyberpaths' power: If they have access to any data, could hack into any system or attack any technological item or system, then a 'villain' who recruited them would have a weapon of mass destruction at their mercy. Because – strictly speaking – the 'all access' cyberpaths are meta-heroes, they could also trigger weapon-systems or override electronic defence mechanisms. Some villains, for example, in *Ghost in the Machine*, present a fatal and entirely digital threat. Here we find another parallel to hacker figures, described by Steinmetz as follows: 'Believed to have incredible powers of technological manipulation, hackers are seen [in pop culture] as contemporary equivalents to trickster figures of the past, such as Loki in Nordic mythology or the Greek Dolos.' (2016, p. 7) Additionally, even though less divine yet powerful, the 'internet of things' gives them access to anything from fridges, microphones and household devices but also to city infrastructures and space programs to mess with. This also means they need to be recruited for a purpose, no matter if 'good' or 'bad', and their all-access skills need to be controlled. A closely connected example, even though strictly speaking not a cyberpath, would be Sky/Daisy/Quake in *Agents of S.H.I.E.L.D.* (2013–2020), who is a hacker genius and later evolves to an 'inhuman' able to influence the frequency and vibration of the world around her. She too finds herself being coaxed in different directions due to her special skill set and she wants to find out more about her past. So does Hana Gitleman who is researching the ominous 'company' that trained her under false pretences. Interestingly, players of the *Heroes* ARG were invited to join her in her quest: following her digital traces, they found data on various online platforms and homepages, often being directly addressed as internet users who are potentially hackable themselves. While the *Heroes 360 Experience* will not be explored further at this point, it is noteworthy that similar 'games with data' have become a contemporary pastime (for example, the cicada 3,310 puzzles) and are a reality of the current (social) media landscape. Prominent examples are campaigns by Google and the German Intelligence Agency, the BND, who have employed comparable tactics to recruit skilled IT personal and hackers with the 'Google foobar challenge' and the 'Follow the White Rabbit' (2021) campaigns. In these cases, like in the *Heroes* ARG, users were invited to investigate and follow hints throughout the web and beyond – almost becoming gamified cyberpaths in real life. Without further elaborating on these campaigns, what was futuristic or superhuman a decade ago now hardly qualifies as such, which may be why more recent iterations have gone back to portraying human hackers (for example *Mr. Robot* (2015–2019)) and why examples like *YOU* (Netflix 2018) emphasise that similar actions are now entirely mundane and potentially dangerous.

At the time of writing this chapter, *Alphas* does not, it would seem to appear, have a particular interest to scholarly circles. The show is listed in some encyclopedic lists such as 'Weird Detectives' (Green, 2019; Romanko, 2019) and even then mostly as reflections on the depiction of people on the autistic spectrum. As Walker (2017) writes, 'Set in a fictional world where people possess unique powers that alienate them from society (in the same vein as the X-Men) a professor leads a special team to investigate incidents and crimes involving the titular Alphas'. He then continues to find that, 'On the professor's team is Gary, played by Ryan Cartwright, a young man with high-functioning autism who has the Alpha ability to see and manipulate electromagnetic signals like a living computer'. What stands out here is the interesting order of character descriptors. The show calls Gary's ability 'transduction' and his social skills are a constant issue (even though not played for laughs as hard as they are, for example, famously with Sheldon Cooper in *The Big Bang Theory* (Lorre & Prady, 2007–2019). Ben Saunders made the argument that even early technopathic narratives emphasised the heroes' techno-dependency as having a downside: 'technology [is] desired as a source of power, but feared and resented, as the cause of a crippling dependency for those who rely upon it.' (2011, p. 110) For Iron Man this lies in the chest plate's tendency to malfunction in Saunder's analysis; for Gary this means that his brain needs to be able to process the received data, rendering him a savant with an isolated talent and a plethora of issues.

Generally speaking, such perceived weaknesses seem necessary to soften the all-encompassing power of cyberpaths. A new media cyberpath without limiting factors would, quite frankly, be a boring hero or villain for that matter, so that they need to be either hunted like Hana or literally disabled like Gary. Additionally, Gary's ability can be hindered by heavily encrypted signals, as he stated in episode 'The Unusual Suspects'. This was exemplified in the earlier episode 'Rosetta' when Gary trustingly explains how his power works to the non-speaking Anna Levy. After it turns out that Anna is the leader of a terrorist organisation, she uses this information to incapacitate Gary with a DDoS attack on a signal he was focusing on at the time. There are also smaller restrictions to his skill, such as not being able to receive Nokia signals (apparently these run on a different platform) but besides this, he can receive any and all signals on electromagnetic wavelengths, such as cellphone signals, television broadcasts, and Wi-Fi frequencies. On the flipside to this, his autism is depicted as a protection against other powers. For example, when the mental pushes of Nina Theroux don't work on Gary. An Alpha herself, usually, Nina can influence anyone to do or say she wants. But because her ability works much like hypnosis and depends heavily on direct eye contact, Gary's social dyslexia protects him from being influenced by her. Similarly, Eric Letrobe cannot read Gary's micro expressions or body language because he moves so erratically, protecting Gary's thoughts form Eric's mindreading abilities.

For cyberpathy to be of a narratological use it can thus be presented as a dangerous meta-power, a driving force for action to unfold, a frightening Damocles sword that is either used for good or potentially weaponised. New media contexts such as mobile data, the internet and social media networks enhance these traits even further, giving cyberpaths access to the most private and public spaces alike and emphasising how most areas of our lives are tightly interwoven with wireless technology.

Showing/Seeing the Wireless Action

Aside from the storytelling aspects explained earlier, a central question becomes apparent: how these powers come to live on screen, and how the cognitive processes are translated into visible action. Depending on such things as the decade and production budget, characters mentally receiving or transmitting data is sometimes shown just by their eyes glazing over and them telling others what they are doing – this resembles messenger or herald speech which first found credence in Greek drama. These made it possible to present events at locations different from where the chorus happened to be or re-enact: wars, crimes, miracles, all of which were not really feasible to act or stage in the theatre – in short, there were methods to present that which cannot be shown or realised due to then-technical limitations. Similarly, showing supernatural or alien skills often needed to be circumvented, either by dialogue or by only showing their effects. As cyberpathy and similar abilities have been present in comic books, anime and graphic novels, which of course don't have the same restrictions of what can be visualised, their creative visualisations have paved the way for their filmic and televised counterparts. For Hana, the *Heroes* creators have used a mix of different approaches (affected and effects). The visual and aesthetic elements that show Gary's ability are contingent on being part of digitally enhanced moving images, as they use fluent hand movements, CGI animation and sound to get his action across.

The example of Hana Gitleman's first appearance in *Heroes* can elaborate on this (see also Ganzert, 2015). In the opening scenes of Season 1, Episode 16 the audience sees a very agitated and, unfortunately, nuclear-charged man named Ted Sprague (Matthew John Armstrong) hiding in a wooden hut 'somewhere in the Nevada dessert'. Out of the blue he gets contacted via a chat message and gets even more confused when he notices that his internet connection is down. Closeups make sure that the viewers understand the apparent issue and the effects of some power at play. His screen also reveals the information that his chat partner is called 'Wireless' who then proceeds to show him schematics of a needle gun that matches the shape of a scar Ted and many of the *Heroes* characters have on their necks. Wanting to know more he asks 'Wireless' to meet him. Almost instantly after that a woman in a leather jacket enters his hideaway, introducing herself as Hana Gitelman and that she has the ability to mentally receive and give out digital information without an internet connection – hence 'Wireless'. She also displays the scar on her neck that matches his, before asking Ted to help her destroy the people who did this to them: 'I can find them, Ted. You can nuke them'.

Ted and the TV audience can gather from this 'call to action' that she has a specific goal, but neither have a real indication as to why she is so dead set on destroying 'the company'. Hana becomes a transmedia guide for viewers – who are also online media users – in *Heroes*' elaborate transmedia universe (Ganzert, 2015). In an additional graphic novel, published online before this scene aired, viewsers could read that Hana is a transmedia superhero and one who can tap into any wireless device through her altered brain waves. Engaged viewers could have downloaded four short graphic novel issues solely on Hana's background story in the Mossad and on the run after her abilities emerged and she became 'wireless'. Interestingly the drawn representation of her skill's first manifestation is similar to the computer-animated version we encounter with Gary in *Alphas*.

This moment in her origin story receives a whole page in the graphic novel and means to illustrate the intense information overload that rushes into her consciousness, causing her visible distress and pain. So much so, that her handler Noah Bennett decides to knock her out with a punch. When she wakes up in her bed a little later her powers have manifested, and she is able to answer Noah's question via a wirelessly sent text message – and she is ready for her first mission. In this mission in Tanzania, she encounters some boundaries of her skill – in the form of a rifle – causing her to say: 'My ability is more suited for the urban jungle than this one. Getting passwords. Stealing data. That sort of thing.' ('Wireless Part 3', p. 4) In the novel's third part she also recalls a scenario in which she was deprived of any accessible device – her satellite phone gone and the laptop shut down – which feels somewhat implausible: Hana's ability is not device-based, and if her satellite phone had worked at that location before, there has to be a satellite phone network that she would be able to tap. It can therefore be argued that the graphic novels show her being affected by the data, or lack thereof, whilst the TV series mostly shows her effect on user interfaces.

To allow the viewers to get a glimpse into Gary's worldview, the TV series shows interfaces like circles or bubbles in Gary's eyeline, which he reads like a screen and interacts with like a touch screen interface. The latter is a slightly contradicting choice, or one clearly 'made for TV', as a primarily mental ability like technopathy tends not to depend on physical movement. But these movements and his action(s) are an essential part of the production design's staging, making his subjective worldview a shared screen experience. Reinerth and Thon summarise this aspect as follows: '*Alphas* [...] makes a point of audio-visually providing "direct access" to the particular ways in which its "superhuman" protagonists perceive the world. During its first episode (S01E01, "Pilot"), the show already offers fairly spectacular – or at least very clearly marked – subjective representations of Gary Bell's ability to "see" all sorts of wireless communication (which includes the ability to compute large amounts of data and focus on specific strands of it; [...])' (Reinerth & Thon, 2017, p. 7) What Gary sees are waves of bright colours (mostly light blue) that surround him. Bubbles or circles appear that contain video footage or images, and these are accompanied by random numbers and code. The camera is often positioned vis-à-vis from him allowing the viewers to see his face and gestures when he accesses the data. When he has found the item he is looking for, the camera perspective jumps to an over-the-shoulder-shot and the viewers can share his POV on the files presented to him. But even then, the camera is slightly moved to the side, so that the hand movements remain visible as Gary's gestures are the sole notable action in the shot. The character's press photos also showed him mid movement using his right hand in thin air looking at something off camera, or in a pinching gesture indicating a zoom – the tiniest, almost intimate movements convey his actions that can have huge effects and consequences for both him and those around him. This is established in the series' pilot episode, when he is shown sitting at his mother's kitchen table sifting through the data supporting one hand with the other while navigating. This approach continued throughout the entire show. It becomes especially noticeable when Gary is under stress or pressure and his movements become faster and more energised.

Hana on the other side is not shown using her hands to navigate the data and we also do not see schematic blurry data streams in front of her. Instead, we mostly get to see the effect of her powers on other people's interfaces when documents are opened, or search words appear in the search bar without anyone typing. This is also very useful, as Hana made information appear on the viewers' devices in the matching ARG for the original show. Hana was the player's main contact, who sent them emails and text messages that led to hidden functions on websites or that let them witness a chat between her and child superhero Micah Sanders (see further). Hana, or 'Wireless', 'is less a character moving through the *Heroes* universe as she is a facilitator of the causal interactions that take place in the ARG'. As Ruppel (2012, pp. 303–309) states, Hana is a character that was 'unique in that she was introduced and developed entirely as a cross-sited character, one whose exploits are charted across the Web, SMS messages, email and graphic novels, occasionally appearing in the television show as well'. Hana therefore becomes a character that could be accessed at multiple sites on various platforms, following *Heroes* fragmented narration principle (Ganzert, 2021), which ensured that the audience was enticed to collect data fragments of Hana and her information as if they were practising cyberpathy as well. The focus on the interface, rather than code, is a main difference between hackers and cyberpathy's presentation in film and TV. In a media context of multiple screens, the audience can easily understand the sensory effect this skill has and the different levels of communication and data can be comprehensively visualised in a cyberpathic aesthetic scheme.

In *iBoy* we can see an amalgamation of the aesthetic choices described here, most of the digital processes happen internally without physical movement or mostly eye movement. Yet for dramatic effect Tom can use his hands when his power becomes a weapon, 'shooting' data force at an opponent's leg, for example. His cyberpathic POV is similarly to Gary's view of light-blue, blurry lights indicating fast movement of information and wireless connections of devices and users. Like Aiden Pearce, the main avatar in Ubisoft's *WATCH_DOGS*, the viewer is included into Tom's technologically advanced view at the world. The game may have also served as an aesthetic predecessor for *iBoy*, as in both instances virtual connections that the protagonist focusses on light up or turn yellow for the audience to focus upon, too. When the camera doesn't take Tom's POV, it shows his data access similar to Gary's as a curved overhead projection, and it mostly stays on the interface level.

This may be another reason why this power's aesthetic is very close to the audience's everyday experience, too, when touch screen gestures are used to navigate through the streams of data by Gary, or when characters move their heads as if wearing VCR head gear while sifting through the data they receive. They are also extremely comparable to scenarios in which these actions are carried out by not-super heroes, hackers, agents and such like. Advanced technology is a hallmark of popular characters everywhere from a spy's equipment to any space-based narrative – the important common theme is that all media are subject to ageing. The once avant-garde technology of early James Bond movies seems charmingly retro today and the technology influenced by Hana clearly uses the aesthetics of the Web 1.0 and not-yet-smart phones. Gary's cyberpathy has held up a little better since 2011 – the five-year difference between the two shows clearly makes a difference. The fact that the first iPhone was released by Apple in 2007 suggests that the developments are directly reflected in the 'new media superheroes' and their actions, gestures and data representation. Finger movements such as 'swiping' or 'zoom pinching' on smartphone touchscreens are a great example for this. They have enabled uses to experience changes in the way that media are used, up to the point that they are now seemingly entirely normal in today's world. They also allow deductions regarding our relationship with new media devices, as, for example, Mowlabocus writes that the use of the smartphone and especially '[t]he mastery of the swipe… is our adult selves attempting to momentarily wrestle control back from a system that we barely understand; a system many of us feel disempowered by, in spite of being told that we are masters of our destiny' (Mowlabocus, 2016, pp. 16–17). Technology and data by far exceed our understanding of this new media approach and by quite literally 'handling' the interface the users enact a degree of control or infrastructure management. The fictional users of large data streams then also enact control through these gestures, be it in science fiction formats on big screens like in *Minority Report* (Spielberg, 2002) or in the superhuman cyberpathic instances as they are discussed here. When Gary is shifting his attention somewhere else in the data, he is often seen to make said familiar gestures that 'new media' has introduced to the audience's experience.

New? Media? Superpowers?

As mentioned earlier in this chapter, the use of the term 'new media' may be irritating, partly because in the so-called 'internet of things', (almost) all items are connected to the internet and thus become hackable. Therefore, technokinetic characters who can influence machines are a close relative to the 'new media superheroes', or rather, the *wireless* heroes that take over their domain as the devices go online. It is therefore also interesting that *Heroes* displays a media historic development with one of its characters. Early in the series Micah Sanders is a school kid with classic technopathy. He is initially portrayed as being able to 'talk to the machines' – but only when he touches them. In season 3, he can do it with merely his hand hovering close to the target technology, possibly because he has grown up and further honed his skill. He also carried a PDA (a 'Personal Digital Assistant' – the early 2000's version of a smartphone) that he was able to use to control security cameras, sprinklers and computer systems by only touching it, creating a machine–human hybrid device as part of his actions. Had *Heroes* been produced only a few years later we can assume many of Micah's abilities would have been reminiscent of the smartphone technology that started with the iPhones launch in 2007. In fact, five years later in the series' reprise, *Heroes Reborn* (Kring, 2015), a teenage-Micah returns as a hooded figure who calls himself the 'Hero Truther' – a figure similar to 'Eyes Only' in *Alias* (Abrams, 2001–2006) or 'GabeH.Coud' in *Homeland* (2011–2020) – and his abilities have in fact developed parallel to digital developments and media inventions of the time.

There has been a sort of a trend showing those who wield the power to control the data streams as either heroes or villains, but clearly not regular people or 'just' the tech-support sidekick. What the characters do online (for the sake of brevity and clarity, this chapter would call them 'interventions') is often also related to acts of cyber activism that many viewers have either partaken in or at least know of. Cyberpath-activism can be considered another sub-trope in this development, making it a sight for much different action than that of Gary or Hana. Micah uses his abilities to mobilise a resistant movement and call protesters to action – the fact that he can address any user on any device with his message is his strength. Again, this is a clearly marked technological advancement that enters into the fictional design of these characters. For example, 'Eyes Only' used classic TV broadcast disruption to spread his content – so this reflects the next shift from mass media to personal devices.

All Access Action

The characters described in this chapter are therefore both supernaturally skilled and close to the audience, making them distinctly different from the specialist hacker type who is an expert known to talk a lingo only few understand. These 'back-end' characters still exist of course, yet the user-based superpowers dealing with surfaces, content and messages mostly are those who are the elevated version of an audience's everyday experience. And even though they are still far and few between, this strengthens the argument that cyberpathic action or superheroes are symptomatic of our time, overwhelming amounts of data and all. The German research group on 'TV series as reflection and projection of change' focused on TV series' capability to reflect change in media and vice versa provoke such change themselves. As they suggest, 'In the course of digital media change, the contemporary television series is becoming more and more a transmedia phenomenon exceeding the limits of its own media. Series detach from the televisual flow, move to other media platforms and enrich their narratives through inter- and transmedia extensions and additions.' This key observation can be transferred to our cyberkinetic action heroes as well. And the same is reciprocally true. The cyberpaths' abilities are transmedia as they both work across platforms and devices and develop over multiple iterations and realisations. They integrate everyday technology, software and user gestures on an enhanced level stressing their importance and ongoing development.

The new media superheroes are therefore self-reflective of the media in which they appear, or rather of the transmedia landscape both in fictional storytelling and new, personal and social, media. Superhero franchises are prone to be extended across media and even across diegeses. The cyberpaths are all access action heroes, who can be anyone from an awkward young man to an agent from a strong line of female fighters – while '[t]he typical image of the hacker is [still]an electronic thief curled over a computer double-fisting cans of Mountain Dew, stealing credit card numbers, and, if many portrayals are to be believed, wearing a ski mask in the privacy of their own home' (Steinmetz, 2016, p. 3). The Cyberpaths are often portrayed as struggling with the amount of data that almost attacks them (at least temporarily), yet realistically both Gary and Hana don't even have contact with a fraction of the wireless data that would surround them when the shows aired and even more so today. This chapter's examples from 2005 to 2011 can be considered historical status-quos of the then 'new media', not Sci-Fi's projections of a technological future to come but state of the art. They are important pieces in building the trope as it, for example, presented itself in *iBoy*, and it will be very telling when new heroes of the cyberpathic kind appear, allowing us to reflect on recent developments in the media landscape and using what is so common to us for their more or less heroic purposes. And of course, what kind of actions they will cause or prevent, carry out, or use to fight or struggle with remains tantalisingly out of reach as this chapter comes to print.

References

Abrams, J. J. (2001–2006). Alias. USA: ABC.
Brown, J. A. (2017). *The modern superhero in film and television: Popular genre and American culture*. New York, NY: Taylor & Francis.
Coleman, E. G. (2013). *Coding freedom: The ethics and aesthetics of hacking*. Princeton, NJ: Princeton University Press.

Deamer, K. A., Lieu, E., & Lonsdale, L. (2014, May 30). Superhuman alphas: Heightened senses. *Journal of Interdisciplinary Science Topics*, *2*, 5–8.
Ganzert, A. (2015). 'We welcome you to your heroes community. Remember, everything is connected'. A case study in transmedia storytelling. IMAGE, media convergence and transmedial worlds (Part 2).
Ganzert, A. (2021). Das fragment als serielles Prinzip in heroes. In V. Cuntz-Leng, V. Fröhlich, & S. G. Einwächter (Eds.), *Serienfragmente*. Wiesbaden: Springer.
Green, P. (2019). *Encyclopaedia of weird detectives: Supernatural and paranormal elements in novels, pulps, comics, film, television, games and other media*. McFarland.
Kring, T. (2006). *"Heroes"*. New York: NBC.
Kring, T. (2015). *"Heroes reborn"*. New York: NBC.
Lorre, C., & Prady, B. (2007). *"The big bang theory"*. New York: CBS.
Hatfield, C., Heer, J., & Worcester, K. (Eds.). (2013). *The superhero reader*. Jackson, MS: University Press of Mississippi.
Maslon, L., & Kantor, M. (2013). *Superheroes!: Capes, cowls, and the creation of comic book culture*. New York, NY: Crown/Archetype.
Masullo, P. A. (2019). Anthropogenesis and technopathy. *Thaumàzein | Rivista Di Filosofia*, *7*, 77–107. doi:10.13136/thau.v7i0.103
McSweeney, T. (2020). *The contemporary superhero film*. Columbia University Press.
Mowlabocus, S. (2016). The 'mastery' of the swipe: Smartphones, transitional objects and interstitial time. *First Monday*. doi:10.5210/fm.v21i10.6950
Penn, Z., & Kranow, M. (2011–2012). *"Alphas"* New York: Syfy.
Reinerth, M. S., & Thon, J.-T. (Eds.). (2017). *Subjectivity across Media: Interdisciplinary and Transmedial Perspectives*. New York: Routledge.
Romanko, K. A. (2019). *Women of science fiction and fantasy television: An encyclopedia of 400 characters and 200 shows, 1950–2016*. Jefferson, NC: McFarland.
Rosenberg, R. S., & Coogan, P. M. (2013). *What is a superhero?* New York, NY: Oxford University Press.
Saunders, B. (2011). *Do the gods wear capes?: Spirituality, fantasy, and superheroes*. London: A&C Black.
Spielberg, S. (2002). *Minority Report*. Los Angeles: 20th Century Fox.
Steinmetz, K. F. (2016). *Hacked. A radical approach to hacker culture and crime*. New York, NY: NYU Press.
Walker, C. D. (2017, August 16). Autism on television done right. Retrieved from https://medium.com/@CDWalker/autism-on-television-done-right-1eebab3bd4bd. Accessed on February 8, 2021.

Chapter 6

Hard Bodies in Virtual Worlds: Assessing the Reception of Abby's Spectacular Body in *The Last of Us Part II* (Naughty Dog, 2020)

Dean Bowman

Abstract

Games are rapidly becoming a site where cultural ideas are explored and consumed and have recently become an arena for debate around representations of gender. This chapter draws attention to key debates occurring in the field of video games that are also applicable to film studies. This interdisciplinary approach demonstrates the relevance to game studies of a rich vein of scholarship on the gendered action body in film studies. Drawing on research by Yvonne Tasker (1993, 2015), Lisa Purse (2011) and Jeffrey Brown (2011), this chapter seeks to unpick the tensions around gender and violence in the reception of *The Last of Us Part II* (Naughty Dog, 2020), particularly regarding the surprisingly vehement backlash against the unconventionally muscular deuteragonist Abby.

This chapter asks what happens when the 'spectacular' and 'hard' bodies of the action heroine enter the soft virtual world of the video game. A focus on whether Abby's body is realistic in the reception of the game leads to a discussion of the ontological status of games as a virtual medium. I argue that the process of motion capture and the real-world reference of CrossFit athlete Colleen Fotsch trouble the conventional dichotomy that understands the medium of games as virtual and film as indexical. Throughout, I use the more ambiguous and ambivalent historical reception of the body of Lara Croft as a useful point of contrast. I argue that the obsessive, hysterical response to Abby's muscular body is indicative of larger tensions between conservative 'hardcore' fandoms and the industry's recent drive for progressive change. By denying Abby's authenticity such players also deny female access to traditional masculine pursuits and identities, whether that be bodybuilding or gaming. This is because virtual female action stars, just as much as their real-world counterparts such as Linda Hamilton, trouble the gendered norms that underpin both second-wave feminist accounts of muscular women and the audience of hardcore video game players. As Fron, Fullerton, Morie, and Pearce (2007) critique in their article 'The Hegemony of Play', a double standard therefore exists in which such women must justify the reality of their musculature through a kind of 'proof of process'. Ultimately, I conclude that a similar demand is made of the emergent female audience of gamers, who are continuously made to justify their right to play in a traditionally male space.

Keywords: Hegemony of play; *The Last of Us Part II*; hardcore gamers; hardbodies; motion capture; Lara Croft

This is a chapter on an action-adventure video game in a book about action cinema and, I hope, by the end of this piece I will have demonstrated the validity of such an inclusion. Certainly, Alexander Galloway's (2006, p. 3) assertion that action is the defining characteristic of games as a medium demonstrates that they provide an apt point of comparison. Galloway contends that not only does action occur in video games at an often unrelenting pace, as players run, jump, and shoot their way through hostile environments, much like the typical action cinema hero that Yvonne Tasker (1993) explored in her book *Spectacular Bodies*, but that the quality of the action itself is usually under the control of the player. Indeed, for Tasker a key concern of action cinema is much the same as many video games: 'the movement of the body through space' (2015, p. 5). Games have, since Tasker's book, evolved into perhaps the most important visual media of the current world system, a point supported by Galloway who argues that games act as 'an allegory for the algorithmic structure of today's informatic culture,' and considered as such, can help us to 'render social realities into playable form' (2006, p. 17). Indeed, by doing so they create a space for reflection on the very realities they simulate. Similarly, Casey O'Donnell has eloquently made the case for considering the close links between games and culture:

> Games, play, and culture are enmeshed and entwined in ways that intimately implicate one another. Games produce culture. They reflect it back. They shift it. Mainstream games in particular contribute to and reinforce hegemonic cultural projects.
> (O'Donnell, 2014, p. 407)

However, though it is clear that mainstream games reflect the cultures that produce them, it does not follow that they only 'reinforce hegemonic' cultural values. *The Last of Us Part II* (Naughty Dog, 2020) is as 'mainstream' as a game can be given its role as a prestige first-party release by a major platform holder, Sony, backed by a colossal marketing push. In spite of this, it is my belief that *TLOU2* (as it shall be written henceforth) is deeply embedded in emergent counter-cultural, anti-hegemonic positions, especially regarding gender and violence (two topics addressed by this book). There are many aspects of *TLOU2* that would serve such an argument – for instance, the central character, Ellie, is queer and Lev is a young trans man struggling against dogmatism, which makes the game an important text amidst growing interest in the field for queer theory (Ruberg & Shaw, 2017). However, in this piece I want to analyse the unconventionally muscular deuteragonist Abby, who has produced a surprisingly vehement backlash in the hardcore player base.

This chapter attempts to demonstrate that in the paradoxical claims from a subset of gamers that this is the worst story ever written (Dr Uckmann, 2020) and the game's many plaudits, (including being nominated for a record number of 13 game BAFTAs), there is clearly some other motivation at play in the fandom's negative response and much of this is centred on Abby and her body. Indeed, the obsessive, hysterical response to Abby's body, of which the various comments in this Twitter thread is indicative (Dr Uckmann, 2020), speaks to larger tensions between conservative 'hardcore' fandoms and the industry's recent drive for progressive change, overlapping with similar events that have been playing out in action cinema and its scholarship. One intervention this chapter makes is to bring film and game studies further into conversation, since I attest that work by Yvonne Tasker (1993, 2015), Lisa Purse (2011) and Jeffrey Brown (2011) can help unpick the tensions around gender in the reception of this game. Focusing on arguments around the gendered action body, this chapter then asks what happens when the 'spectacular' and 'hard' bodies of the action heroine enter the virtual world of the video game?

The Murder of Joel Miller and the Symbolic Death of the Male Gamer

The Last of Us Part II is the long-awaited sequel to the beloved and critically acclaimed *The Last of Us* (Naughty Dog, 2013), which saw gruff middle-aged smuggler Joel Miller reluctantly act as guardian to the smart-Alec teenager Ellie on a journey across post-apocalyptic America to a group of survivors known as the Fireflies. Ellie was deemed exceptional due to her immunity to a zombie-like plague caused by a mutation of the parasitic *Cordyceps* fungus crossing into human populations, and the intention of the Fireflies was to manufacture a cure from her. Over the course of this long journey, Joel and the player controlling him build a considerable bond with Ellie who becomes a surrogate for Joel's daughter who tragically dies in the game's opening scenes. Joel cannot accept that Ellie will be killed in the process of making a cure and, in direct violation of Ellie's wishes, kills the surgeons about to operate on her, and with them the last hopes for a cure for humanity, and escapes with her unconscious body. The finale sees Joel swear to Ellie that the doctors merely sent her home, thus establishing their ongoing relationship on the foundations of a profound lie, undercutting the ostensible optimism of the ending.

Fast forward five years and Joel and Ellie are happily living in the town of Jackson, a peaceful walled community with the feel of a romanticised frontier township and have just about started to mend the aforementioned breach of trust. The further adventures of Joel and Ellie that some gamers hoped for was not to be, since the sequel significantly begins with the outrageously violent murder of Joel at the hands of a small group led by Abby Anderson, the daughter of the surgeon killed by Joel, an event that becomes the primal scene for the gritty and sophisticated study of the futility of revenge that the game becomes. Backlash against *TLOU2*, largely related to Joel's murder, included boycotts, review-bombing and regular death threats to seemingly anyone who touched the game during production or tried to defend it post launch (Glennon, 2020 catalogues some of these). Self-professed fans of the first game set up a petition on *Change.org* that gathered 55,236 signatures angrily bemoaning how the developers 'forced us to use the character that killed off Joel' (Miller, 2020), in reference to Abby. Demonstrating a sense of entitlement common amongst extreme fandoms, the petition had the hubris to call for a complete rewrite claiming:

> ...this was a massive disrespect for every fan of The Last of us [*sic*] franchise that had to wait an entire 7 years for the sequel. We deserve better than this, we paid 60$ and we are entitled to make a change.
>
> (Miller, 2020)

Such is the level of identification between hardcore fans and Joel that the petition's initiator appropriated his identity as a pseudonym, making it seem like Joel himself was railing against the injustice of his death from beyond the grave. Fan outrage is bound up in the perception that Neil Druckmann, the creative director and writer of *TLOU2* as well as vice president of developer Naughty Dog, is a mere 'social justice warrior' (an internet pejorative deployed by those on the alt-right to dismiss the efforts of those speaking out for marginalised identities). Druckmann, himself Jewish (an identity he explores with tremendous insight and subtlety through Dina's character in *TLOU2*), has become a high-profile champion of diversity in the games industry in the years following *The Last of Us* and has publicly proclaimed a desire to represent and normalise different kinds of characters in his games (Makuch, 2012).

The player is certainly not supposed to be happy about Joel's death; indeed, time spent with him through the first game means that the player feels the loss deeply, alongside Ellie. Joel's actions at the end of the first game, outlined earlier, can be read allegorically as a commentary on entitled male heroism, in which the hero always 'gets the girl'. This trope is dominant in most action films and video games; only here it is spectacularly subverted so that the macho hero isn't saving the damsel from unambiguous evil, but selfishly dooming the world to protect his own desires and values. When Joel carries Ellie's body from the hospital, he effectively effaces her decision, stripping away her agency even as the scene renders her body a passive burden to be carried to safety. As the player we are made complicit in that action, whether we agree with it or not, because unlike

Hard Bodies in Virtual Worlds 77

many games which sport alternate endings to cater to a range of player desires, *The Last of Us* forces Joel's decision on us just as much as it does Ellie. With these events in mind, we might read the motivating force behind the petition to change *TLOU2* as an attempt to rescue Joel from Neil Druckmann's narrative scalpel just as Joel once 'rescued' Ellie from the surgeon. Rather than seeing Joel's actions as morally ambivalent at best, selfish at worst, this fan reaction casts them as heroic within the bounds of a patriarchal ideal, in which the vulnerable female body should be protected by male strength, and male decisions are assumed to trump those of the female. Gamers behind the petition ultimately ignored the game's subtle critique of the very patriarchal impulses that drove their own actions in making it.

In another move that angered fans, Joel is also used at the beginning of *TLOU2* to motivate the female character's vengeance in a way that gender flips the trope of 'fridging' (the practice, first discussed in relation to comic books but a familiar trope in all media, of killing a female character to motivate the male hero's quest for revenge). Here, it is the Abby's brutal murder of Joel that motivates Ellie's quest for revenge. This kind of motivation is what Purse (2011) refers to as a 'trigger', an event that justifies and explains the honing of the action body and that 'often takes the form of a physical or psychological trauma' (2011, p. 33). The image of Joel lying dead on the floor, deployed frequently by detractors on social media as shorthand for a moral injustice, is also a trigger motivating the fan reaction outside the game. This means that the game already contains an implicit critique of the petition as a poorly considered response to the event of Joel's death, just as much as Ellie's quest for vengeance is morally condemned in the game's narrative logic. Joel's death at the hands of Abby is not only an important continuation of the narrative trajectory of the first game but also a highly symbolic act of dethroning the male protagonist as the normative vehicle for the player's entry into the game world because Joel's death clears the way for us to play as not one, but two strong and resourceful female characters.

The clever narrative conceit of *TLOU2* is that we first see the events of the game through the eyes of Ellie as she pursues Abby, before switching halfway through to control Abby and playing through the same period of three momentous days through her perspective. The switch point is the moment Ellie tracks Abby to the Seattle aquarium and murders Abby's friends Owen and Mel (who is pregnant). The bleak climax of Ellie's part of the story finally places her beyond the moral pale, allowing the player the initial emotional pretext to begin the process of forgiveness towards Abby (another trigger), whose flesh we take on for the next 10–15 hours. Through Abby's eyes we recall the death of her surgeon father and the loss of the dream of a healed world, as well as the brutal fallout of Ellie's current actions – cleverly condemning the acts already committed by the player, which we must now guiltily reflect upon. Those players who did not simply give up after Joel's death and angrily sign the petition are likely to at least understand, if not fully condone, Abby's actions, a concept that felt impossible in the opening scenes. Through its looping narrative the game perfectly enacts the tragic spiral of revenge and masterfully orchestrates both the player's sympathies and morality in a manner that is rarely pulled off in the greatest works of literature or film.

Female Hard and Soft(ware) Bodies in Action Games

In the body of Abby, players not only see the slayer of their hero and a symbolically castrating figure but also an affront to the traditional gender boundaries on which their patriarchal attitudes depend. Abby's body is what the youth would describe as 'hench' – bulky, broad shouldered and muscular (but still not in a manner that is so extraordinary as detractors complain). Her body is what Jeffrey Brown describes as a 'hardbody' a 'hardware, hard-as-nails heroine' who 'indicates a growing acceptance of non-traditional roles for women and an awareness of the arbitrariness of gender traits' (2011, pp. 20–21). For Brown the hardbody transcends and troubles the typical passive/active dichotomy of Laura Mulvey's (2009) classic and persistent model of the male gaze, in which female characters are made to be passive and looked at, since it 'does not exist solely to please men, it is a body designed to be functional' (Brown, 2011, p. 25). For Brown the gaze is transformed through the hardbody and turned back upon the male spectator as a 'glare' based on 'an aggressive, angry, and knowing use of looking' (2011, p. 18).

The legacy of critical readings around Lara Croft, a notorious video game *femme fatale*, demonstrates that the nature of this glare is not always transparent. As argued by scholars like Helen Kennedy (2002), high-profile heroines like Lara Croft are controversially ambivalent. They are seen by some as post-feminist icons of empowerment for a growing audience of female gamers, and others as a product of the superficial girl power movement of the late 1990s; still objects of the male gaze that merely paid lip service to empowerment. There are uncomfortable rhetorical links between the grounds on which Abby has been rejected by fans and the manner that second wave feminists initially rejected the hardbodies of female action heroes (not to mention Lara Croft). Historically these characters have been, not unproblematically, considered 'women in drag' and dismissed as merely 'a way for male authority to revel in a form of threatening female sexuality, and to control it' (Brown, 2011, p. 15). Brown notes how the female action hero troubles second-wave feminism to its core. In many ways, the second wave depends upon an inversion of the same strict gender binary as the patriarchy it opposed, most embodied in the idea of the male gaze which depends upon the fixity of male and female as discrete and opposed entities.

In such a schema, women are unable to wield the power of the gaze or the muscle already so inseparably associated with the male, leading to an impasse in which an 'overly simplified, pessimistic, dualistic, and paranoid view of cultural subordination' ultimately casts women as 'powerless, cultural dopes' (Brown, 2011, p. 21). Contrary to this, one important characteristic of the project of third-wave feminism, established by Judith Butler's (2006) seminal *Gender Trouble* and informing Tasker's (1993) considerably more nuanced readings of female action heroes, is the notion that gender is as much performed and socially framed as it is biological and, therefore, can be understood as a fluid continuum rather than a fixed binary system. Under this schema, women are at least capable of fighting back because the gaze and the muscle are no longer the sole domain of the male in absolute terms and can be appropriated and critically repurposed, as Abby does throughout *TLOU2*. This is an example of what Tasker punningly calls 'musculinity', a portmanteau that redefines a 'physical definition of masculinity in terms of a developed musculature' and shows that it 'is not limited to the male body within representation' (1993, p. 3).

Since Lara Croft, a glut of female protagonists, less problematically presented in terms of sexual display, have taken to the virtual stage. These include Alloy, the heroine of *Horizon: Zero Dawn* (Guerrilla Games, 2017) and Jesse Faden of *Control* (Remedy Entertainment, 2019). Whilst these protagonists happen to be empowered females without the games being particularly interested in the issue of their gender identity, in *TLOU2* I argue that the two female protagonists have their gender mobilised as part of a much more intentional attempt to challenge the exclusion of marginalised identities within the sphere of video games. Gamers who complain that the emphasis on such marginalised identities is inherently political, or merely motivated by a kind of 'social justice' agenda, conveniently ignore the much more common process of casting the player as a white male protagonist, which is so persistent in games that one journalist has memorably called it 'the curse of the scruffy white male' (Kaiser, 2014) Far from being the result of a patriarchal agenda, such identities are perceived as natural and normal to male gamers who have been long thought of as the core audience of video games (Fron et al., 2007). This is because terms like maleness and whiteness act as entrenched cultural norms that are so frequently evoked that they have become natural, which is after all the function of ideology. As Purse (2011, p. 71) reminds us, despite the incredible uptick in female action heroes, the white male hero is still the 'archetypal' norm against which all other bodies are read.

Just as the action film is characterised as a masculine mode of exhibition, so too games action is aligned to the perceived masculine fanbase of the medium (Fron et al., 2007). In the face of this, Jesper Juul (2012) was among the first scholars to point out a sea-change he terms a 'casual revolution', with emerging new female audiences that the industry is still struggling to accommodate. Shira Chess' (2017) *Ready Player Two* explores this audience in depth, showing how female gamers have been typically alienated from the medium due to its historically aggressive positioning as a male pursuit. Given the inevitable tensions between established and highly conservative traditional audiences and emerging new demographics, video games have quickly become one of the key sites of struggle in the so-called 'culture wars' around intersectional identities (Chess, 2017, p. xiii). Evidence of this traumatic process can be seen in the events of 2014 collectively termed 'GamerGate'. This was a Twitter hashtag that grew into a sexist cyber-harassment movement, interpreted by many as a violent backlash from a long-established audience of hardcore, white, male players being confronted by a cultural Other within a medium they had always assumed was theirs alone (Kuchera, 2014; Ruffino, 2018). Such players were said to belong to the traditional 'hardcore' fanbase of gamers, a dominant audience persona that

Janine Fron et al. (2007, p. 7) argue that the industry sees as 'the "de facto" target demographic for its goods' and have defined as:

> An adolescent male sensibility that transcends physical age and embraces highly stylized graphical violence, male fantasies of power and domination, hyper-sexualized, objectified depictions of women, and rampant racial stereotyping and discrimination.
> (Janine Fron et al., 2007, p. 7)

Fron et al.'s concept of the 'hegemony of play' points out a tight recursive link between the prevalence of violent, action-oriented video games and their hardcore male audiences. The industry is thus closely structured around the very type of audience it actively produces via products with highly homogenous characteristics (and highly homogenous male characters, of which Joel is one), creating a situation in which 'alternate products of play are marginalized and devalued' (2007). As game studies emerged as a disciplinary field, many assumed that the male audience was the natural state of the industry, rather than an audience constructed through a series of historical moments as many have shown since (Chess, 2017; Kirkpatrick, 2015; Kocurek, 2015). Indeed, as little as 10 years ago claims were made by foundational game studies scholars Espen Aarseth (2004) and James Newman (2004) over Lara Croft's body not mattering to them in slightest when they play *Tomb Raider* (Core Design, 1996), demonstrating that the assumptions exposed in the hegemony of play have historically also seeped into scholarship. As Aarseth demonstrates:

> The dimensions of Lara Croft's body, already analyzed to death by film theorists, are irrelevant to me as a player, because a different-looking body would not make me play differently... When I play, I don't even see her body, but see through it and past it.
> (Aarseth, 2004, p. 48)

Newman agrees, arguing that when the player inhabits a character, they become a mere token; a purely functional 'sphere of action' (2004, p. 129). Aside from the clearly problematic nature of two male game scholars writing off the issue of gender representation from their own position of privilege, this supposedly 'gender-blind' reading speaks to a tendency in early game studies known as 'ludology'. This was a formalist position that largely dismissed the wider cultural contexts of play and, with it, the entire sociopolitical sphere, a point made rather well recently by Soraya Murray who, like me, sees here an attempt to 'wrest video games from narrative-based interpretation... (with its attendant representations)' (2017, p. 133). Esther MacCallum-Stewart (2014), whose article attempts to unpick some of the complexities and ambiguities of gendered readings of Lara Croft, notes that Aarseth's attempt to 'disavow' her gender paradoxically draws attention to it, and through the very use of her as an example highlights 'her irrefutable position as a woman already considered out of place' in a medium dominated by male heroes and male commentators.

This 'out-of-placeness' of the female action body is a key context for both the reception of female action stars as addressed by Purse and Tasker, as well as in fan reactions to Abby that dismiss her muscular body as 'unrealistic'. For instance, a lengthy, polemical Twitter thread (Dr Uckmann, 2020), sees dozens of players attempting to present their dislike for the game based on the quality of the writing, even as dozens more explicitly make comments about Abby's body type being unrealistic (the ultimate insult for a game that trades on naturalism). These two concepts become utterly conflated in this exchange in a way that binds together the progressive quality of the narrative with the unconventional qualities of Abby's body, both of which are then rejected as inauthentic. Such a response illustrates perfectly how the female 'hardbody' is thought to be incompatible with the hardcore fandom. The impulses driving this disavowal of Abby and the similar ease with which Aarseth (2004) and Newman (2004) can discard Lara's representational layer are both indicative of a conservative interpretive gesture; an attempted escape from the critical tradition of feminism and cultural studies that had been gaining significant traction in the academy and in game studies.

Given the rhetoric of presence (a more advanced form of immersion in which the player feels embodied in the virtual world) in much video game marketing, criticism and scholarship (See Calleja, 2011 for a thorough overview of the importance of these terms), it is perhaps unusual that game studies has neglected the actual role of the body in all its specificity for so long (except to insist that it doesn't matter as in the case of Lara). The dominance of highly formalist ludological approaches demonstrates one potential cause of this neglect. This is a situation that is only recently being addressed by works tackling games from the intellectual traditions of affect theory (Anable, 2018) and phenomenology (Keogh, 2018), as well as (re)making the case for the relevance of cultural studies (Murray, 2017). This chapter may helpfully point video game scholars to an existing body of work (pun intended) that is sympathetic to these new trends towards the study of embodiment in their own field. After all, if action cinema is 'defined by its persistent and detailed attention to the exerting body' (Purse, 2011, p. 2), such a body is doubly central in the video games because they function precisely through such a process of embodiment, in which the controller as interface allows us to manipulate our own body double (or avatar) on screen. However, the next section will demonstrate a double standard in which female protagonists are expected to prove their abilities more rigorously than their male counterparts.

Proof of Process: Authenticating the Hard Virtual Body Through Motion Capture

Female athletes and bodybuilders who dedicate themselves to sculpting their bodies into the hardbodies suitable for action are constantly under pressure to legitimise and evidence their labour in ways that men rarely are because a muscular male frame is accepted as normal, natural and therefore beyond question. Even when muscular action stars were critiqued as a form of 'hysterical masculinity' (Tasker, 1993, p. 80), it was never the reality of the male's muscles themselves that was being questioned, but the excessive nature of the display. For instance, Brown demonstrates how widely reported Linda Hamilton's training regimen was as though to pre-empt the inevitable disbelief that would be met in the audience because her 'bulging biceps and striated shoulders in a black undershirt' placed in question 'the naturalness of muscles as markers of sexual difference' (Brown, 2011, p. 32). This double standard of legitimisation is something that we might call 'proof of process', a burden of proof that falls to women to demonstrate their ability and right to play in a male space, whether that space be real or virtual.

Thirty years later and Abby appears in a military-style vest like the one that Linda Hamilton once sported, designed to display bulging biceps. Such an allusion indicates that games are going through a similar cultural moment of struggling to accept female action heroes as that moment in 1980's action cinema. Abby is deliberately linked to her predecessors as a point of cross-media solidarity. Her bulky torso is similarly provocatively positioned for the male spectator, not under the logic of the male gaze, but Brown's confrontational 'glare', an empowered female hardbody that turns the male gaze back on itself. This shows that, real or virtual, the appropriation of muscles by female stars is challenging the assumptions around genders and what they are capable of that patriarchal gender roles are built upon. As Tasker writes of female bodybuilders: '[they threatened] not only current socially constructed definitions of femininity and masculinity, but the system of sexual difference itself' thus making explicit 'the extent to which both sex and gender constitute the body within culture' (1993, p. 141).

Yet Brown's linking of the 'hardbody' and 'hardware' opens a potentially paradoxical space for this study, since the female bodies on display in *TLOU2* are also the immaterial virtual bodies of software, although the effects and affects they produced on social media were anything but soft. The hardbody of the action heroine is also simultaneously the soft(ware) body of the digital and virtual world of the computer, and if we recall Lev Manovich's (2002) claims of new media to be endlessly fluid, and subject to easy manipulations, her 'realism' within this medium is rendered uncertain. Abby's body in *TLOU2* is highly constructed given it is designed in 3D imaging software driven by computer algorithms, rather than the more commonly understood indexical realism of cinema, which refers to a realism that cannot help but mechanically capture (index) the reality in front of it – no matter how ultimately staged that reality is. Although ontologically speaking the digital world of the video game, like animation, is always constructed from scratch, it is rarely constructed without reference to or input from the real world, often using very tangible processes.

One such process that imbues Abby with authenticity is motion capture technology, where specialised sensor suits, camera rigs and software arrays allow a real-world actor's proportions and movements to be scanned into the computer to act as a model for a character. Naughty Dog are global leaders in this technology, and they typically take its use much further than other studios, staging entire scenes to give their games an actorly and cinematic quality. In terms of motion capture, Abby is a composite of three women: Laura Bailey (movement and expression capture), Jocelyn Mettler (face model) and Colleen Fotsch (body model). Fotsch is an accomplished CrossFit athlete (Baines, 2020) and is wholly responsible for Abby's physique, thus acting as a real-world guarantor for its claim to authenticity. By linking Abby to Fotsch as a reference in such a way that the technology of motion capture confers upon the soft virtuality of game development some of the hard indexicality of cinema, but it also provides a similar 'proof of process' comparable to Hamilton's training regime.

The use of Fotsch as a kind of literal body double reveals the complaints of hardcore gamers that Abby is not realistic to be hollow attempts to contain her threat to traditional, binary gender norms that see muscles as natural to one body and aberrations on another. Those trying to deny Abby's authenticity as a character, and therefore disempower her as a potential role model to female gamers, attempted to dismiss her muscles on the grounds that they are impossible without the use of steroids (Dr Uckmann, 2020), an accusation that was even extended to Fotsch herself (Bayonetta_, 2020). Action films frequently partake in what Purse calls strategies of containment that 'work to contain the threat embodied by the presence of the physically powerful woman' (2011, p. 81). Such strategies include excusing female strength through fantasy or humour to 'set the potentially culturally disturbing possibility of female agency and physical power at a distance from our everyday contemporary reality' (Dr Uckmann, 2020). Claims about steroids can be understood in these same terms, as a dismissive attempt to simultaneously undermine the labour undertaken by Fotsch in the honing of her real-world hardbody, as well as the team of creatives at Naughty Dog who carefully crafted its virtual equivalent in Abby.

Counterarguments made against this position in the popular press (Baines, 2020) sought to tackle the issue of steroids and Abby's authenticity by rightly pointing out that the game takes pains to ground the character realistically in the world. When players take over Abby's body after playing in Ellie's skin for so long the difference is striking. Abby *feels* bulky and this is communicated not just through the visual representation of the character model but in a certain sense of heaviness programmed into the game via its physics engine. Whilst Ellie is lithe and resourceful, Abby solves her problems by direct force – something which is communicated with an entirely different skill set made available to the player that emphasises her physical prowess. Far from decorative, Abby's appropriated musculature is directed in very purposeful ways not only in the moment-to-moment experience of play but is narratively justified within her overall program of revenge and survival. Indeed, our first view after taking control of Abby is the incredibly well-equipped gym just outside her quarters. Abby lives in an organised community based in a sports stadium seemingly structured around military ideals of strength and self-discipline, where she has both the means to spend five years honing her hardbody into an instrument of vengeance and more than enough motivation to do so following the murder of her father.

This discussion demonstrates that the virtual soft body of polygons is in fact more complex, manufactured, sculpted (literally) and spectacular as the bodies

Tasker analyses in the action genre, but is also grounded in real-world processes and references. Rather than merely virtual, the bodies in action games must also be considered extremely physical – not least in the effect they have on players. Perhaps it would be best to think of the term 'virtual' here not in its common understanding as 'not real' but in its philosophical sense of being 'in potential', for instance, in the manner Deleuze and Guattari (2013) make of the term in which the virtual speaks to the range of potential emergent outcomes implicit in an assemblage. This would place it in line with Purse's notion that action narratives are very often 'narratives of becoming', in which action sequences '[articulate] the protagonist's physical and emotional trajectory towards achieving full occupation of the heroic action body' (2011, p. 33). In broader cultural terms the debate surrounding Abby's body and its claims to the 'real' demonstrate a similar struggle for becoming in women who refuse to be bound by conventional gendered terms regarding the shapes of their bodies and the uses those bodies can be put to (or are allowed to be put to).

Conclusion: A Precarious Permission to Play

In action cinema and especially in games, both male-dominated mediums, the issue of representation still looms large and, as Lisa Purse argues, demands a critical exploration of the 'different kinds of bodies that are permitted, celebrated and denigrated' (2011, p. 54). Such a project is overdue in game studies. My reading of Abby not only demonstrates the relevance of concepts from film studies developed by Tasker, Purse and Brown but also discredits Aarseth and Newman's argument that the type of body the player inhabits matters little to the true experience of play. Rather we can see the aesthetic, representational frame, and rule-bound actions mesh tightly together in Abby's design. Additionally, the debate initiated by Abby's body illustrates that, as much as we might want them not to, in the wider culture such representational surfaces still matter deeply to many.

Ultimately, the idea that virtual female action stars must justify their presence through a kind of proof of process just like their cinematic counterparts links to a similar demand made of the emergent female audience of gamers, who are continuously made to justify their right to play in a traditionally male space. As Shira Chess argues, the gradual broadening of the audience for video games driven by imperatives of profit has resulted in female players gaining a kind of 'permission slip to play' through their act of consumption, but notes that such slips 'are powerful yet ephemeral' and that 'buying into a culture is not the same as being an authentic part of that culture' (2017, pp. 127–128). By denying Abby's authenticity the players who reject *TLOU2* also implicitly deny real females access to traditional masculine pursuits and identities, whether that be bodybuilding or gaming. *TLOU2* radically rejects this view and unequivocally answers the call from Purse to open a 'space for women to be active in action cinema [and video games] without their presence being qualified' (2011, p. 91).

References

Aarseth, E. (2004). Genre trouble: Narrativism and the art of simulation. In N. Wardrip-Fruin & P. Harrigan (Eds.), *First person: New media as story, performance and game*. Cambridge, MA: MIT Press.

Anable, A. (2018). *Playing with feelings: Video games and affect*. Minneapolis, MN: University of Minnesota Press.

Baines, T. (2020, July 4). 14 reasons Abby's arms are realistic, actually, in the Last of Us Part II. *Thumbsticks*. Retrieved from https://www.thumbsticks.com/14-reasons-abbys-arms-realistic-actually-the-last-of-us-part-ii/. Accessed on July 12, 2021.

Bayonetta_. (2020). Abby's real body model Colleen Fotsch is she on steroids. Gamefaqs. Retrieved from https://gamefaqs.gamespot.com/boards/202466-the-last-of-us-part-ii/78645762. Accessed on July 12, 2021.

Brown, J. A. (2011). *Dangerous curves: Action heroines, gender, fetishism, and popular culture*. Jackson, MS: University Press of Mississippi.

Butler, J. (2006). *Gender trouble*. New York, NY: Routledge.

Calleja, G. (2011). *In-game: Immersion to incorporation*. Cambridge, MA: MIT Press.

Chess, S. (2017). *Ready player two: Women gamers and designed identity*. Minneapolis, MN: University of Minnesota Press.

Core Design. (1996). *Tomb Raider*. Eidos Interactive.

Deleuze, G., & Guattari, F. (2013). *A thousand plateaus*. London: Bloomsbury Academic.

Dr Uckmann. (2020). Tweet from Neil Druckmann. *Twitter*. Retrieved from https://twitter.com/Neil_Druckmann/status/1310360785353277440. Accessed on July 15, 2021.

Fron, J., Fullerton, T., Morie, J. F., & Pearce, C. (2007). The hegemony of play. In *Situated play: Proceedings of digital games research association 2007 conference* (pp. 1–10). Presented at the DiGRA, Digital Games Research Association (DiGRA), Tampere, Finland, pp. 1–10.

Galloway, A. R. (2006). *Gaming: Essays on algorithmic culture*. Minneapolis, MN: University of Minnesota Press.

Glennon, J. (2020). 2020's most controversial video game reveals the worst thing about fandom, inverse. Retrieved from https://www.inverse.com/gaming/last-of-us-2-goty-abby-controversy. Accessed on July 15, 2021.

Guerrilla Games. (2017). Horizon: Zero Dawn. Sony Interactive Entertainment.

Juul, J. (2012). *A casual revolution: Reinventing video games and their players*. Cambridge, MA: MIT Press.

Kaiser, R. (2014). The curse of the scruffy white male: Why representation matters in video games. IndieWire. Retrieved from http://www.indiewire.com/2014/07/the-curse-of-the-scruffy-white-male-why-representation-matters-in-video-games-23990/. Accessed on January 5, 2018.

Kennedy, H. W. (2002). Lara Croft: Feminist icon or cyberbimbo? On the limits of textual analysis. *gamestudies.org*, *2*(2). Retrieved from http://www.gamestudies.org/0202/kennedy/. Accessed on November 18, 2019.

Keogh, B. (2018). *A play of bodies: How we perceive videogames*. Cambridge, MA: The MIT Press.

Kirkpatrick, G. (2015). *The formation of gaming culture: UK gaming magazines, 1981–1995*. Basingstoke: Palgrave Macmillan.

Kocurek, C. A. (2015). *Coin-operated Americans: Rebooting boyhood at the video game arcade*. Minneapolis, MN: University of Minnesota Press.

Kuchera, B. (2014). The year of GamerGate: The worst of gaming culture gets a movement, Polygon. Retrieved from http://www.polygon.com/2014/12/30/7460777/gamergate-2014-just-the-worst. Accessed on March 25, 2015.

MacCallum-Stewart, E. (2014). "Take that, bitches!" refiguring Lara Croft in feminist game narratives. *Game Studies*, *14*(2). Retrieved from http://gamestudies.org/1402/articles/maccallumstewart. Accessed on November 14, 2019.

Makuch, E. (2012). Naughty Dog: Games don't need males on cover to sell. *GameSpot*. Retrieved from https://www.gamespot.com/articles/naughty-dog-games-dont-need-males-on-cover-to-sell/1100-6401457/. Accessed on July 15, 2021.

Manovich, L. (2002). *The language of new media*. Cambridge, MA: MIT Press.

Miller, J. (2020). Remake the storyline of The Last of Us Part II, Change.org. Retrieved from https://www.change.org/p/sony-remake-the-storyline-of-the-last-of-us-part-ii. Accessed on July 15, 2021.

Mulvey, L. (2009). *Visual and other pleasures* (2nd ed.). Basingstoke: Palgrave Macmillan.

Murray, S. (2017). *On video games: The visual politics of race, gender and space*. London and New York, NY: I.B.Tauris.

Naughty Dog. (2013). The last of us. Sony Computer Entertainment.

Naughty Dog. (2020). The last of us part II. Sony Interactive Entertainment.

Newman, J. (2004). *Videogames* (2nd ed.). London: Routledge.

O'Donnell, C. (2014). On Balinese cockfights: Deeply extending play. *Games and Culture*, *9*(6), 406–416.

Purse, L. (2011). *Contemporary action cinema*. Edinburgh: Edinburgh University Press.

Remedy Entertainment. (2019). Control. 505 games.

Ruberg, B., & Shaw, A. (Eds.). (2017). *Queer game studies*. Minneapolis, MN: University of Minnesota Press.

Ruffino, P. (2018). GamerGate: Becoming parasites to gaming. In *Future gaming: Creative interventions in video game culture* (pp. 104–119). London: Goldsmiths Press.

Tasker, Y. (1993). *Spectacular bodies: Gender, genre, and the action cinema*. London: Routledge.

Tasker, Y. (2015). *The Hollywood action and adventure film*. Chichester: Wiley Blackwell.

Part 3
Intergenerational Action

Chapter 7

Dark Fathers and Damaged Sons: The Paternal Betrayal of *Jason Bourne*

Toby Reynolds

Abstract

The *Jason Bourne* series of films (2002–2016) are widely acknowledged with helping to successfully re-invent the action thriller genre in the 2000s by focusing more on motivation and plot than over-the-top spectacle. Featuring a profoundly wounded son figure in the titular character, the films are indicative of an awareness of the vulnerabilities and reactions of a fatherless masculinity within a post-Cold War political reality.

This chapter will argue that Bourne's onscreen pain and subsequent violent responses to his various narrative predicaments are a result of being repeatedly betrayed by a series of older males, in many cases, father surrogates. Bourne's experience of this paternal disruption and betrayal is the key psychological motivating factor, with the films and the story arc of the character only being resolved when both he and the audience finally discover and reconcile the role that his biological father played in shaping his destiny and his life. This 'father hunger' – in effect a need for a continuative masculinity – that Jason Bourne experiences, and that is arguably at the heart of the franchise, will be analysed and explored within the contexts of post-Jungian screen theory. Alongside the deliberately casting of 'quality' actors (such as Brian Cox, Joan Allen, Tommy Lee Jones, David Strathairn) and other formalist elements of the text, archetypal energies and symbolism are also rife throughout the film, and can be, in part, credited with the critical and commercial success of the films. Finally, the films are put in their cinematic context in terms of the influence they subsequently exerted on other action film franchises – particularly *James Bond* (1962 to present).

Keywords: Jason Bourne; betrayal; gender; masculinity; fathers; action franchises

Re-inventing the spy action film for the early 2000s, the *Jason Bourne* film franchise series (2002–2016) has managed to combine both critical acclaim and a healthy box office take (a $1.637 billion take against a budgetary total of $490 million) to become a direct stylistic influence on action films (e.g. the *James Bond* series, in franchise entries from 2006 to the present). Whilst critical and industry focus on the crunchy action sequences and stunts was entirely justifiable and contributed in large to the franchise's success, the psychological and gender aspects of the series have been less well-known, as unusually, for the spy and thriller genre, the *Bourne* franchise has both a strong gender and psychological component to it with regards to the main character's motivations.

This chapter posits that the films essentially chart Jason Bourne (Matt Damon)'s psychological, and eventually familial, quest for Self; his dissociative amnesia being a key narrative driver of the plot. His quest for his identity is intimately bound up with his relationship with his absent father enables us to analyse the films from the perspective of gender, invoking what has been termed 'father hunger', a psychological quest that seeks to re-establish the masculine continuum between father and son (Biddulph, 1995; Bly, 1990). This quest is the over-reaching psychological narrative arc of the films (barring *The Bourne Legacy* [2012]), resulting in Jason Bourne's final psychological realisation of who he is and what he has become. The series is also noteworthy for what can be described as dark, or shadow, patriarchal figures that consistently betray him and collude in plotting to kill him in order to protect both secrets of the state and the government agency Bourne originally worked for (the CIA). This paternal betrayal of a wayward son is also a key narrative device within the films and provides much of the underlying motivation for the action sequences that entranced audiences. This patriarchal masculine betrayal of the wounded son figure gives rise to father hunger. Jason Bourne not only has to discover and remember who he is, but he also has to re-connect with the masculine continuum via a father figure in order to do this, even though this is a profoundly troubling and negative experience for him. There are also direct onscreen references to fathers and families throughout the films. Jason Bourne's CIA assignments often involve killing men who are fathers in order to carry out his missions, but when confronted, his conscience stops him. Before moving into closer textual analysis of the films, I will firstly examine the figure of the father in more depth, and how his onscreen presence is mediated.

The Father and the Son in Cinema

Theorists such as Bruzzi have described the cinematic father as treated '"a bit like air" – omnipresent but rarely talked about' (2005, p. xi). This paradox can be seen as a fruitful area of enquiry, given that the father is coming under increasing focus and attention in action films. In contemporary film, the audience is often confronted with multiple, and crucially, different cinematic images of the father and, concomitantly, of what has been termed 'father hunger'. These contemporary images contradict past perceptions of the father as a largely one-dimensional and under-analysed presence within films dealing with masculinity. From a post-Jungian developmental perspective, psychologically speaking, a male child's identification with a father figure (which is sometimes not necessarily the biological antecedent) is held to be essential to masculine identity, experiencing a fundamental identity difference between himself and the maternal. As Stevens (1994, p. 69) states: 'At this point, the presence of a father figure can prove crucial, enabling the boy to move from a self-concept based on mother identity to one based on identification-with-the-father'. The young male then begins to realise that he is profoundly different from his mother, not least because of his sexual organs. At some point in his development, he realises that he must learn, absorb and know from his father in terms of experience and worldly wisdom. This is not necessarily as Freud and psychoanalysts describe, as an enemy and rival, but more as a gender 'bridge', into the world of men and masculinity that his own, slowly activated father archetype directs him towards. It can be said that the teleological journey of the son towards manhood is ultimately to transcend the father (both the father archetype and the biological father), a major difference from a psychoanalytical perspective. This is a more optimistic outlook, than perhaps a classical Freudian perspective, with both the father's individuation and the child's development psychologically potentialised.

As a bridge/evolution of the male child's increasing sense of himself, the presence of the father, or father figure, is perceived and viewed as a crucial one (Biddulph, 1995; Bly, 1990; Herzog, 1983). Consequently, father hunger is said to result from a sundered or broken link with the father, with the son becoming an adult male, but a male that has not properly known or learnt from his father, with the masculine continuum being interrupted. Furthermore, if we also subscribe to the performative interpretation of masculinity, fatherhood can therefore be said to both function and be performed (Butler, 1990; Pomerance & Gateward, 2005) in both arenas of this gender hegemony, with filmic imagery reflecting these performances. If we link this with the men's movement theories of the critical central role that the father performs within the masculine continuum, then cinema can be seen as accurately divining cultural perspectives in gender relationships.[1] When surveying the figure of the adult son within film, there is an almost Biblical dimension to gender relations in that the son very often has to deal with the sins of his father (e.g. *Lone Star*, 1996), effectively becoming a conduit for the consequences of the father, and being affected in fundamental ways because of paternal actions. This is a key narrative feature of the *Bourne* franchise, where the actions of the father result in violence and drama for the son, which, by the end of the final film, is explored in depth. The *Bourne* franchise gradually reveals the truth

---

[1] In-depth criticism of the mythopoetic men's movement groups' foregrounding of the father as being central to masculine identity have come from a number of sources, including Andrew Samuels (1993) and David Tacey (1997).

about Bourne, and his father Richard Webb, whose past actions have entrapped his son. Bourne struggles over four films to free himself from his father's shadow, as well as a series of deadly patriarchal figures who are shown to consistently betray Bourne. As Hamad states: 'Fatherhood has become the dominant paradigm of masculinity across the spectrum of mainstream U.S. cinema' (2014, p. 1). As this chapter proves, this paradigm is reflected within the action/thriller genre, which is, at first glance, not a genre that necessarily lends itself to paternal gender contemplation.

It is worth reflecting upon the treatment of masculinity, or more accurately, masculinities in action films in terms of the focus on the male body, rather than the male psyche (Tasker, 1993). In 1980s action films, the male body, replete with vast musculature (Arnold Schwarzenegger, Sylvester Stallone, Dolph Lundgren) was the main site at which action and masculinity was measured and depicted. Tasker, for example, neatly identifies the onscreen male body as the site of both masculine strength and masculine fear: 'Anxieties to do with difference and sexuality increasingly seem to be worked out over the body of the hero. The male body (usually replete with muscles) is an arena whereby contemporary anxieties are played out on screen' (1993, p. 236).

As the 1990s progressed, filmic action masculinities became more anxious, and more fractured, fragile, and vulnerable to being wounded, as demonstrated by heroes such as John McClane (Bruce Willis) in the *Die Hard* series (1988–2013). This increasing masculine vulnerability was in sharp contrast to 1980s depictions of action heroes with their comically enmuscled bodies and deliberately large phallic guns, rocket launchers and other destructive equipment. By the 2000s, it appeared that traditional action films needed a fundamental re-boot, exemplified by the *James Bond* spy series, whose 2002 outing, *Die Another Day* was a dismal critical failure, despite it performing relatively well at the box office. Betraying an almost surreal lack of contemporaneous geopolitical awareness, *Die Another Day* managed to both rehash and reinforce the more ridiculous aspects of the series' mise-en-scene, plot twists and thematic concerns (giant space lasers, invisible cars and cliched villains) to the overall detriment of the film and the series. Compared to the flailing Bond franchise, the first film of the Bourne series, *The Bourne Identity* (2002), successfully tapped into post-9/11 ambiguity, anxiety and anger surrounding American foreign policy, and how it was carried out. As Klaus Dodds contends:

> Since he burst onto the screens, this hyperkinetic amnesiac assassin has been widely credited with challenging the generic standards associated with James Bond and spy-/action-thrillers more generally. Played by Matt Damon, a public critic of the James Bond character, the Bourne series raises troubling questions about the use of violence and the excesses of national security managers

who decide that this former U.S. soldier and trained assassin is himself a security threat and needs to be terminated.[2]

(2010, p. 22)

By marrying claustrophobically close wobble-cam cinematography (borrowed from both documentaries and echoing the more realistic American TV shows like *Homicide: Life on the Street* [1993–1999, NBC]), and employing realistic stunts and acting, *The Bourne Identity* depicted a much darker and ambivalent world of spies, violence and betrayal, where any botched mission by an agent was liable to result in the execution of the spy, rather than any protection from the spy agency. As Gaine suggests (2011, p. 159): 'Generically, Jason Bourne (Matt Damon) shares much with James Bond and other secret agents such as Jack Ryan and Harry Palmer, but the trilogy expresses discomfort with the role of the spy as an unproblematic agent of his government'. By the end of the film, Jason Bourne is no nearer to finding out who he actually is, but he has managed to survive his former CIA employers' best attempts to kill him to protect their highly classified 'Treadstone' assassination programme, a crucial part of the series' overarching narrative and storyline. This deliberately downbeat and unresolved ending has two purposes; one, it leaves an opening for a sequel and the possibility of a successful franchise; and two, it also does not complete Jason Bourne's psychological journey.

The Bourne Identity (2002)

The Bourne Identity opens with a French fishing boat in the Mediterranean discovering what appears to be a corpse in the sea. When it is revealed to be an unconscious American with two bullet wounds in his back, the skipper performs the necessary surgery to save the patient, and we are introduced to the main character. When a secret microchip displaying a mysterious numerical code is shown embedded under his skin, we sense that there is much more to this figure than is first revealed. The spy thriller territory is firmly established as the film progresses and the character discovers that he is the owner of a safety deposit box that contains money, several passports and a pistol. The name 'Jason Bourne' is on one of the passports and we also discover that Jason Bourne suffers from traumatic retrograde amnesia, presumably induced by him being shot. When he pays Marie Kreutz (Franka Potente) $20,000 to drive him to Paris to check the address contained in one of his documents, his search for Self has started in earnest. A parallel narrative twist (presumably linked to our protagonist's past) involving a mid-level CIA officer Conklin (Chris Cooper) and his boss Ward

---

[2]Damon went public with his opinions on the character of Bond, declaring in a *GQ* magazine interview (8 July 2007) that: 'Bond is part of the system. He's an imperialist and a misogynist, and he laughs at killing people, and he sits there slugging martinis. It'll never be the same thing as this, because Bourne is a guy who is against the establishment, who is paranoid and on the run'.

Abbott (Brian Cox) is one of the first of many dark father figures who appear throughout the film franchise.

After Bourne and Marie are ambushed by a mysterious killer who jumps out of the window to his death rather than confess to anything, they are then pursued by the French police, immersing us in a car chase that manages the difficult task of appearing both realistic and thrilling. With the action switching back and forth between Bourne and his former employers, we gradually come to realise that Bourne is part of the 'Treadstone' programme, a CIA 'black ops' operation that trained deep-cover assassins who were on call, and located worldwide whenever the CIA needed someone killed. Through a series of cleverly edited memory-specific flashbacks and diegetic detective work, Bourne starts to remember that he was tasked with killing Nykwana Wombosi (Adewale Akinnuoye-Agbaje), an African politician who was CIA-backed but deeply unpopular in his own country, and threatened to expose the CIA's involvement with his country's politics. When Bourne covertly enters Wombosi's yacht in the Mediterranean at night to kill him and complete his mission, Wombosi is playing with his children. This sight of a vulnerable father spending time with his offspring is enough to make Bourne hesitate. Unfortunately for Bourne, this reluctance nearly gets him killed as Wombosi grabs his own gun and shoots Bourne twice in the back, thus completing both our understanding of how Bourne came to be found in the sea. Despite, or even because of, this psychological realisation, Bourne is now determined to find out more about his previous life, and his employers. His psychological search for Self is now threatening to endanger his employers, and they dispatch another one of his Treadstone compatriots, the Professor (Clive Owen) to kill him and end the growing existential threat that he represents. Dodds summarises this situation neatly:

> Shockingly, as it turns out, a man trained, programmed, and authorized to maim and kill is 'cast out' by his corrupt superiors. He is disposable. The security covenant has been broken and these entanglements of power, money, and security increasingly endanger Bourne, as he recovers slowly his memory.
> (2010, p. 22)

After thwarting the Professor's attempts to kill him whilst hiding at Marie's brother's house (another father and his children), Bourne finally manages to contact his employers directly and arrange a meeting, the two main narrative threads coming together at the film's conclusion.

This climactic meeting back in Paris is deeply psychologically significant for Bourne due to the harsh revelations of Conklin; Bourne begins to relive crucial memories which contextualise his situation. Conklin, for his part, snarls at Bourne: 'You're US Government property. You're a malfunctioning $30 million-dollar weapon! And you're a total goddamn catastrophe!' Whilst this is a large part of the truth about Bourne's identity, more crucially there is a dehumanising element to it. This dehumanising attack on Bourne's identity is characteristic of what can be described in post-Jungian film theory as the *shadow senex*. David Tacey, a post-Jungian gender theorist, pithily summarises the power that the shadow, or negative, senex can have on younger men: '...bosses and employers assume the role of the negative senex or devouring father, leading men into a spiralic condition of performance anxiety, where the emotional rewards are very few' (1997, p. 124). This 'devouring father' is a key emerging feature of the older men appearing in the Bourne franchise. Whilst Bourne digests and processes his true identity, Conklin attempts to kill him, but Bourne manages to escape both him and the agents who follow in a thrilling pursuit and shootout. The film ends with the dark father figure turning on his progeny for any failure. On Ward Abbott's orders, Conklin is executed, and the Treadstone programme shut down; Abbott is shown appearing in front of the Senate oversight committee and mentioning a new covert programme, Blackbriar. The final scene shows Bourne reunited with Marie in sunny Mykonos, a deliberately sharp contrast to the mainly rain-swept streets and grey clouds that dominated the mise-en-scene throughout most of the film. Bourne is shown as recovered from his ordeal, and in a psychologically healthier place than before, despite not having fully recovered his memory. It is implied that Bourne's conscience and compassion, alongside his deadlier skills has saved him, and he looks ready to move on with his life. He confesses to Marie that he still doesn't know who he is, but that he wants to be with her. What is different about this particular thriller is that, as Dodds puts it (2010, p. 23): 'Bourne's quest to recover his sense of identity and evidence of his recent past, challenges the political and moral geographies of the national security state', a state of affairs that is not viable in the long term, but a state of affairs that leads onto another chapter in the franchise. Bourne's quest for his Self has begun in earnest, and luckily for the audience and the studio, this means more films in the franchise.

The Bourne Supremacy (2004)

The events of *The Bourne Supremacy* take place two years after the first film, with Bourne and Marie now in a serious relationship and living in Goa, India. Whilst things appear relatively normal, Bourne is plagued by flashbacks and disturbing visions of his previous life, signs that his psyche is not ready to leave him alone. Meanwhile in Berlin, a new character, CIA Deputy Director Pamela Landy (Joan Allen) is coordinating a potential sting operation to locate a corrupt CIA agent who stole $20 million seven years ago. The operation goes badly wrong; both her undercover agent and Russian source are killed, and crucial data stolen. An unexploded bomb, with Bourne's fingerprints on it, is discovered in the building where the killings took place. Unaware that he is in the process of being framed for the murders and theft, Bourne and Marie are attacked by a Russian assassin, who kills Marie and leaves Bourne for dead in an Indian river. Haunted by Marie's death, and fearing that the CIA are again after him, Bourne starts his own investigation, neatly parallelling his own psychic quest to uncover his true identity. With the action moving to Germany and Russia, Bourne gradually uncovers a darker aspect to his past; he killed Russian politician Vladimir Neski and his wife, and made it look like a murder-suicide. Neski was trying to uncover who stole the $20 million, with the trail leading back to Ward Abbott, who stole the money in conjunction with a Russian oligarch. Longing for a surrogate father (or fathers) is not without its dangers, it seems. Fathers, including surrogate father figures such as Abbott, can overwhelm the adult son, leading to potentially limited psychological growth and to burden the son with personal complexes. Whilst Abbott is not shown as being in direct contact with Bourne, he has, nevertheless, overseen and taken a deep interest in Bourne's transmutation into a human weapon, which is what the CIA wanted. In effect, this knowledge of Bourne (the CIA has access to his psychological profile, family history and everything significantly psychic about him) is very much what a father would do in raising a son in his own image. It can be said that there is a strong surrogate familial aspect to the CIA, but unfortunately in Bourne's case, the dark father, or negative senex, has, yet again, corrupted and exerted a malign influence over his surrogate or substitute sons. Abbott and his colleagues have 'raised' Bourne to be a killer, and weaponised him to aid them in their goals. The corrupting function of the paternal is indicative of another dark aspect of the father figure, and one that is made clear within the Bourne series, with Tacey (1997, p. 163) identifying another feature of the dark senex: 'The negative senex rules best when our psychic energy is not available to challenge him'. Bourne is in the unenviable position of being unable to resist the pull of the senex, his amnesia being both a psychic barrier against further trauma, but also a barrier against knowing too much, despite wanting to. However, by betraying Bourne, Abbott inadvertently causes his own downfall, with the powerful feminine, represented by Landy, laying a trap once she realises the holes in her colleague's story. When finally confronted by Landy, Abbott blusters: 'I'm not a traitor. I've served my country...In the end, honestly, it's hubris. Simple hubris. You reach a point in this game when the only satisfaction left is to see how clever you are'. He desperately tries to justify his actions, yet Abbott's suicide tells a different story as the senex is brought down by his own greed. Unfortunately for Bourne (but luckily for audiences who enjoy action and plot twists), he is driven by a gnawing sense of conscience that impels him to attempt to put right what has been done wrong. This moral quest leads to more car chases, shoot-outs and other staple action film tropes. The senex's (Abbott's) betrayal ultimately affects his surrogate son, Bourne in distinctly harmful ways. Bourne ends up wounded in several places and is barely able to move without being in pain as evidenced by the ending of this instalment. This physical pain is reflected in his emotional and psychic pain with Bourne finally realising that he must atone for his past actions. With his conscience pricking him, Bourne makes contact with the Neski's daughter, Irena, and apologises, confessing his crimes. This is an unusual twist, unseen in most action thrillers, and a scene that purportedly was inserted against the studio's wishes, but with the support of both the director, Paul Greengrass, and Damon himself. As Gaine eloquently puts it (2011, p. 162): 'Not that he is absolved. As the trilogy emphasises culpability, Bourne's rediscovery of responsibility is also a reclaiming of morality'. This act of confession and attempted atonement also leads to a psychological reward of sorts. With Bourne surviving Abbott's betrayal, there is one final twist, courtesy of Landy. In a phone conversation Landy tells him his true name, David Webb, and a date of birth. Bourne's adventures, wounds, trials and dark psychological journeys have earned him, and the film's audience, a further clue as to his true identity, and he has taken his first steps to becoming psychically whole.

The Bourne Ultimatum (2007)

Taking place almost immediately after the second film, Bourne must avoid capture by Moscow police and get out of Russia. Bourne escapes and decides to go off-grid again to avoid attention. A month and a half later, Landy has exposed Treadstone and Ward Abbott's taped confession to the CIA Director, Ezra Kramer (Scott Glenn), another dark father figure. Meanwhile, a British journalist, Simon Ross (Paddy Considine) meets an informant who tells him about 'Blackbriar', a covert surveillance programme mentioned briefly at the end of the first film by Abbott. Ross's phone call mentioning 'Blackbriar' is detected by the CIA and draws the attention of Vosen (David Strathairn), Blackbriar's head. Bourne is aware of Ross and arranges to meet him at Waterloo station where, despite Bourne's best efforts, Ross is gunned down by a CIA assassin. Following the trail and aided by Nicky Parsons (Julia Stiles) from the first film, Bourne tracks down a lead to Spain, and then Tangiers where he is nearly killed by another assassin. Travelling to New York, and helped by Landy, Bourne starts to recover his memory when confronting Dr Albert Hirsch (Albert Finney), yet another negative senex figure, who is a behaviour-modification specialist integral to the success of the Treadstone programme. Hirsch's involvement with both Blackbriar and Treadstone is, like Abbott, deeply reminiscent of a dark paternal in that he works with Bourne/Webb's psyche, subjecting him to brutal evaluations and harsh psychological techniques with the goal of weaponising him. During Hirsch's programme, and told via flashbacks, Bourne/Webb effectively undergoes a psychic rebirth and emerges as his present-day self, a deadly weapon that is controlled by older men, and used for dark and violent actions. Crucially, Bourne realises that he volunteered for the programme and that he was in the military prior to the CIA. However, before he can question Hirsch further, Bourne is attacked and forced to flee to the roof of the building where he confronts Paz (Edgar Ramírez), an agent whose life he spared earlier and who has the opportunity to kill him. In a moment of psychological truth, he forces Paz to question and reflect upon what they have both become in the service of the CIA and the old men who run it. 'Look at us. Look at what they make you give'. As Dodds (2010, p. 23) states, Bourne's '... survival depends on resisting particular constellations of power and security and in so doing offers a redemptive model of conflicted masculinity, which uses violence in a selective and knowing manner-Bourne kills fellow professionals and apologizes to victims and their families'. At this point in the film, Vosen unexpectedly appears and shoots at Bourne. Dodds describes the significance of this scene to the narrative:

Bourne and Vosen represent different manifestations of 'manpower'. Both assume the role of masculine protector. Both enjoy the loyalty and support of others, in particular women. But Bourne's masculinity is more conflicted; he is concerned about the welfare of others and even apologizes to the families of victims.

(2010, p. 32)

In terms of gender and psychological journeys, Bourne has started to confront his father hunger and his search for his identity as they effectively mesh into one, and he is getting closer as to why he volunteered for the Treadstone programme in the first place. Bourne falls into the East River, mimicking a deep plunge into his own subconscious, framed by the camera, and edited to encourage us to think that he dies. A postscript shows us Landy reporting Hirsch, Vosen and Kramer to the authorities and their subsequent arrest and closure of their black-ops programmes. The film concludes with Nicky smiling at the news that Jason Bourne's body has not been found yet, despite a three-day search. The film then cuts to a freeze frame of Bourne's river plunge, and he is shown as swimming and likely surviving. Bourne is depicted as having taken a number of courageous steps in his psychic quest to discover his former identity; his confrontation of the dark senex in the forms of Abbott and Hirsch has yielded partial results and uncovered some of what he needs in psychological terms. However, the continuing psychological ambiguity and ambivalence about Bourne's identity is, in many ways, crucial to keeping the franchise going. Too neat of an ending to this narrative device would imply that the films had concluded, and as we see in the next section, there is still one more reveal to come.

Jason Bourne (2016)

The final film of the franchise, *Jason Bourne*, is a direct sequel to *The Bourne Ultimatum*. With the final film's poster boldly proclaiming 'You know his name', potential audiences are given a strong sense that this will be the conclusion of the franchise. The poster also marks the return of Matt Damon following his absence from *The Bourne Legacy* (2012) which starred Jeremy Renner as agent Aaron Cross; *Jason Bourne* having little direct connection to *The Bourne Legacy*. With a steely gaze looking out of the poster, and deliberately framed in a harshly monochrome chiaroscuro close-up, it is intimated that in this film Bourne finally discovers the truth about himself. More importantly, for fans of the franchise, we also get to discover his family and its connection with the intelligence community and its operations, with the overarching question of his identity finally answered.

Taking place 12 years after the events of the first three films and reflecting the passage of real time since the release of the last film, Bourne is still living off-grid, surviving by working as a bare-knuckle boxer on the Greek border. He has largely recovered his memories, his amnesia fading into the background as he survives and stays off the radar. However, fate (in the shape of Nicky Parsons from the previous films) has other plans for him. Having left the American intelligence services, she has switched sides in geopolitical terms, and is now working with a loose-knit hacktivist whistle-blowing collective led by Christian Dassault (Vinzenz Kiefer), no doubt inspired by real-life figures Julian Assange, Edward Snowden, and Chelsea Manning. When Nicky's hack into classified CIA files to expose their black-ops programmes is realised, a new set of shadowy antagonists emerge. These include Cyberservices Division Chief, Heather Lee (Alicia Vikander), and yet another dark patriarchal father figure in the shape of CIA Director Robert Dewey (Tommy Lee Jones) who is in the process of setting up Operation Iron Hand, a more ruthless version of Operation Blackbriar. When Nicky discovers that Bourne's deceased father, CIA analyst Richard Webb, was instrumental in setting up Operation Treadstone, but crucially did not want his son joining the programme, she sets out to find Bourne and give him one of the last pieces of his identity puzzle. Travelling to Athens, Nicky tracks down Bourne, but the CIA have also sent an assassin, known as the Asset (Vincent Cassel) who holds a personal grudge against Bourne, as he was captured and tortured after Bourne leaked the details of Blackbriar to the media.

During violent anti-government riots (strongly echoing the real-life riots that took place in Athens during the austerity period), Nicky and Bourne are chased and attacked by their enemies. They manage to escape, but not before Nicky suffers a fatal wound. Here, the Bourne films are similar to the James Bond franchise is that the wounded and dying feminine seems to be a regular trope, with any women connected to Bourne/Webb suffering a violent end or fate (Marie and Nicky). Before dying, Nicky gives Bourne a locker key which allows him to access the hacked files that partially detail his father's role in Treadstone. Again this moment is psychologically significant, and again, very similar to the James Bond franchise, in that the wounded feminine is sacrificed for continuation of the masculine. The feminine can be argued to represent vulnerability in a way that the masculine cannot; if the masculine allows itself to be open, it is almost certainly potentially wounded or compromised by the actions of the feminine. Heather Lee is an exception, but it is also arguable that she is effectively masculinised and shows little overt femininity, and therefore not put at risk.

Following the few remaining clues available to him, Bourne tracks down Dassault in Berlin where he learns his family history contained in Nicky's encrypted files, but in doing so inadvertently alerts the CIA to his location where they send another assassination team. Fleeing to London, Bourne tracks down one of his father's colleagues, Malcolm Smith (Bill Camp), a potentially more positive older male role model, and finally learns the truth about his father and that the terrorist attack that killed him. The more difficult truth to face, however, is that the terrorist attack that motivated Bourne/Webb to join the CIA to avenge his father, was, in fact, orchestrated by Dewey and carried out by the Asset. Avoiding the CIA hit squad that kills Smith, Bourne/Webb is helped by Lee who disagrees with Dewey's methods and directs Bourne to a technology convention in Las Vegas. Here, Dewey is meeting with Aaron Kaloor (Riz Ahmed), a tech entrepreneur who was secretly funded by the CIA in his early days. Dewey wants to access to enhance Operation Iron Hand with Kaloor's flagship app, Deep Dream which would allow embedded real-time mass surveillance. When Kaloor refuses, Dewey, perhaps the ultimate shadow senex figure in the film franchise, plots to have the Asset kill both him and Lee, whose betrayal he has discovered.

Bourne foils both assassination attempts and confronts Dewey in a pivotal moment of the film. This is appropriately filmed in shadows with little light illuminating the main characters; here Dewey calmly states: 'Took a long time to get here Jason', the double meaning (psychologically and physically) abundantly clear. With the shadow senex finally confronting the younger man, Dewey challenges Bourne/Webb with the truth about his father not having the mettle to make the program work, but acknowledging that his son, Bourne/Webb, did. That the senex figure has betrayed both Webb father and son is characteristic of the shadow father, and Dewey's calm statement about Bourne/Webb's actions is shocking, truthful and disturbing: 'Thirty-two kills Jason. Everyone of them made a difference. People all across this country are safer because of what you did.' This chilling assertion of 'end justifies the means' philosophy is characteristic of post 9/11 *realpolitik* thinking, shorn of any particular ideological meaning. The events of 11 September 2001 when the Al-Qaeda terrorist network deliberately crashed planes into the World Trade Center in New York marked a change in attitude towards external threats to the USA in that post 9/11, George W. Bush launched a 'War on Terror'. This counter-terrorism policy was, in turn, argued to mark the growth in infringement of civil liberties (Howell & Lind, 2009) and the adoption of harsher measures against perceived enemies which was broadly supported by the American public (Nacos, Bloch-Elkon, & Shapiro, 2007).

When Bourne/Webb, the son figure, tries to articulate another means of achieving the same goal (presumably) of keeping the country safe, Dewey smirks and asks the penetrating question: 'And how's that working out for you?' This exposes Bourne/Webb's attempts to choose another, more peaceful path, as potentially futile and naïve. Dewey goes on to give Bourne/Webb another harsh truth; 'You're never going to find any peace. Not until you admit to yourself who you really are. (Pause). It's time to come in, Jason. It's time to come in'. This 'coming in' is common in spy and action films and refers to the process or action of being accepted back into the fold of the intelligence agency from which a character is estranged or previously rejected from. 'Coming in' can be a dangerous choice for an agent, and in Bourne/Webb's case, a potentially deadly one, as Dewey's verbal offer is, in reality, an attempt to stall for time whilst his aide Jeffers (Ato Essandoh) races to reach his boss and save him from Bourne/Webb. When Jeffers tries to save his boss, Bourne/Webb kills him, is wounded by Dewey, who in turn is shot dead by Lee, an interesting example of the strong (and masculinised) feminine gaining both revenge and ascendancy on the dark masculine, which is counter to the fate of Marie Kreutz and Nicky Parsons.

Bourne/Webb then chases after Asset, and in a deeply symbolic location of the sewers under Las Vegas, they engage in a shadowy, brutal, visceral, and bloody fight to the death, with Asset taunting Bourne/Webb: 'You're a traitor. You've always been a traitor. It's in your blood', presumably making a direct reference to Bourne/Webb's father. It is this final insult that inspires Bourne/Webb to overcome his opponent and break his neck, killing him. When Lee tries to entice Bourne/Webb back to the CIA with promises of making it into the organisation he wants it to be, he refuses and walks away, to disappear once again, his psychological and gender journey complete and presumably at peace with finally knowing, and accepting, who he is. With this downbeat ending, the franchise is at an end as well, with the dark father figures who caused the various conflicts with the figure of the son, defeated for now.

Conclusion

The Bourne film franchise clearly depicts the discovery of Bourne/Webb's father (crucially, no mother or other family members are mentioned), as being fundamental to his gender identity, the so-called masculine continuum (Biddulph, Bly, et al.). This father hunger (Stevens) expresses itself as an unconscious desire to know in the first film and is catalysed and gradually brought to consciousness by his struggles with his disassociative amnesia. It is both deliberate and ironic that the initial trauma that Bourne/Webb undergoes is prompted by his reluctance to execute Wombosi whilst he spends time with his son, the father showing himself as symbolically vulnerable. As Bourne/Webb gradually starts to discover who he really is, his struggle to know both his father, his real name and recover his memories becomes conflated with the bigger geopolitical picture in terms of the CIA and its various clandestine operations in the post-9/11 world. As Vosen states in a stark conversation with Landy about the dangers the United States faces and the need for the Treadstone and Blackbriar assassination programmes: 'You've seen the raw intel...you know how real the danger is. We need those programs now'. Mixed in with this, and providing the films with suitably dangerous and identifiable villains, are the shadow father figures of Abbott, Hirsch and Dewey, dangerous to the son in that they betray and wound both their surrogate family (the CIA) and their surrogate sons; not only Bourne/Webb but also the other participants in Treadstone and Blackbriar. The figure of the son, in this case Bourne/Webb, is wounded both physically and psychically during the films, by older men who act as toxic surrogate father figures. What makes Bourne/Webb different from the other assassins is his amnesia, and subsequent conscience; as Gaine states (2011, p. 162): 'Bourne's search for his identity and his past, including his guilt, ultimately serves to rehumanise him'. Ultimately, Bourne's psychic wound points the way for him to become whole again.

References

Biddulph, S. (1995). *Manhood: An action plan for changing men's lives* (2nd ed.). Lane Cove, NSW: Finch Publishing.
Bly, R. (1990). *Iron John: Men and masculinity* (2nd ed.). London: Rider.
Bruzzi, S. (2005). *Bringing up daddy: Fatherhood and masculinity in post-war Hollywood*. London: British Film Institute publishing.
Butler, J. (1990). *Gender trouble: Feminism and the subversion of identity*. London: Routledge.
Dodds, K. (2010). Jason Bourne: Gender, geopolitics, and contemporary representations of national security. *Journal of Popular Film and Television, 38*(1), 21–33.

Gaine, V. (2011). Remember everything, absolve nothing: Working through trauma in the Bourne trilogy. *Cinema Journal*, *51*(1), 159–163.
Hamad, H. (2014). *Postfeminism and paternity in contemporary U.S. film: Framing fatherhood*. Abingdon: Routledge.
Herzog, J. (1983/2013). *Father hunger: Explorations with adults and children*. Hove: Routledge.
Howell, J., & Lind, J. (Eds.). (2009). *Civil society under strain: Counter-terrorism policy, civil society and aid post-9/11*. Hartford, CT: Kumarian Press.
Nacos, B. L., Bloch-Elkon, Y., & Shapiro, R. Y. (2007). Post-9/11 terrorism threats, news coverage, and public perceptions in the United States. *International Journal of Conflict and Violence*, *1*(2), 105–126.
Pomerance, M., & Gateward, F. (Eds.). (2005). *Where the boys are: Cinemas of masculinity and youth*. Detroit, MI: Wayne State.
Samuels, A. (1993). *The political psyche*. London: Routledge.
Stevens, A. (1994). *Jung: A very short introduction*. Oxford: Oxford University Press.
Tacey, D. (1997). *Remaking men: Jung, spirituality and social change*. London: Routledge.
Tasker, Y. (1993). *Spectacular bodies: Gender, genre and the action cinema*. London: Routledge.

Chapter 8

Beyond Actions: Remodelling Heroine-Hood in *The Grandmaster*

Jasmine Yu-Hsing Chen

Abstract

This chapter examines how the breakthrough of Zhang Ziyi's depiction of a female kung fu master in *The Grandmaster* (2013) transforms the figure of the heroine in Chinese action films. Zhang is well known for her acting in action films conducted by renowned directors, such as Ang Lee, Zhang Yimou and Wong Kar-wai. After winning 12 different Best Actress awards for her portrayal of Gong Ruomei in *The Grandmaster*, Zhang announced that she would no longer perform in any action films to show her highest respect for the superlative character Gong. Tracing Zhang's transformational portrait of a heroine in *The Grandmaster* alongside her other action roles, this analysis demonstrates how her performance projects the directors' distinctive gender viewpoints. I argue that Zhang's characterisation of Gong remodels heroine-hood in Chinese action films. Inheriting the typical plot of a daughter's use of martial arts for revenge for her father's death, Gong breaks from conventional Chinese action films that highlight romantic love during a woman's adventure and the decisive final battle scene. Beyond the propensity for sensory stimulation, Gong's characterisation enables Zhang to determine that women can really *act* in action films – demonstrating their inner power and ability to create multi-layered characters – not merely relying upon physical action. This chapter offers a relational perspective of how women transform the action film genre not merely as gender spectacles but as embodied figures that represent emerging female subjectivity.

Keywords: The Grandmaster; Zhang Ziyi; heroine-hood; characterisation; kung fu film; female subjectivity

The final scene of *The Grandmaster* (2013) shows Gong Ruomei, also known as Gong Er (Zhang Ziyi), recalling how her father had taught her *baguazhang* (literally meaning 'eight trigrams palm'), a well-known form of Chinese kung fu, when she was young. An overhead shot shows one of the film's most beautiful scenes, as her *baguazhang* movements create a semi-circle in the heavy snow on the ground; accompanying the montage, a voice-over says, 'What I learned from my father wasn't skill (*zhao*) so much as ideation (*yi*)'. The idea of ideation, by Wayne Wong's definition, refers to a specific configuration of the presence and the absence that contains powerful emotion in tranquillity. Wong's translation of *yi* as 'ideation' is more accurate than the English subtitle as 'a code of honour' (Wong, 2018).

As the heroine in this action film, Gong's final image is poetic and focuses on non-actional ideation more than fighting movements. Gong's words also reflect the director Wong Kar-wai's vision for the creative potential of Chinese action film: the synthesis of the abstract ideals and the extraordinary martial arts performance aims to create an insightful moment of quietness, not emotional excitement (Wong, 2018). This vision also shapes Gong as a heroine with a strong, unique subjectivity rather than a simple action film female character who falls in love and follows heroes.

The plot of *The Grandmaster* focuses on the Wing Chun grandmaster Ip Man (Leung Chiu-wai). However, Gong Ruomei is significant as the only female character to challenge the male masters in the film. Shortly before the Second Sino-Japanese War (1937–1945), the northern grandmaster Gong Baosen (Wang Qingxiang), visits the south to celebrate his retirement. He was accompanied by his appointed heir Ma San (Zhang Jin) and his daughter Gong Ruomei. During his stay, Ip Man, a master of Wing Chun style of kung fu in Southern China, defeats Gong Baosen in a contest. Gong Baosen's defeat prompts Gong Ruomei to demand a match with Ip. She finds herself having a crush on Ip, following their duel in the gold pavilion; a lavishly decorated brothel frequented by the region's kung fu masters. The unspoken attraction between the two remains unrequited as the Sino-Japanese War erupts. The war devastates Ip's family and livelihood, and then the film shifts focus to Gong Ruomei. Gong Ruomei, after learning the death of her father following a confrontation with Ma San, returns to her hometown in Japanese-occupied north-eastern China where she vows to avenge her father's death. Having drifted apart for more than a decade, Ip and Gong eventually meet again in Hong Kong and recall their previous relationship.

There are four versions of *The Grandmaster* in circulation. Despite the variations, the core story is of the kung fu masters' personal vicissitudes as they struggle with radical sociopolitical changes due to the war. There are three versions of the film that screened in 2013: A Chinese version of 130 minutes mainly targeting audiences in Hong Kong, China and Taiwan, a version that was debuted in February 2013 at the Berlin International Film Festival running at 123 minutes and a version distributed by The Weinstein Company (US), running at 108 minutes. The European and the US versions have different arrangements of narrative and story sequence, and both eliminate some details to cater to the target audience's preference. In 2015, a 3D version lasting 111 minutes was created with a structure like the US version. The longer Chinese version (130 minutes) includes more details of Gong's characterisation.

My analysis of the film will be primarily based on the 3D version, while specifically addressing some points from the Chinese version to fully consider the heroine-hood presented in the film. This chapter shows how *The Grandmaster* transcends external kung fu movements and presents a woman's hidden affection, struggle to make difficult decisions and the challenges of daily life using cinematic subtext.

Although Zhang Ziyi and other lead actors such as Leung Chiu-wai and Chang Chen trained extensively in the specific Chinese kung fu form before acting in *The Grandmaster*, the film features much more than extravagant fighting. In comparison to the typical ending of protagonists' sensory-stimulated fighting in numerous Chinese action films, Gong's revenge encounter is placed in the middle of the story, while Zhang's most impressive performance occurs after the revenge. As the only female kung fu master in the film, Zhang's virtuosic performance won her multiple Best Actress awards. Following these achievements, Zhang announced that she would no longer perform in any action films. She claimed that all team members involved in *The Grandmaster* collectively helped her polish the performance to make Gong an insuperable character. Thus, she stopped performing as other martial heroines to show her highest respect for the superlative character Gong (Sun, 2013). Zhang's decision raises the question of how the characterisation of Gong is distinctive from existing characters and how Gong remodels heroine-hood in Chinese action films.

This chapter examines how the breakthrough of Zhang's portrayal of Gong transformed the role of female characters in Chinese action films. Zhang is well known for her acting in action films led by renowned directors, including *Crouching Tiger, Hidden Dragon* (2000) directed by Ang Lee, *House of Flying Daggers* (2004) directed by Zhang Yimou and *The Grandmaster* (2013) directed by Wong Kar-wai. Tracing Zhang's transformative portraits of female action heroes in *The Grandmaster* and her other action films, this analysis demonstrates how her performance projects the directors' distinctive gender viewpoints. By drawing on interviews of the actor, descriptions of her and analysing her performances, this chapter not only considers the meaning of her character's physical movements but also how the inner tension of characters' personalities are expressed in the quieter, more mundane scenes. Such tension is closely related to the philosophical connotation of kung fu. I argue that Zhang's performance as Gong remodels the roles of heroines, daughters and women in Chinese action films. Although *The Grandmaster* initially follows the typical plot of a daughter using martial arts for revenge, Gong shatters the conventional genre pattern that highlights romantic love during a woman's adventure and the final decisive battle scenes. In her performances, Zhang embodies womanhood and gender in ways that defy the character model of women in typical Chinese action films and enables the actress to fully showcase her talent and subjectivity through the filming process.

Gender Subjectivity and Women in Chinese Action Films: Surveying the Field

The idea of subjectivity, in the context of Western philosophy, is thought to have its roots in the Enlightenment. In Enlightenment thought, the idea of subjectivity, and therefore subjecthood, centres on a free, autonomous individuality that is unique and rational (Mansfield, 2020). Enlightenment philosophy, particularly that of Immanuel Kant, often bases notions of subjectivity on a gender-neutral unitary and universal subject, but numerous feminist philosophers rightfully argue that these notions are conceptually dependent on the female subject as the 'shadow' (Gatens, 1991, p. 5). While the male subject is constructed 'as self-contained and as an owner of his person and capacities' (Gatens, 1991, p. 5), the female subject is constructed as 'prone to disorder and passion, as economically and politically dependent on men. ... She is indistinguishable from a wife/ mother' (Gatens, 1991, p. 5). In short, women are framed as more bound to the limits and will of their bodies than men. The female subject position is linked to fleshy continuity, rather than to an autonomous and individualised 'soul' or 'mind' (Battersby, 1998, p. 10). It is women's capacity to give birth that is the basis for the bounded body-subject model and similar paradigms of self–other relations based on that model (Tyler, 2000). Feminist theorists like Simone de Beauvoir have challenged the presumptions that women's subjectivity is the mere inferior negation of that male subjectivity. In *The Second Sex*, de Beauvoir places the female body at the centre of her philosophical investigation of gender by asserting that the body 'is not a *thing*, it is a situation: it is our grasp on the world and the outline for our projects' (de Beauvoir, 2009, p. 46). Following this radical new understanding of womanhood, Nick Mansfield has reviewed popular theories of subjectivity over the last 30 years and concluded that they all reject the idea of the subject as a completely self-contained being on the basis that the subject is constructed, made within the world. This assumption of a bounded subject is still apparent in discussions of gender and sexuality (Mansfield, 2020). Therefore, how women break through the gender roles constructed based on their bodies and fertility choices is an important manifestation of female subjectivity.

Responding to women's social status as the second sex in the Chinese context, based on Confucianism, women's gender roles further require them to support the family and detach from personal social life. Confucianism has long been the dominant social ideology in China, and the values of the Confucian family are based on gender separation of male and female and the division of domestic and public spaces. Women's mobility, freedom and social life are highly restricted (Lu, 2019). Confucianism has assigned three roles to a Chinese woman: 'the sexual object and possession of the man, the child-bearing tool to carry on her husband's family name, and the servant to the whole family' (Gao, 2003, p. 118). Such conservative values have been challenged during the twentieth century, especially with the rise of the film industry as it allowed women to perform different gender roles on the big screen and enact these possibilities for themselves off-screen.

During the 1950s–1970s, Hong Kong was a major production centre for Chinese action movies. With the industrialisation and modernisation of Hong

Kong, the reappearance of heroines in action films in the late 1960s to the early 1970s was often regarded as an empowering symbol of women's capacity for social mobility at that time (Kar, Bren, & Ho, 2004; Yip, 2017). Women commonly retain certain masculine attributes and are viewed as an extension of excessive masculinity in Hong Kong action films (Lo, 2005). However, the real transgressive aspect of these heroines is their skill in performing multiple gender identities, including female masculinity, an appropriation of mainstream male norms, as well as feminine masquerades, a conscious exaggeration of femininity (Yip, 2017). Throughout the history of Chinese films, a heroine is often a distinctive figure in the male-dominated martial arts world, as she 'is not only the action hero but also the subject of desire, she can eventually become the mate of the man she loves' (Dai, 2005, p. 89). Likewise, in Chinese action films, women are either portrayed as more gender-neutral, or their bodies are made hyper-visible to suggest the mysterious power of sexuality in a way that appeals to male desires. Defying each of these, Zhang Ziyi's performances in Chinese action films utilise both the female body and female sensibilities to garner new and alternative symbolic meanings under the gaze of different directors.

This chapter offers a relational perspective of how Zhang's portrayal of Gong transforms the Chinese action film genre from one merely treating gender as a spectacle into one where women are embodied figures that echo the emergence of female subjectivity. As stated in the literature review, how women break through and defy gender roles is a powerful site of female subjectivity. Action films usually treat the heroine's kung fu as mere skills for defence and attack, thereby foreclosing how kung fu is a subjective journey of learning oneself. The process is especially meaningful for women, because, in a patriarchal society, they are often viewed as weak and in need of protection. Learning kung fu not only increases women's physical mobility but also their emotional and mental autonomy, making them more independent and powerful. Thus, more than physical skills, kung fu is an attitude that deeply affects a martial arts master's personality traits, choice-making and the sublimation of their mentality. As such, the matured interiority of Gong's character also remodels the conventional representation of kung fu as merely 'flashy fighting' in action films.

More Than Actions: The Characterisation of Gong Ruomei

Wuxia and kung fu are two main genres within Chinese action films. One key distinction between the genres is their stylistic differences. *Wuxia* films feature supernaturalism through fantastical swordplay or conventional martial arts movements based on traditional Chinese opera. Kung fu films, on the other hand, feature authenticity and realism through hand-to-hand combat (Wong, 2018, p. 202). The aesthetic value of kung fu films is commonly questioned by film critics and scholars, as many of the rapid productions are characterised by 'a disjointed storyline, ridiculous acting, excessive violence and shabby quality' (Yu, 2012, p. 13). With its multi-layered characters, *The Grandmaster* is a kung fu film that does more than stimulate the senses through fight scenes, as is evident in Zhang's transformation during the filming. Zhang practised martial arts for six months to play Jen in *Crouching Tiger, Hidden Dragon*. During the practice and filming, she had one simple goal: to validate Director Lee Ang's decision to cast her as Jen. Training to play Gong was more challenging for Zhang, but it helped her gain more commitment to the role and build her confidence, giving her more complex goals (Sun, 2013). Because Gong has more restrained calmness and desolation than Jen, embodying Gong enabled Zhang to realise that women can really perform in action roles – demonstrating their inner power and depth – rather than merely carrying out physical fighting and flat dialogue.

To understand Zhang's characterisation of Gong, it is important to investigate her training for the role. Well before filming began in 2010, the vision of *The Grandmaster* originated in 1996. Director Wong Kar-wai requested leading actress Zhang to learn different styles of *baguazhang* to fully capture the techniques from various angles. *Baguazhang* differs from Chinese kung fu styles like *bajiquan* (literally 'eight extremes fist') and *xingyiquan* (literally 'form-intentioned fist') that feature linear, masculine and powerfully explosive movements. Instead, it stresses circular and flowing water-like movements and the reconciliation of masculinity and femininity. In this manner, it embodies the cosmology of the eight trigrams (*bagua*), which are eight different symbols that form and correspond to the changing ways of the *yin* and *yang*. The two forces are commonly characterised as male (*yang*) and female (*yin*), hard and soft, forceful and submissive (Dillon, 2013, p. 371). *Baguazhang* represents this mix of masculine and feminine forces, as these trigrams share commonalities but focus on different aspects of duality.

Even though Zhang was considered an experienced actor, she appreciated the demanding and authentic kung fu training. Despite her background as a dancer professionally trained in Chinese folk dancing, learning *baguazhang* was challenging for Zhang. Nonetheless, Zhang became obsessive about the practice of *baguazhang* as she believed it was necessary to undergo a physical transformation to wholly represent the character (Fang & Zhu, 2013). *Baguazhang* features a unique combination of softness and rigidity. The training requires attention to leveraging force and softening one's movements yet being extremely persistent when attacking (Xing & Li, 2007). The actions should show relaxation in exertion and decisiveness in calmness. The featuring of *baguazhang* in the film serves as a symbol for Gong as a strong-minded woman. Not only does she excel in outward movement skills but she also has a determined mind. For example, before Gong's encounter with Ma, Ma attempts to push down the Gong family servant, Old Jiang (Shang Tielong), but Gong silently supports Jiang's back with her palm. This simple and subtle action of support symbolises Gong's inner strength and will to save the legacy of the Gong family.

Zhang's years of practising *baguazhang* prepared her for the action sequences and cultivated her internal strength to engage with Gong's spirit and attitude toward life. Comparing Gong to the character Jen Yu in *Crouching Tiger, Hidden Dragon*, Zhang's performances show her confidence and ability to be more than a mere action-movie actress. *Crouching Tiger, Hidden Dragon* was Zhang's first action film, which she began as a college student at the Central Academy of Drama in Beijing. At that time, she had little professional acting experience, so she channelled the brilliance, youthfulness and curiosity of her age into the role. She put more effort into learning the martial arts and less effort into understanding how to analyse a scene, a line or the rhythm of the performance. Thus, Yu appeared like 'a wild horse galloping on the grassland, completely letting go' (Yuan, 2015, p. 418). After a decade of acting experience, Zhang aimed to accurately control the emotion and remove any unnaturalness in her performances. She thus thought that portraying Gong was a process of diminishment and excluding superfluous actions (Yuan, 2015, p. 419). Zhang indeed creates a heroine who is an excellent kung fu master and not merely in physical skill. Her performance of Gong also captures the inner, spiritual journey of kung fu, as the heroine abandons the techniques and commits to her choices to honour her family despite the resulting loneliness. Zhang's kung fu training provided her with the emotional capacity and understanding to emphasise Gong's invisible depth more than visible actions.

The change in Zhang's performance style from unreserved to multi-layered is related to director Wong's insistence on implicitness and an insightful visual narrative. Wong's directorial style highly relies on actors' impromptu performance, as the shooting usually commences without a script. More specifically, during filming, Wong tends to give actors a general direction of the scene rather than a fixed script (Bettinson, 2014, p. 1). This directorial style provides actors greater freedom to perform based on their reception of the character. During the editing process, Wong deliberately eliminates sections that contain excess emotional or sensory stimulation. He only retains footage that demonstrates the actor's inner affective tension with moderate external actions. For example, when filming the scene where Gong's father was killed by his apprentice Ma San and Gong takes the train back to attend the funeral, Zhang sobbed uncontrollably and went into a frenzy over the thought of her father's death. Zhang was satisfied with her performance of Gong's grief and indignation in that scene, and Wong could tell that her rage was strong enough to convince audiences she could be a killer. Yet, Wong finally decided to completely cut this emotional outburst, only keeping the footage where Zhang represented Gong's sadness with a calm expression. The screenwriter Xu Haofeng believed that Wong shows his insight through choosing the most critical line or expression in the actor's eyes, and omitting the rest, no matter how impressive (Lv & Xu, 2013). This editing philosophy transcends the belief that the genre of Chinese kung fu film is 'replete with bloody, violent, formulaic, action-driven narrative and visual sequences' (Ongiri, 2002). *The Grandmaster* demonstrates how an action film can also be a valuable artwork that does not simply feature fight sequences. In Wong's action film, he demonstrates that even the duel should be a process of controlling both external movement and sensory emotions. In place of establishing wide-angle shots, close-up shots of characters speaking or viewed from a fixed position are used.

In contrast to the crucial fighting scenes in *Crouching Tiger, Hidden Dragon* and *House of Flying Daggers* that occur in an outdoor space so that actors can show off their martial arts skills, the fight scenes in *The Grandmaster* are mainly in indoor or narrow spaces. For example, the master Ip Man and Gong Ruomei's father Gong Baosen compete over breaking a cake in their hands. When Gong Ruomei worries that her dual with Ip will destroy the delicate décor in the Golden

Pavilion, a lavishly decorated brothel frequented by the region's martial artists, Ip claims that kung fu is about precision, so if anything gets broken, he loses the fight. At the very end of the 3D version, a post-credits scene shows how Gong demonstrates her 64 hands technique to Ip within the short time between a door opening and closing. Within such a short time, it is unlikely that Gong really demonstrates all the techniques. What the brief scene does show, implicitly, is the depth of Gong's inner self and mastery of ideation. In *Crouching Tiger, Hidden Dragon* and *House of Flying Daggers*, Zhang's main scenes feature her elegant martial arts movements. Despite the high quality of her characters' skills, men treat them like objects they want to conquer and project their male desires onto these women. To a certain extent, these women with high martial arts abilities all end up submitting to men's superior physical strength. In terms of mental strength, however, Gong in *The Grandmaster* challenges the trope of a woman being inferior to, or desperately needing, a man. For one, Gong is the master whom Ip always wants to ask for advice. Even when Gong chooses to show Ip her 64 hands technique, the composition of the scene does not emphasise her actions and skill (*zhao*) but rather uses lighting techniques and close-ups of Gong's face to highlight her abstract understanding of how to apply ideation (*yi*). Even with a personality as strong as the men in the film, Gong's image in the movie is neither masculine nor gender-neutral. Instead, she exhibits unique plasticity to inhabit both masculine and feminine features without reverting to displaying her sexuality and her body in ways just to appease men. This portrayal of Gong transgresses the usual role expectations of women in Chinese action films by hinting at her complex inner self. After the short demonstration, with Gong's back turned to Ip, she flashes a complacent smile. She restrainedly but clearly shows the value of a woman's confidence in the male-dominated martial arts world. Such humble confidence from a woman is especially notable for an action movie as it gives her character inner depth and does not simply emphasise actions.

Beyond Revenge: Daughterhood With Female Subjectivity

In addition to Zhang's performance of Gong, her other characters, Jen Yu in *Crouching Tiger, Hidden Dragon* and Mei in *House of Flying Daggers* showcase complex female roles, in particular, the social role of a daughter. Jen Yu runs away from an arranged marriage while Mei is a pseudo-daughter who shoulders the responsibility of getting revenge for a father figure in her life. These female characters, Jen and Mei, are, on the surface, strong-minded and brave like Gong, but their lives still come to be framed by men. Jen's subjectivity is defined by her impulsion and romantic, naïve imagination of *jiang hu*, an imaginary martial arts world that 'connotes the image of a wandering life' (Chan, 2004, p. 301). Jen later realises her recklessness in abandoning her obligations; she then commits suicide after being reunited with her secret lover. Compared with Jen, Mei lets her fate be decided by her daughter role to an even greater extent. To avenge her pseudo father's death, Mei joins an assassin community in which she, among numerous women, must obey their masculine female leader's command. While Mei's sole goal is to kill the enemy who took her pseudo father's life, her life takes another turn when she falls in love. She leaves the assassin community, and later she sacrifices her life to save her lover at the end of the film. Both Jen and Mei's tragic fates are deceptive; while these women appear to distance themselves from the patriarchal structure, they are tightly bound to it. After these women complete their romantic relationships with men or avenge their fathers, their lives immediately come to an end, as if their lives are meaningless without a man to define them.

Unlike Jen and Mei, Gong is an independent woman who actively chooses to live her life on her terms after achieving revenge for her father, even though her life alone proves even more challenging than the fight for revenge. Gong seeks revenge not simply to kill but to maintain the justice and honour of the kung fu spirit. This spirit is threatened when Gong's father is killed by his disciple Ma San. Gong is also unique in that while, conventionally, a master only teaches males, Gong's father raised her as a son and secretly taught her *Baguazhang*. Her background also distances her from typical female characters who superstitiously believe in fate. In the Chinese version of the film, while all her father's old friends urge Gong to forgo the revenge, as Ma has a Japanese military force behind him, Gong still insists she must reclaim what belongs to her family, the kung fu. Pursuing revenge is Gong's decision, even though this decision goes against her father's last wish. She knows that her father wants her to have a peaceful life, not one full of revenge, but Gong believes that 'if I do not revenge his death, I will never be at peace'. Her father's old friends persuade her to accept that her father's death may be God's will, but Gong replies vehemently: 'I am God's Will'. Gong's determination shines through in this scene, setting her apart from other female characters like Jen and Mei who fold under the weight of patriarchy. Despite the great pain of losing her father, Gong retains her autonomy and strength and thereby resists the traditional passivity of Chinese women to continue pursuing revenge.

Gong is one of the very handful female kung fu masters in her era, and she is the one who deliberately follows the kung fu honour code. After her father's funeral, Gong goes to Ma San's house despite senior male masters discouraging her to do so. Although she harbours great resentment, she does not directly break into Ma's room but says: 'I respect you as a brother-in-arms' but 'you cannot hide forever'. By controlling her grief and anger here to not to break into Ma's room, Gong acts on her belief that kung fu reflects more of a person's integrity than physical techniques. However, Ma takes advantage of a sexist etiquette rule to refuse the duel. The rule holds that an engaged woman does not belong to her birth family, and at this point in the film, Gong is engaged to a man who is out of the kung fu circle. Ma thus claims that Gong is disqualified from taking revenge for her father, which puts Gong in a dilemma: to forfeit revenge or her engagement. This dilemma eventually becomes 'the core of her rebellious femininity', and she 'goes beyond the doctrine of male apprenticeship and becomes a remodelled female grandmaster loyal to her authentic self' (Tan, 2019). To avenge her father, Gong chooses to give up the right to get married, pass on her skills and have children. Her choice also illustrates her refusal to abide by the dominant

Confucian expectations of women. Gong understands her sacrifice, suggesting that kung fu gives her more life meaning than anything man could ever. After Gong defeats Ma, he claims that he has returned what he obtained from the Gong family. Gong replies, 'let's be clear, you didn't return it to me, I took it back myself'. This line highlights Gong's self-awareness of her autonomy and her right to uphold the dignity of kung fu. Her courage to actively claim her agency is rare in the era in which the film is set, as is a woman who has forged her independence in the male-dominated sphere of kung fu. Beyond physical destruction, Gong's spiritual pursuit for revenge shows a determination to maintain a master's code of honour, thereby staying true to kung fu as a practice of cultivating an honest self and upholding one's integrity.

Zhang said that the characterisation of Gong was built up little by little through the filming process. Sometimes Zhang encountered contradictory points within herself and the character, but she always ended up understanding and accepting the character (Fang & Zhu, 2013). Zhang believes that the ideation of kung fu is a kung fu master's realm and understanding about the world, people and things. Wholehearted concentration in the art can turn the practice of kung fu into a way to communicate with self, even if only for a few moments. Such momentary self-communication connects the present aura, air and a master's physical and mental state. In turn, playing Gong gave Zhang access to many feelings she had never experienced (Qin, 2013). Zhang claims that she became more focused and tough by embodying Gong, which explains why and how the character has enriched her life and career so deeply (Qin, 2013). During the filming of *The Grandmaster*, when Zhang became the subject of celebrity gossip for her affair with a couple of rich businessmen, she was quoted as saying the tenacity that she learned from playing Gong helped to mentally sustain her (Sun, 2013). Almost like a symbiotic relationship, Zhang and Gong shape and influence one another; the ways in which Zhang embraced and processed the contradictions between herself and Gong is what allowed Gong to transform her as well.

Gong actively chooses to accept both her revenge and her perspective of herself. As one of a handful of female masters at that time, Gong is conscious of the consequences of her activities and how they add meaning to her identity. By showing self-awareness of her social role and subject position, it is evident she understands that her actions will further mark her as a social outcast, unable to wholly be herself with women or men. Accepting this fate, she still chooses to do what is most important to her. Her sacrifice demonstrates her commitment to her subjectivity, understanding that not following her heart would reduce her to the social role she is expected to play.

Resisting Sexual Objectification: The Woman's Romance in *The Grandmaster*

The focus on Gong's interior self and transgression of gender norms remodels the typical representation of the heroine's body and romance found in numerous Chinese action films. Commonly, action films include a dramatic romance between the hero and heroine to attract the viewer's attention. In *Crouching Tiger, Hidden Dragon*, Jen's young female body is clearly an object of the male gaze that projects men's sexual desire. Jen refuses her arranged marriage and is secretly in love with Lo (Chang Chen), who is a desert bandit, with whom she shares a romantic love scene in the middle of the Gobi Desert. After Jen is drugged by her jealous martial arts mentor Jade Fox (Cheng Pei-pei), who has traded her sexuality and innocence in pursuit of more refined skills, she similarly uses her sex appeal to seduce the master Li Mubai (Chow Yun-fat). Jen is portrayed as an immature woman with an incredible gift, unworthy of other male masters' respect because she uses her sex appeal to her advantage. Similarly, in *House of Flying Daggers*, Mei is almost raped by her old lover Captain Leo (Lau Tak-wah) and is later killed by him when she chooses to follow her true love Captain Jin (Kaneshiro Takeshi). Different from traditional Confucian values that treat women's seclusion within, and devotion to, the family as a virtue, these women project romantic imaginations of mobility, which are diverse in a manner that foregrounds their subjectivity. Yet, the adventurous heroine's romantic love tends to revolve around their bodies as sex objects to be conquered by men in these films.

The characterisation of Gong in *The Grandmaster* repudiates this genre convention, as Gong's favourable impression of Ip Man and vice versa cannot be simply described as a romance or love interest. Their connection is built on their devotion to kung fu and their appreciation of each other's talent. For instance, Gong invites Ip to the Golden Pavilion, which usually only serves men, to have a contest. When Gong first directly faces Ip in the Gold Pavilion, the scene shows courtesans dressed in shiny cheongsam while Gong sits in the centre wearing a plain and neat cheongsam. She has not accepted Ip's defeat of her father three days ago. At the gilded, high-class brothel, Gong and Ip sit on opposite sides of a long table. Both Gong and Ip are quiet and solemn. However, even though their faces are calm, in Zhang's words, their hearts are 'turbulent' with emotions (Sun, 2013). The turbulence of their relationship is further clarified in the following scene, in which Ip and Gong engage in a duel as if it is a delicate courtship, exuding a sense of attachment. Their relationship dynamic goes through subtle changes based on their appreciation of each other's kung fu. Gong initiates their interaction and impresses Ip with her capacity and compelling temperament. After Gong tactically wins the contest, Ip asks if he can visit her in her hometown to further compare notes, and Gong promises that she will be waiting for his arrival. Their relationship never surpasses kung fu; it is their mutual appreciation of each other's skill and personhood that opens space for Gong to show her inner self.

Even with the demanding fight sequences, Zhang said the most challenging scene to perform was Gong's farewell to Ip in Hong Kong after the war. In fact, during the filming of the scene, Zhang did not 'act', and instead naturally and accurately expressed what she wanted to say (Yuan, 2015, p. 420). Before her last meeting with Ip, she carefully puts on beautiful makeup, though she has been sick and very pale for a while. In interviews, Zhang explained that her expressions of Gong's feelings were like freezing water that slowly melted and flowed down. The water was still cold, but one can sense the warmth and emotion hidden behind it

(Yuan, 2015, p. 420). The three-year long filming process made Zhang feel that the characterisation of Gong was an inseparable part of her life and that she understands Gong's every decision wholeheartedly (Fang & Zhu, 2013). During the filming, Zhang gradually realised that Gong is only calm on the surface, hiding the tears in her heart (Fang & Zhu, 2013). Director Ang Lee praised Zhang's performance of Gong's confession to Ip as the key moment that earned her the Golden Horse Award for Best Leading Actress, particularly as her seemingly calm words that speak to the audience's restless emotion (Interview Team, 2013). When Gong told Ip that 'I had had you in my heart', the past perfect tense designates that they will never have another chance to progress their relationship and their kung fu through one another. Her words complement her regrets of missing a dearest friend, yet she does not regret her decision for revenge. Alongside Gong's onscreen journey, the process of learning kung fu and restraining her affection put Zhang on her own self-searching journey.

Epilogue

The heroines that Zhang has performed indeed reflect maturation as an action star, from *Crouching Tiger, Hidden Dragon* to *The Grandmaster*. The representation of gender in *The Grandmaster* not only advances Zhang's performance to new heights but also advances the Chinese action film genre. Gong's characterisation shows both immense strength and vulnerability, sometimes by being silent and expressing loneliness at the idea that no one can understand her. Even though she is determined to abandon her affection for her fiancé and Ip, she is nostalgic for the old days. The characterisation of Gong transcends the typical female romantic love interest by featuring her spiritual communication with Ip through kung fu and her regret of lost time with Ip. The short-lived fate of their relationship gives her an irreplicable quality. It is in these ways that the film provides a new standard for representing gender with such nuance in Chinese action films.

Much more than a master in skill, Zhang's heart-melting performance pursuing her revenge shows that she embodies the philosophies of kung fu. Her portrayal of Gong shifts the sole focus from fighting action to also showing the spirit of kung fu. The real challenge, the film suggests, begins after the fight when it is time to face oneself. Playing Gong empowered Zhang to believe she 'can do better than just kicking ass', and thus realised she wants to take on characters with depth that likewise showcase her depth as an actress (Headlee & Zhang, 2013). *The Grandmaster* strives past current choreographic and cinematographic portrayals of action and stasis in Chinese action films (Wong, 2018). This change opens space for Gong to be a three-dimensional character that expands and enriches the potential for heroines in action films.

References

Battersby, C. (1998). *The phenomenal woman: Feminist metaphysics and the patterns of identity*. Cambridge: Polity.

Bettinson, G. (2014). *The sensuous cinema of Wong Kar-Wai: Film poetics and the aesthetic of disturbance*. Hong Kong: Hong Kong University Press.

Chan, S. (2004). Figures of hope and the filmic imagery of *Jianghu* in contemporary Hong Kong cinema. In E. Cheung & Y. Chu (Eds.), *Between home and the world: A reader in Hong Kong cinema* (pp. 297–330). Hong Kong: Oxford University Press.

de Beauvoir, S. (2009). *The Second Sex*. London: Jonathan Cape.

Dillon, M. (2013). *China: A cultural and historical dictionary*. London: Routledge.

Fang, Y., & Zhu, Y. (2013, January 6). Zongshi zhilu: zhuanfang Liang chaowei, Zhang Ziyi ji muhou tuandui [The Road of the Grandmaster: The Interview of Leung Chiu-wai, Zhang Ziyi and the Backstage Crew]. *Southern Metropolis Daily*, p. RB01.

Gao, X. (2003). Women existing for men: Confucianism and social injustice against women in China. *Race, Gender & Class, 10*(3), 114–125.

Gatens, M. (1991). *Feminism and Philosophy: Perspectives on Difference and Equality*. Bloomington: Indiana University Press.

Headlee, C. (Interviewer), & Zhang, Z. (Interviewee). (2013, August 22). Grandmaster Ziyi Zhang: I Can *Do Better than just kicking ass*. [Audio radio]. Retrieved from https://www.npr.org/transcripts/214483001

Interview Team of the Golden Horse Awards. (2013, November 24). Li Kangsheng yadaoxing chengdi, Zhang Ziyi xiansheng Zheng Xiuwen [Li Kang-Sheng Won best actor award with no doubts; Zhang Ziyi Won a narrow victory over Zheng Xiuwen]. *Liberty Time*.

Dai, J. (2005). Order/anti-order: Representation of identity in Hong Kong action movies. In Morris, M., Li, S. L., & Ching-kiu, S. C. (Eds.). *Hong Kong connections: Transnational imagination in action cinema*. Hong Kong: Hong Kong University Press.

Kar, L., Bren, F., & Ho, S. (2004). *Hong Kong cinema: A cross-cultural view*. Lanham, MD: Scarecrow Press.

Lo, K.-C. (2005). Fighting female masculinity: Women warriors and their foreignness in Hong Kong action cinema of the 1980s. In L. Pang & D. Wong (Eds.), *Masculinities and Hong Kong cinema*. Hong Kong: Hong Kong University Press.

Lu, W. (2019). Gender and social life in imperial China. In *Oxford research encyclopedia of Asian history*. Retrieved from https://doi.org/10.1093/acrefore/9780190277727.013.201.

Lv, Y. (Interviewer), & Xu, H. (Interviewee). (2013, February 5). Yidai zongshi bianju Xu Haofeng fangtan [The interview of Xu Haofeng, the scriptwriter of *The Grandmaster*]. Interview Transcript. Retrieved from http://www.niubo.cc/article-445-1.html

Mansfield, N. (2020). *Subjectivity: Theories of the self from Freud to Haraway*. London: Routledge.

Ongiri, A. A. (2002). "He wanted to be just like Bruce lee": African Americans, kung fu theatre and cultural exchange at the margins. *Journal of Asian American Studies*, 5(1), 31–40.

Qin, W. (2013, January 8). (Interviewer) Zhuanfang Zhang Ziyi: Sannian kunnan yishiran [The interview of Zhang Ziyi: Three years of difficulties have been relieved]. ifeng.com. Interview article. Retrieved from http://ent.ifeng.com/movie/special/grandmasters/zhangziyi/#pageTop

Sun, L. (2013, January 18). Zhang Ziyi: woxiang kandao Yu Jiaolong yu Gong Er xiangfeng de changing [Zhang Ziyi: I want to see the scene where Jen Yu meets Gong Er]. *The Beijing News*, p. C10–C11.

Tan, Y. (2019). "I Revolt, therefore we are to come": Imaginary M/other in the assassin and the grandmaster. *Concentric: Literary and Cultural Studies*, *45*(2), 27–54.

Tyler, I. (2000). Reframing pregnant embodiment. In S. Ahmed, J. Kilby, C. Lury, M. McNeil, & B. Skeggs (Eds.), *Transformations: Thinking through feminism*. London: Routledge.

Wong, W. (2018). Action in tranquillity: Sketching martial ideation in *The Grandmaster*. *Asian Cinema*, *29*(2), 201–223.

Xing, C., & Li, M. (2007). *Zhonghua wushu* (Chinese martial arts) I. Shenyang: Liaohai Press.

Yip, M. (2017). *Martial arts cinema and Hong Kong modernity: Aesthetics, representation, circulation*. Hong Kong: Hong Kong University Press.

Yu, S. (2012). *Jet Li: Chinese masculinity and transnational film stardom*. Edinburgh: Edinburgh University Press.

Yuan, L. (2015). Zhiming zhinian: zhuanfang Zhang Ziyi [The age of knowing the destiny: The interview of Zhang Ziyi]. In A. Wong, G. Pan, & Z. Li (Eds.), *Wang Jiawei de yinghua shijie (Wong Kar-wai's world of film)* (pp. 418–421). Hong Kong: Joint Publishing.

Part 4
Politics and Race

Chapter 9

'Always Bet on Black': Wesley Snipes – Action Star

Shelley O'Brien

Abstract

Wesley Snipes has had an extensive career on the big screen starting out as part of the New Black Cinema movement in the 1990s working with Spike Lee and Mario Van Peebles. His roles have been incredibly varied covering drama, comedy, action, thriller, horror and Science Fiction: he has played everything from jazz saxophonist to paraplegic and drag queen to vampire, as well as recently appearing as character actor D'Urville Martin in Eddie Murphy's critically acclaimed *Dolemite Is My Name*. However, despite his versatility as an actor and his popularity in action films such as *Demolition Man* and the *Blade* Trilogy, Snipes has been, surprisingly, the subject of minimal analysis unlike, for example Schwarzenegger and Stallone. Unfortunately, he has also fallen foul of the direct to video curse from around 2005 as well as being sentenced to three years in prison for tax evasion. However, this should not negate Snipes' contribution to cinema, especially in the genre of action. Snipes can be a commanding presence given the right script and direction – as an expert martial artist he is lithe and agile; he has strong facial features and a powerful voice, plus the ability to deliver the wisecracking humour which often goes hand-in-hand with action performances. The aim of this chapter, then, is to focus on Snipes as an action star and, more specifically, his significance as a black action star, examining several key films which have helped to develop his onscreen persona and performance style.

Keywords: Wesley Snipes; film; action; black; gender; actor

Remember Wesley Snipes? One of the most successful film stars of the 1990s? It is easy to forget just how dominant Snipes was as a presence in cinema during this decade because his work in the 2000s fell victim to the direct-to-video curse and, in 2010, a prison sentence for tax evasion which also had a negative impact on his career. His screen roles have been incredibly varied covering drama, comedy, action, thriller, horror and science fiction. He has played everything from jazz saxophonist to paraplegic and drag queen to vampire. Yet he is usually thought of as the black star of a run of action films during the 1990s which saw him become, for a time, almost as popular as Arnold Schwarzenegger and Sylvester Stallone.

Despite his misfortunes, it is notable that Snipes started to make a strong comeback with *The Expendables 3* (2014) starring alongside Stallone. More recently he has given critically acclaimed comic performances as character actor D'Urville Martin in *Dolemite Is My Name* (2019) in which he almost stole the film from Eddie Murphy and *Coming 2 America* (2021) once again with Murphy. It is therefore apparent that his talent has not faded away, and he is once again showing his versatility as an actor in a range of different roles. However, although his breadth of work is impressive and warrants further study, this chapter will focus on Snipes' most significant action roles as well as appraising his success as a major action star of the 1990s. It will seek to rectify the current lack of analysis of Snipes' onscreen persona and, also, interrogate the significance of his blackness using key examples of his work made during this decade.

The 1990s is a significant period for black images on screen as, finally, it seemed there was a real breakthrough in giving a more full and three-dimensional representation to both characters and actors on the big screen. The films of Spike Lee and others, in what has often been referred to as the New Black Cinema movement, went some way towards change and progress into how black representations appeared onscreen. Also, black actors such as Denzel Washington, Will Smith, Whoopi Goldberg, Laurence Fishburne, Halle Berry and Samuel L. Jackson continued to make their mark during this time, and it was alongside them that Wesley Snipes became a major actor in the industry. Notably, though, he was the only black star to carve out an action career to rival Schwarzenegger and Stallone. This is not without significance and, arguably, it is related to Snipes' onscreen persona and performance style which is distinctive and worth examining in more detail.

Discussing his early career in an interview with *Total Film* magazine (March 2021) Snipes said that: 'Basically, to win the affection of the few females in the neighbourhood you had to have some swag…so street dancing was where it's at…All that took me to a performing arts high school, and there they introduced us to the real art form of drama and dramatic acting. And that's where it all started'.

The street dancing clearly had an influence on Snipes' ability to move in a dynamic and agile manner onscreen in conjunction with his skill in a range of martial arts which he studied from an early age. As noted on the Martial Tribes Website, 'Snipes already was a professional martial artist after training since the age of 12 and earning a fifth dan black belt in Shotokan Karate and a second dan black belt in Hapkido (Martial, n.d.). He also has training in Kung Fu, Brazilian Jiu-Jitsu and kickboxing.'

Equally, though, the drama training he received in his formative years was a key element in beginning his career as an actor. His first film role was in Michael

Ritchie's *Wildcats* (1986). He was 23. He followed this with an appearance in the TV show *Miami Vice* and, notably, opposite Michael Jackson in the official video for *Bad* which was directed by Martin Scorsese. This would prove to be a turning point in his early career. The director Spike Lee apparently saw his appearance in *Bad* and this eventually led to Snipes playing dramatic roles for Lee in *Mo Better Blues* (1990) and *Jungle Fever* (1991). His performances were well received by critics, especially as the wonderfully named Flipper Purify in the latter film, but he also made a major impact in Abel Ferrara's *Kings of New York* (1990) playing a detective alongside Christopher Walken, and as the ruthless drug lord Nino Brown in *New Jack City* (1991) directed by Mario Van Peebles.

These four films marked Snipes out as a significant screen presence who had real versatility and charisma, as well as paving the way for his blossoming action career beginning with *Passenger 57* (1992). Furthermore, in the same year, he starred as Sidney Deane with Woody Harrelson in the sports comedy/drama *White Men Can't Jump* which not only capitalised on his agility but also showed off his comic timing – both of which were to become important features of his work in his action films. His third film in 1992, *The Waterdance*, also extended his dramatic range when he played a paraplegic in a nuanced and underrated performance.

When considering how wide-ranging these roles are, it is evident that Snipes could have continued his career in this way indefinitely. However, it was his strong screen presence in *Passenger 57* which shifted him further into the realms of action and it took some time before he returned to a broader spectrum of screen roles. Although *Passenger 57* received mixed reviews, it did well at the box office and Snipes' performance as John Cutter, an undercover security operative, was praised and subsequently led to him being cast in further action films. Whatever the limitations of the script, the film does have several excellent action sequences which showcase Snipes' physical skills along with his assertive and pithy delivery of dialogue, in particular his response to the self-important terrorist, Charles Rane, in the film's climax on a plane:

>Cutter: Charlie, ever played roulette?
>Rane: On occasion.
>Cutter: Take my advice. Always bet on black!

This exchange is notable on two counts. First, it showcases Snipes' ability to infuse superficially humorous conversation with meaning and, second, it is referencing his blackness in a way which signifies that he will triumph in this violent game of one-upmanship. It is also worth noting that Snipes' blackness is rarely made an issue of in his action roles, although there is usually a rather wry acknowledgement of it by Snipes himself in films such as *Rising Sun* (1993). Drew Ayres (2008, p. 41) states in relation to action films more generally: 'Surprisingly reflexive, often addressing the audience with an ironic knowledge of its own spectacular and repetitive nature, the action film is a rich site for the complex interaction of narrative, spectacle and masculinity'. Here, this 'reflexive' and 'ironic knowledge' is being played out in a way which recognises Snipes' blackness as being significant for his onscreen persona and yet, at the same time, insignificant in relation to the narrative and spectacle in the films. Indeed, this seemingly contradictory idea is apparent in most of his films and will be explored further in this chapter due to its importance when discussing Snipes' action performances.

To explore this distinct onscreen persona further, it is first necessary to describe Snipes' external appearance. Performance analysis normally uses this as a starting point to enable a more incisive analysis not only of the character being played but also of the actor's specific acting style. Physically Snipes is not particularly tall – around 5 feet 9 inches in height – but this does not detract from his onscreen presence for several reasons. First, his body is muscular but leaner and not overly 'pumped' like Schwarzenegger or Stallone. He has well-defined abdominal and pectoral muscles and no chest hair – which would seem to be obligatory for action stars to show off a sculpted physique built for fighting. It is a body honed through the rigorous techniques of martial arts training which, as noted earlier, was complemented by his dance training. As Ayres (2008, p. 45) asserts, '... just as muscularity implies rigorous and painful training, so too does martial arts skill. It is simply a matter of muscles versus motion, and both inform the narrative structure of the hardbody action film.' This is certainly true of Snipes' action roles in which he often showcases his martial arts training, and it also contributes to the image of masculinity he presents onscreen.

However, what really makes Snipes stand out is the fact that his style is 'traditional martial arts mixed with Bronx street-fighting' as noted in a brief piece on the Martial Tribes Website 'Why Martial Arts made Wesley Snipes a Movie Star'. The piece continues:

> He is a maverick, and some people may not appreciate his lack of following traditional styles, but what he makes up for is some incredible fight scenes that almost appear natural and unrehearsed. Snipes often combines a number of very different traditions to come up with a unique style that then is attributed to the character themselves.

Second, and linked to these points, Snipes walks in a manner which is both confident and commands attention. His measured, compact strides contrast with sudden bursts into running, jumping and fighting which shows that he is more of a combination of the so-called 'hardbody' and the technically excellent martial moves associated with Jackie Chan or Jet Li. Indeed, his physical skills are far more fluid and balletic than anything Stallone or Schwarzenegger perform on screen, and due to his mixing of fighting styles he is also distinct from Chan or Li. Snipes' physique and physical agility, therefore, are major signifiers of his difference from these other famous action stars.

Finally, his face is well-proportioned with a chiselled bone structure. He has full lips and a broad smile and large, almond shaped eyes which are extremely expressive. Although his voice is deep and distinctive, his vocal pitch and dynamic range is extensive and adjustable to the onscreen situation, depending on what mood needs to be expressed. It is worth noting here that Snipes is adept at quick-fire delivery of dialogue much like Eddie Murphy, so it is no surprise that they have worked well together in comedy films.

Accordingly, then, these are key physical attributes which begin to show how Snipes carved out his own niche in the world of Hollywood action movies and, in 1993, his career was starting to peak in terms of audience appreciation, box office and critical success when he starred opposite to Stallone in the sci-fi/action film *Demolition Man*. The poster images for *Demolition Man* are significant too because they give equal weight to Snipes and Stallone – both photographed in profile with Stallone on the left and Snipes on the right with identical billing status. The film did extremely well at the box-office and it cemented Wesley Snipes as a major action star, so it is worth looking at his performance as Simon Phoenix in more detail.

The plot revolves around a maverick cop, John Spartan (Stallone), and a psychopathic crime boss, Simon Phoenix (Snipes), who are both sentenced to freezing in a cryogenic penitentiary in 1996 – Spartan for his destructive excesses (hence, nicknamed the Demolition Man) and Phoenix for his extreme crimes. While in cryo-stasis both men are subject to rehabilitation through 'synaptic suggestion'. When Phoenix is thawed for a parole hearing in 2032, he escapes. Spartan is then unfrozen to try and capture him. 2032 is a very different place, seemingly a utopia with model citizens, and cops who do not know how to deal with violent crime. The ensuing action is mostly played for laughs, although there is social commentary amidst the humour related to class hierarchy, power and corruption. Dr Raymond Cocteau's (Nigel Hawthorne) apparent benevolence as the architect of this future utopia is revealed to be fake. He has had Phoenix programmed while frozen to become an expert in martial arts, computer hacking and torture, in a plan to get rid of resistance leader Edgar Friendly (comedian Denis Leary) and his followers.

Phoenix is introduced in a pre-credits sequence where Spartan is pursuing him, as he has threatened to kill numerous hostages in a large factory building. When they finally come to blows and we see Phoenix more clearly, he is wearing a checked leather jacket and black and white-striped trousers. His hair is dyed blonde with shaven sides and earrings in each ear and, notably, he has one brown eye and one blue eye. It is a distinctive, if somewhat comical, appearance and Phoenix is immediately presented as a giggling maniacal figure – he lights a cigarette with a blow torch and trots out line after line of scornful dialogue before a brutal fist fight with Spartan. There is no martial arts finesse here and it is presented like a typical Stallone fight which is more about brute strength rather than coordinated athletic precision. The scene ends with Phoenix being dragged away by cops mockingly shouting at Spartan 'See you sweetie, honey, sugar!' This introduction to Phoenix sets up his character traits for the rest of the film and showcases Snipes' ability to deliver rapid fire comical dialogue amidst all the violence and mayhem.

When we next see Phoenix, he is at his parole hearing – strapped into a metal upright gurney – where he automatically translates everything the prison warden says into Spanish. When told to 'Stop it!' he answers with a half-smile. Asked if he has anything to say regarding his parole, he looks slowly to one side before saying determinedly, 'Yeah. I do'. He says the password (which has been programmed into him) to release the metal cuffs, which starts the next action sequence. This time, though, Phoenix defeats his opponents easily with martial arts moves and a weapon he appropriates from one of the guards. He despatches one guard swiftly with powerful high-kicks and, during the action, uses his catchphrase for the first time 'Simon says...' – in this case 'die' – before he subdues the other guard with rapid punches to the torso and finished off with a body slam and a violent stomp to the chest. The mixture of gallows humour and brutality continues as Phoenix spots the warden cowering behind the metal gurney and bellows 'Yoo hoo!' to him with a large grin on his face. He approaches with his characteristic steady stride, pinning the warden to the bars and removing his eyeball with a pen (not shown onscreen) to use as an identification scanner. As Phoenix makes his escape, a voice in the elevator says, 'Be well', as he looks at the eyeball and replies ironically, 'You too'.

The entirety of the sequence is shot and edited in such a way that it allows the audience to witness not only Snipes' physical skill but also his acting style which has an easy confidence to it. Rapid cuts accentuate his movements, and the camera maintains focus on Snipes showing to good effect the fact that he can command attention effortlessly with his modulating vocal pitch and subtle use of facial expression, while also setting the tone for the action sequences which follow. Furthermore, the mixture of hand-to hand combat, mocking humour and intimidation allows him to retain the upper hand for most of the film.

After Phoenix escapes from the cryo-prison, he is clothed in an orange string-vest, denim dungarees, heavy boots and leather wrist bands, which are all topped off with orange-blonde hair. This rather comical appearance works with the over-the-top quality of the character and his behaviour. The scene begins with him hacking into a public computer looking for the latest weaponry to arm himself with and it also contains one of the many pop culture references in the film when he shouts, 'C'mon Hal, where are the goddamn guns', referring to the off-kilter talking computer in Stanley Kubrick's *2001: A Space Odyssey*. It has already been established that swearing is a criminal offence in 2032 and each time he spews more expletives, the computer issues him with more fines. He also becomes aware of his new synaptically suggested skills saying, 'Damn! I'm possessed. Wonder if I can play the accordion too!' It is all played for laughs but it also reinforces the character traits which have already been established and cues the audience into laughing with him. Eventually, he is confronted by six cops, but they are completely unprepared for the way that Phoenix both talks and acts towards them. Phoenix proceeds to demolish all of them with a variety of different dexterous moves and blocking techniques. He is ordered to lie down but, instead, he swaggers towards them saying, 'What's this? Six of you. Such nice tidy uniforms. Oh, I'm so scared. What? You guys don't have sarcasm anymore?' As he moves back to the computer, one of the cops again tries to arrest him, but Phoenix, making another withering quip, activates an anti-graffiti programme in the wall which apparently kills a cop standing next to it. He then proceeds to deliver a series of martial arts blows and avoids a bullish charge by one cop who crashes through a plate glass window, leaving Phoenix to strike a matador pose and shout 'Ole!' He continues with his unconventional blend of fighting styles including palms to the face, headbutts, slaps, boxing punches and kickboxing expertise. Unimpressed by the lack of any real competition during the chaos, he walks away shaking his head and mutters 'Stupid'. Realising that the whole thing has been watched by the police in the station via a camera lens in the wall, Phoenix shouts at them, 'Simon says...everybody's dead!' Even though this is seen back at police headquarters, such is his presence through the camera that the whole police squad back away from the screen.

Yet again, Snipes' energy and charisma dominate here, as well as providing the audience with an opportunity to witness his fighting skills alongside his wisecracking brand of humour. It is notable that Snipes is different in comparison to Stallone in both his movement and speech. Snipes fires off numerous one-liners and engages in choreographed fights which rely on his ability to move swiftly and with great agility, whereas Stallone's style is more reliant on slugging it out, using guns, and a deadpan delivery of humorous dialogue. Stallone is even cast as a sort of relic from the past – referred to as 'A brutish fossil' and 'a muscle-bound grotesque' by the police commissioner – as if commenting on his previous film roles.

Ed Guerrero (1995, pp. 395–396) asserts, when writing about the representation of black men on screen, that 'Stallone's biggest money-making ventures have resulted from formulaic, epic struggles with black men, from the Rocky cycle, with Carl Weathers and Mr. T, through *Demolition Man* (1993) and the dystopian, punked-out super villain played by Wesley Snipes'. The implication here is that somehow the film is all about Stallone and his 'struggle' with a black villain. Stallone certainly has plenty of humorous lines, as well as taking part in some explosive action sequences, but Snipes matches him scene for scene throughout and seems to thoroughly enjoy himself as a 'super villain' who revels in terrorising people and takes any opportunity to cause bedlam. Arguably, it was Snipes as Simon Phoenix who was just as responsible as the presence of Stallone for the film's strong box office performance. It is difficult to imagine the film working as successfully without his scene-stealing work within the film. As noted earlier, Snipes' race is not commented upon at all in the film. It could be easy to write this off as insignificant in terms of the narrative or, as Guerrero argues, it is about Stallone having black opponents or the black male inevitably cast as a villain. However, it seems more complex than this in *Demolition Man*. Yes, Snipes is cast as the criminal, but he certainly had not been typecast as such before, or after, making this film. Also, there is a definite pleasure in aligning with Phoenix causing mayhem because of how Snipes plays the role. Rather than encouraging an audience to hate him, his quick wit, fighting skill and overall demeanour make him a captivating character. Indeed, Phoenix is presented as a disruption to a society which has become a sanitised, mostly white, middle-class parody of itself and, therefore, there is an interesting dynamic at play here. There is a definite feeling of wanting Phoenix to disturb this bland future existence and, as a black male in a very white world, he succeeds. He even vocalises this by the end of the film, telling Cocteau, 'You can't take away people's right to be assholes'.

As the film progresses, there are more spectacular action sequences and he continues to add to his wicked yet funny image by referring to a museum's The Hall of Violence as 'Home Sweet Home'. He also makes a quip about Rambo, and he has a lengthy fight with Spartan whilst spouting a constant barrage of one-liners and pop culture references, whilst revelling in the carnage and destruction that he brings to the building, destroying the place in the process. This continues through to the end of the film, calling the people of the future a real-life version of the iconic American sitcom family, the Brady Bunch, saying 'The world has become a pussy-whipped, Brady Bunch version of itself'. When holding a massive gun, Phoenix refers to Pacino's Scarface by shouting, 'Say hello to my little friend', and even the serial killer Jeffrey Dahmer somehow gets a look in with him proclaiming, 'I love that guy!' Clearly, this is in keeping with the style of the film generally, but it is also indicative of Snipes' performance style. Indeed, in this film, Phoenix is played as a sort of cocktail of Nino Brown, Flipper Purify, Sidney Deane and John Cutter. As with all star images, Snipes, in *Demolition Man*, was constantly maintaining but also adding to his tics and traits and therefore developing his individual onscreen persona, which is quite different, for example from that of his black contemporary, Will Smith, as well as distinct from other action stars such as Stallone or Jackie Chan. And it works.

After the success of *Demolition Man*, Snipes made more comedies such as *To Wong Foo, Thanks for Everything! Julie Newmar* (1995) where he played a drag queen, as well as dramatic roles in films such as *One Night Stand* (1997). However, most of his output consisted of action films and thrillers such as *Boiling Point* (1993), *Rising Sun* (1993) in which he was top-billed with Sean Connery, *Drop Zone* (1994), *Money Train* (1995), *Murder at 1600* (1997) and *US Marshalls* (1998). Apart from a couple of exceptions, none of these films did particularly well at the box office or in critical terms, although it is worth noting that none of this failure was ever attributed to Snipes' performances and he is often cited as being one of the good things about them. All this changed when he made the vampire-themed movie *Blade* in 1998 and Snipes attained major box office success once again.

Directed by Stephen Norrington and based on the Marvel Superhero comic, *Blade* received mixed reviews on release but has since gained a cult fan following and reappraisal. As the first black superhero to be developed into a cinematic figure *Blade* has possibly gained greater significance after the success of, for example, *Black Panther* (2018). Snipes (as first choice for the role) is perfect casting due to his being able to seamlessly stitch together a terrific and magnetic onscreen presence, unique fighting skills and his gift for comedy. Although the release of *The Matrix* (1999) seemed to eclipse some of the special effects seen in *Blade*, the film still stands on its own merits with its exciting, violent action sequences and Snipes' performance as the eponymous character.

The plot revolves around Blade who is a 'daywalker' – a vampire hunter who is a hybrid human-vampire. Blade works with his old friend Whistler (Kris Kristofferson) who both supplies Blade with a set of unique weapons at his disposal whilst maintaining his supply of a special serum that enables him to live longer and avoid drinking human blood. He is fighting a battle for humanity against vampires who are a mixture of so-called 'pure blood' elders led by Dragonetti (Udo Kier) and 'turned' younger vampires. The most vicious and arrogant of these younger vampires is Blade's main adversary, Deacon Frost (Stephen Dorff).

Snipes makes Blade into a tough, likeable hero who cares about his friend Whistler and protects others from Deacon Frost and his vampiric cronies. Looking more closely at his performance as Blade, we can see that there are important details which contribute to his already established screen persona. Described by Tia C.M. Tyree and Liezille J. Jacobs (2014),

> He can leap, fight, and shoot well. He soars as he jumps, has superhuman strength, and can quickly heal. He wears sunglasses, black clothing, keeps a sword attached to his back. He is muscular, cool, tough... (p. 15)

We are first introduced to Blade in the opening sequence of the film where all these traits are in evidence. Although Snipes continues to showcase his martial arts moves – this time enhanced with wire work – he is also adept at using a variety of weapons with great style. The look of the character fits Snipes' onscreen persona like a glove – a long black leather coat, black t-shirt and trousers, and heavy boots, combined with wraparound sunglasses, a cropped hairstyle with shaved sides and black tattoos, plus a pencil moustache all contribute to the 'cool' and 'tough' appearance that the character demands. His specially made sword, kept in a scabbard on his back, adds further to this striking look. Then, of course, this is enhanced even more by Snipes' portrayal of Blade. The teeth-flashing grin, sonorous voice and delivery of humorous dialogue are retained from previous performances, but this is quite a long way from Simon Phoenix. It is a more controlled performance in line with the character.

The opening scene takes place in an underground rave club for young 'turned' vampires run by Frost. As they dance, sprinklers in the ceiling open spraying blood onto the revellers. One female vampire has taken a human along for part of this blood feast, but as the vampires prepare to attack, Blade appears and a momentary hush descends. Someone breaks the silence with, 'It's the daywalker!' He stands still, looks at the crowd before him, smiles and then begins to blast them to pieces with his pump action shotgun loaded with anti-vampire bullets. He has a good supply of small metal stakes which he uses to great effect, by jamming them into the vampires' chests causing them to explode. His high kicks and punches repel his enemies, and a specially made form of *shuriken* – a Japanese hand-held throwing weapon originally used by ninjas – which returns to him like a boomerang. After a good deal of wanton destruction and slaying, Blade corners the vampire Quinn, pinning him to the wall with one of his stakes. As the vampire writhes in agony, Blade moves towards him. Blade sets the vampire on fire, and he mockingly says in his derisory tone, 'Give my regards to Frost!' As the narrative progresses, this tone is maintained, but Snipes also imbues Blade's speech with a certain amount of gravitas when he speaks seriously and enunciates words with both precision and clarity. This clearly makes Blade an erudite, intelligent character, and one who can be both witty and sarcastic in equal measures, whilst still giving him the gravitas that the character deserves.

Crucially, when examining Snipes' performance as *Blade*, unlike his previous action roles, his blackness is a key feature of his character. Tyree and Jacobs (2014) note when writing about Black male superheroes in Hollywood,

> When the average American moviegoer thinks of great cinematic superheroes, many will probably envision Superman, Captain America, Batman, Spider-Man, or Iron Man. Among those who have become the staple visual for the American superhero is the White male... [and yet] ... a small number of films over the last few decades provided an alternate view of the superhero, one with the Black male as a central heroic figure. While these representations were few, they are worthy of investigation, because film works to influence how Blacks are viewed and constructed in the world. (pp. 1–2)

Their statement is worthy of attention because Blade is certainly presented as a 'central heroic figure' and no doubt this has had some impact on how Snipes' star image continued to be constructed during the late 1990s. In the film, it is also made clear that Blade acknowledges his black identity. For example, he visits a shop where he refers to the owner as 'Brother' and exchanges a complex form of hand greeting or 'giving dap' which is a practice originating from black soldiers in Vietnam related to cultural identity. This might seem like a small incident to note but it does have significance because it confirms Blade as being connected to his blackness. It is not overtly mentioned by anyone else in the film apart from one key moment when Blade and Frost finally meet. Frost baits Blade saying, 'C'mon, spare me the Uncle Tom routine, okay?' because he is fighting to save humanity from vampires and yet he is a hybrid. Frost continues his goading of Blade saying, 'You think the humans will ever accept a half-breed like you? They can't. They're afraid of you, and they should be. You are an animal, a fucking maniac'. The fact that he calls Blade an Uncle Tom, and a half-breed, is not only intended to insult and provoke a reaction, but it also draws attention to his blackness in opposition to Frost's own whiteness. Notably, in *Blade*, black is represented as good and white is almost entirely represented as bad.

Tyree and Jacobs (2014) make an interesting point about this idea in their article, arguing that most black superheroes are:

> ...aggressive, cool, and tough and, in return, the films' narratives show Black men who are willing to fight back and use threats to back down their enemies. Besides the superheroes' threatening discourse, their archenemies, mostly White men, threaten them across the films. The threatening discourse of the White archenemies ripens the analysis of these films, because it highlights why the elements of cool pose and tough guise are essential defense strategies used by Black superheroes in their

struggle to construct masculinity against the backdrop of a racist sociopolitical context. (p. 17)

Blade certainly conforms to this description of the black superhero and his eventual defeat of Frost. He not only fights to save humanity, but he also refuses to accept Frost's venomous description of him as 'Uncle Tom', 'half-breed' and 'animal'. Blade, arguably, takes on some of Snipes' own characteristics which relate to the 'cool pose and tough guise' noted by Tyree and Jacobs, along with traits inherited from earlier action roles. This is further supported by James Craig Holte (2001) who refers to Blade as '...an attractive superhero confronting absolute evil...[and]...played enthusiastically by Wesley Snipes, an accomplished black actor...' (p. 2). Holte is suggesting here that Snipes' presence is a key aspect of the character and, therefore, an important part of how the text might be interpreted.

Even more significant when considering Blade as a black superhero, though, is the fact that he triumphs by killing the white villain Frost and taking care of the vampires' immediate threat to humanity. Crucially he does not die at the end of the film, and he also continues to fight the vampires as shown in a brief epilogue. This ending paved the way for the sequel *Blade II* (2002) directed by Guillermo del Toro which was another success at the box office not least because of Snipes' maintaining the character's integrity as a black superhero. As Holte (2001, p. 3) notes, 'It is clear that issues of race as well as gender, along with a postmodern urban setting, provide the creators of the *Blade* series with a context to add depth to the adventures of their hero'. Blade's blackness imbues his character with more meaning. Blackness here does not inevitably lead to sacrifice or death – it is powerful, exciting, attractive and admirable. Indeed, it could be argued that Blade, with his super-cool look, his ability to vanquish his villains, and his use of both his mental agility and physical prowess, clearly marks him as a successor to Richard Roundtree's impeccable performance as John Shaft in the original *Shaft* trilogy (1971, 1972, 1973) whilst paving the way towards those films' own reboots/remakes (2000, 2019).

At the time of writing, it has been confirmed that Mahershala Ali will play Blade in a reboot of the black superhero story. It will be interesting to see Ali's interpretation of the character but, perhaps Snipes' version will be seen to be the definitive one. Without Snipes' striking and successful portrayal of Blade in the character's first screen iteration, Blade might have been consigned to history rather than being revived. In light of this, it is worth noting that the representation of black characters in Hollywood has made gradual progress over time, if not as quickly as it should, or could, have done. Those who continue this movement towards change are following in the footsteps of a long line of key figures in the industry. Wesley Snipes' contribution to this progress should not be underestimated and it is evident that he became a considerable, and commanding screen presence in the 1990s. He had a long run of action films which, although varying in quality, cemented his place as an actor of significance. After examining his performance style and his ability to dominate the screen in this chapter, it is reasonable to argue that appraisal of his work is long overdue. Snipes has not had the accolades of, for example, Denzel Washington, but his acting achievements are certainly worth exploring further.

When examining his career, it becomes apparent that Snipes' longevity as a bankable box office name – despite his spending time incarcerated at a federal prison for tax evasion issues – does not seem to have waned, despite some films becoming DVD-only releases. His career before his sentencing saw him appear in approximately 40 films, of which he was the lead in at least 28 of them. After the incarceration, and up to the writing of this chapter, he has made 11 films, with five billing him as the main star. Even when he appeared in a cameo role or as a guest star – for example, *The Expendables 3*, in which the opening sequence sees Barney Ross (Stallone) and his Expendable-Team consisting of Lee Christmas (Jason Statham), Yin Yang (Jet Li), Toll Road (Randy Couture) and Gunner Jensen (Dolph Lungdren) carry off a daring extraction of Doctor Death (Snipes), a knives specialist and former member of the squad from onboard a moving train – his screen presence is undeniable. As the train speeds along, Christmas frees Doc from his shackles. Rather than thanking him, Doc – with his grown-out, and greying afro – looks straight ahead at a portrait of his captor, an Eastern army general. Then, instead of jumping onto Ross' helicopter to make his escape complete, he runs down the train's roof, kills two soldiers and takes control of the massive canon at the front of the train. The train is hurtling down the track towards the general's army base, and Doc blasts the doors of the fortified building. At the very last moment, with the train about to smash into the fortress, Doc jumps onto the helicopter's undercarriage and climbs to safety. Not once does he utter a word. He is that cool. Whilst the film's ensemble casting does not focus too readily on Snipes' character, it clearly shows that in the pantheon of action stars, his stardom still remains bright. He is a name. He comes to the franchise with a knowingness from both him as an actor and 'us' as his audience. That the opening sequence is set around his grand entrance – sitting behind bars, wearing a grubby white t-shirt and with a mask covering much of his face – clearly demonstrates this.

To conclude this chapter, it is pertinent to briefly discuss Snipes' latest movies. Whilst they may not have had the same box office results or critical reviews as before, Snipes has taken on a variety of roles that demonstrate his prowess as both actor and action star. His gangland warlord Casanova Phillips in *Brooklyn's Finest* (2009) and CIA Agent Marcus Jones in direct-to-DVD filler *Game of Death* (2010) reveal the usual tropes of Snipes' performances in the thriller genres, but he stands out amongst the cast. Moving away and into the horror genre, Snipes finds good solid performances in *Gallowwalkers* (2012), *The Recall* and *Armed Response* (both 2017). His comic timing is clear, as mentioned earlier in both *Dolemite Is My Name* and *Coming 2 America*. Perhaps it will only be a matter of time before he becomes more employable as a character actor, one who can move out of the action hero trappings for which he is justifiably known. What appears obvious though, is this: from super villain to superhero and everything in between, Wesley Snipes has had a fascinating career, and one which is currently undergoing a deserved renaissance. The major action stars of the 1980s and 1990s are getting older. They were replaced by actors like Tom Cruise, Will Smith, Jason Statham,

Vin Diesel and Dwayne Johnson. But all of these are quickly becoming ageing action stars themselves. Perhaps one day Snipes will return as Blade. After all, the final film in the original trilogy does see Blade rising from the (un)dead to keep on stalking his vampiric quarry. Whatever happens to Snipes, it is clear that with his strong screen presence, laconic use of dialogue and terrific agility, it certainly seems to substantiate John Cutter's motto: 'Always bet on black'.

References

Ayres, D. (2008). Bodies, bullets, and bad guys: Elements of the hardbody film. *Film Criticism, 32*(3), 41–67.

Guerrero, E. (1995). The black man on our screens and the empty space in representation. *Callaloo, 18*(2), 395–400.

Holte, J. C. (2001). Blade: A return to revulsion. *Journal of Dracula Studies, 3*(5). Retrieved from https://research.library.kutztown.edu/dracula-studies/vol3/iss1/5

Martial. (n.d.). Retrieved from https://www.martialtribes.com/martial-arts-wesley-snipes-movie-1/. Accessed on July 1, 2021.

Tyree, T. C. M., & Jacobs, L. J. (2014). Can you save me? Black male superheroes in Hollywood film. *Spectrum: A Journal on Black Men, 3*(1), 1–24.

Chapter 10

Dismal Setbacks and Stunning Breakthroughs: A Look at Pam Grier's Career and How It Changed Hollywood

Dahlia Schweitzer

Abstract

While there is no question that women on movie screens are frequently eroticised, with countless shots of heaving bosoms or curvaceous rear ends, action stars do occasionally get a reprieve. Pam Grier, the first female action star, was not so lucky. While Grier's Amazonian status should be celebrated, the dark side of her career should also be noted as a cautionary tale of just how much misogyny and racism lurks behind Hollywood doors and intertwined into American cinema history. This chapter examines how Grier's career forces us to rethink both femininity and racism, as well as action films themselves.

Keywords: Pam Grier; blaxploitation; Quentin Tarantino; *Jackie Brown*; *Foxy Brown*; action; black; Hollywood; Coffy; Jack Hill; Roger Corman; race

While there is no question that women on movie screens are frequently eroticised, with countless shots of heaving bosoms or curvaceous rear ends, action stars do occasionally get a reprieve. Some, like Charlize Theron in *Mad Max: Fury Road* (George Miller, 2015) or Demi Moore in *G.I. Jane* (Ridley Scott, 1997), get a shaved head and a dirt-streaked face, while others, like Linda Hamilton in *The Terminator* (James Cameron, 1984), get a no-nonsense black cotton top, a no-nonsense ponytail and impressive arm muscles. While these roles are an impressive diversion from the norm, Pam Grier, the first female action star, was not so lucky. Despite the fact that Grier 'kicked the door open to future female action…fighting for a just society, killing men with hairpins, broken bottles, shotguns, and steel hangers' (Schubart, 2007, p. 63), she had to do so in lingerie, tiny tops, tight dresses, if not altogether nude.

This dichotomy – a tough as nails vigilante terrorising drug dealers and cops most commonly in the guise of a prostitute with prominently displayed curves – epitomises Grier's career. On the one hand, Grier did break down doors, making room not only for later actresses but also obviously for herself – playing roles that had never been seen before, either for black women or even just actresses in general. However, on the other hand, these roles were almost always accompanied by constant objectification, as well as by physical and/or verbal degradation. While Grier's Amazonian status should be celebrated, the dark side of her career should also be noted as a cautionary tale of just how much misogyny and racism lurks behind Hollywood doors and intertwined into American cinema history. This chapter examines how Grier's career forces us to rethink both femininity and racism, as well as action films themselves.

Introduction to Blaxploitation

Until the rise of blaxploitation cinema, action films (like much of Hollywood) were dominated by white male actors. Inspired by the civil rights movement, the blaxploitation era can best be described as a double-edged sword. Running from approximately 1970–1975, the genre named from a combination of the word 'black' and the word 'exploitation' featured blacks in urban settings and aimed to get box office dollars from a black audience who, as the strategy hoped, would be excited to see themselves on screen in positive and progressive roles at last. Blaxploitation represents a unique moment of diversity in Hollywood, with more black actors, directors, and writers than ever before. Grier herself told *Ebony* in 1976 that 'a lot of people got work and were able to join unions because of those films' (Matza, 1988, para. 13). However, these new roles were often horrifyingly sexualised, frequently featuring pimps, prostitutes, sex, nudity and drug use, demeaning both in terms of visual, as well as narrative, context. As Michael Matza wrote for the *Chicago Tribune* in 1988, 'Depending on your point of view, these films were either a stunning breakthrough or a dismal setback for black performers in the early 1970s' (para. 9). Despite being inspired by the civil rights movement and the growing popularity of figures such as the Black Panthers, political messaging in these movies was often kept to a minimum. Instead, as Ed Guerrero writes in his book *Framing Blackness*, Hollywood just combined 'its traditional moneymaking ingredients of violence and sexploitation' with the 'distorted and grotesque signs and imagery of the urban black underworld' (1993, pp. 94–95). Hollywood, as always, figured out how to capitalise on the zeitgeist while lining its pockets, recognising the profitability of this cultural moment and only too happy to exploit black talent along the way.

Not only did blaxploitation films depict a range of black characters and a range of black urban locations, they also frequently featured white villains oppressing the black community. However, while the narratives often depicted the black protagonist's fight against the white oppressor (literally or metaphorically seen as a fight against the American racist machine), the journey to get from oppressed to triumphant would often be littered with scenes of brutal violence, cruel subjugation and overt sexualisation. For example, one of the films to launch the blaxploitation genre, as well as to bring attention to black culture, was *Sweet Sweetback's Baadasssss Song*, a 1971 film written, co-produced, edited and directed by Melvin Van Peebles. Sweetback, the title character of the film, spends most of the film evading arrest from the police and contending with physical violence. When he is not doing either, chances are his sexual prowess is on display. In her book *'Baad Bitches' and Sassy Supermamas: Black Power Action Films*, Stephane Dunn describes the story of Sweetback's revolt, pointing out how, because 'of its sexual stud protagonist and the prominence of sex as a narrative strategy, some Black Nationalists and Black Power activists embraced it as revolutionary, while others condemned it as counterrevolutionary' (2008, p. 49). Those who condemned it argued that the overt sexualisation of Sweetback reinforced the stereotype of the oversexed Black man, while those who embraced it believed it to be a refreshing contrast to years of asexual Black characters. Despite the mixed critical response, the film's success – grossing $10 million at the box office alone and an additional $4 million in rentals – guaranteed the succession of the black male action hero in films like *Shaft* (Gordon Parks, 1971) and *Super Fly* (Gordon Parks, Jr., 1972), albeit with a vastly toned-down political message.

In 1970, police arrested Angela Davis for providing weapons which were used by Jonathan Jackson in an attack on a California courthouse, charging her with conspiracy, murder and kidnapping. Despite being eventually acquitted on all charges, Davis spent 18 months in jail and became widely known for being an activist for civil rights and other social issues. Inspired by Davis's defiant image, as well as by the creation of the National Black Feminist Organisation in 1973 and, of course, a determination to remain relevant, blaxploitation started to feature bold female protagonists. As Pam Cook explains, 'A popular version of 'women's lib' was celebrated in sexual role reversals in which strong, assertive women, often brandishing weapons, took their destiny in their own hands' (Cook, 1993, p. xvi). At last, room opened up on movie screens for the female action hero.

Before blaxploitation, journalist Mark Jacobson writes, 'black actresses had to be slaves (Butterfly McQueen), sing but not speak (Lena Horne), be demurely professional (Diahann Carroll), sultry and exotic (Dorothy Dandridge) or long-suffering strivers of racial underclass (Ethel Waters, Cicely Tyson etc.)' (1975, para. 1). In blaxploitation films, however, as Lakesia D. Johnson summarises in her book *Iconic: Decoding Images of the Revolutionary Black Woman*, 'women were gorgeous sex objects' while also very much 'not victims of their environment'. Rather, 'they were superwomen who fought black and white criminals, using femininity and sex to lure and eventually destroy their prey' (Johnson, 2012, p. 46). So, while the women were sexualised and objectified, they were still portrayed as invincible and defiant, and, significantly, their sexuality was used as a tool rather than as just a characteristic.

Grier's Career Begins Behind Bars

The most well-known actress of the blaxploitation era, Pam Grier's career began with 'women in prison' films for Roger Corman's company, New World Pictures, and, unfortunately, much of her early work continued to feature her in a prison or as a prostitute. Her first film with Corman and director Jack Hill was *The Big Doll House* (1971), where she plays an angry lesbian prisoner. This was followed by a role as a sadistic lesbian warden in *Women in Cages*, directed by Gerardo de Leon, that same year. In 1972, she was back behind bars for *The Big Bird Cage*, another Jack Hill picture. Similarly, in 1973, she plays another prisoner, but not for New World. This time it was for Eddie Romero and his film *Black Mama, White Mama*, which was originally produced by Four Associates Ltd, Eddie Romero's production company with John Ashley, before being acquired by American International Pictures (AIP). AIP would produce most of Grier's blaxploitation films, starting with *Coffy*, directed by Jack Hill and released in 1973.

Grier finally got a different kind of role in *Coffy*, which established the iconic image of Pam Grier wielding a sawed-off shotgun. AIP's head of production, Larry Gordon, had originally wanted to make *Cleopatra Jones* (Jack Starrett, 1973), a blaxploitation film about a female government agent (masquerading as a fashion model) trying to destroy the drug trade. After losing the rights to *Cleopatra Jones*, Gordon asked Jack Hill to write a similar revenge movie – also with an African American woman as lead protagonist – that could compete in the box office. Hill wrote *Coffy* and brought in Grier, with whom he had already worked twice, to play the lead. Grier-as-Coffy takes down drug dealers in retaliation for the damage drugs have done to her eleven-year-old sister. Her desire for vengeance is further fueled when her friend Carter (William Elliott), an honorable policeman who refuses to play ball for the mob, is severely beaten as a result. Coffy might have been an action hero, but she was one who used her sex appeal just as much (if not more so) than her weapons. Her basic strategy is to use her sex appeal to seduce her targets before killing them or stabbing them in the eye with a bobby pin. She even blows away three sets of male genitals with a double-barreled shotgun. To say the film was a success is an understatement. It was made for $700,000 and grossed $2 million (Variety, 1974, p. 19). The film made her a star, earning Grier a multi-picture contract with AIP.

Foxy Brown and *Sheba, Baby*: Taking Revenge

Her next film, and perhaps the one for which she is most well-known, would be *Foxy Brown* (Jack Hill, 1974), released the following year. Originally intended to be a sequel to *Coffy*, AIP requested the creation of a new character since they were concerned sequels would not do well at the box office. However, even though the protagonists' names are different, the two films are still very similar in concept. In this film, Foxy's boyfriend is murdered by the mob after being exposed by her brother for being a government agent. In order to avenge his death, Foxy goes undercover as a prostitute to infiltrate the mob's escort agency.

Once more, Grier plays a vigilante determined to right the wrongs in her community, but even more so, to avenge the murder of her boyfriend. Foxy fights to bring down evil madam Miss Katherine (Kathryn Loder) and her partner and lover, Steve (Peter Brown), who deal in both prostitutes and drugs.

This notion of 'personal revenge' would prove a persistent theme in Grier's films. While *Foxy Brown*, much like *Coffy*, pits a black underdog against a white villain, the final message is not one of racial liberation or feminist ideology. Rather it is about a black heroine making the villain pay for a personal wrong, and the intimate nature of this personal conflict is emphasised by the fact that it is, again and again, Foxy or Coffy working solo in her own specific fight. There is never a real sense of community support.

Similarly in *Sheba, Baby* (William Girdler, 1975), her last movie with AIP, Grier's character, private detective Sheba Shayne, goes back to her hometown in Kentucky because her father is being harassed by local criminals who want control of his business. Predictably, the stakes are raised when the criminals kill her father. Again, without support from police or the community at large (only from her father's business partner), Sheba identifies the head of the gang (a white man, naturally) and kills him. At least in this particular film, as Linda Gross of the *Los Angeles Times* put it, 'thankfully the racism and violence are minimal' (Gross, 1975, p. 15). Director William Girdler intentionally made Grier's character lighter and more mainstream than her previous roles and there is no explicit sexual element found within the narrative. There is even a hint of 'women's liberation' – for instance, when her father tells her not to get involved in his problems, she insists that she will not 'sit on the sidelines just because [she is] a woman'. Unfortunately, and unsurprisingly, however, Sheba goes undercover as an escort, and the trailer for *Sheba, Baby* ends with an uncomfortably long and lingering shot of her ass, as she walks away from the camera. That's it – that's all we see. We do not even see the back of her head.

Violence, Sexism and Friday Foster

Despite the fact that many aspects of Grier's films are empowering in the sense that she is a badass woman who does not let anyone get in her way, there is a feeling of the same conflicted response that met *Sweet Sweetback's Baadasssss Song* when writing this chapter. Her films and her characters are revolutionary for featuring black urban culture (and black women!), but the repeated violence and sexism definitely feel counterrevolutionary. For instance, any positive victory on the part of Grier's characters is repeatedly coloured by violence against her physical body. Rapes and beatings are frequent in her films, as are the omnipresent racial slurs meant, perhaps, to fuel the conflict between Foxy or Coffy or Sheba and the various white villains, but they also feel as if they are positioned to be just as much against Grier herself.

In one particularly upsetting scene in *Coffy*, mob boss Arturo Vitroni (Allan Arbus) meets Coffy while she is undercover as a prostitute. Her plan is to murder Vitroni while he is unprepared and unprotected. However, the film takes an especially dark turn when Vitroni orders Coffy (as a prostitute) to play out a racist and physically abusive fantasy. He shoves her to the floor, since that is where a 'no-good nigger bitch' should be says, before ordering her to crawl towards him, begging for sex. Coffy complies, but he still spits on her, calling her even more racist slurs. When Coffy fights back, Vitroni's men rush into the room and take her captive. These men later try to kill her, and the only reason Coffy survives is a veritable fluke. As part of her attempt to wreak havoc on the drug dealer King George, she had found his secret drug stash, replacing it with sugar. Luckily, it is this sugar solution which Vitroni's men use when they inject Coffy, planning to sedate her before killing her. However, because of her earlier action, the sedation does not work, and she escapes.

In *Foxy Brown*, the damage done to Foxy by a white man looking to dominate her is even more devastating physically. Miss Katharine sends Foxy, once again undercover as a prostitute, to 'the ranch' as punishment for disruptive behaviour. However, as if as a nod to black women's supposedly 'insatiable' sex drive, Katharine smugly says that Foxy will probably enjoy the abuse in store for her. This kind of demeaning attitude finds its roots in the pervasive stereotype of black women as being 'promiscuous, hypersexual, sexually available and as having "animalistic" sexuality', which goes back to the 'sexualised exploitation of Black women during slavery', as Lisa Rosenthal and Marci Lobel discuss in their work in this area (2016, para. 9). In the horrifying next scene, two white men tie Foxy to a bedpost, where they drug her, beat her, and rape her. Stephane Dunn, in her essay 'Foxy Brown on My Mind: The Racialized Gendered Politics of Representation', writes that the film 'reenacts the historical rape of black slave women and the breaking of spirited slaves through physical abuse by white masters'. Dunn points out that the men's 'devaluation of her black female body and personhood' goes so far as to tell Foxy that 'she is lucky to be getting "it" from them' (2003, p. 80).

While Grier's films became less violent over time (at least for her body), perhaps as she grew to have more agency over their content, the overt sexism remains a constant. Based on the first syndicated comic strip to feature a black female heroine, *Friday Foster* (Arthur Marks, 1975) is the last film that she made with AIP. In it, she plays Friday Foster, a photographer who witnesses an attempted murder. She partners with private detective Colt Hawkins (Yaphet Kotto), and the two of them try to figure out what is happening as people she knows are murdered one by one, and even Friday narrowly escapes being killed. As is par for the course for Grier's films, the police are useless and she is forced to do all the legwork herself (no man to rescue her!), putting herself into danger repeatedly. Even Hawkins is not terribly useful. Significantly, Friday succeeds where others fail. Despite the unconcealed sexism and the oppression by the white patriarchy, the final message is always that, even if her skin is luscious and her breasts are buoyant, Grier's characters succeed as a result of her skill, intelligence and cunning.

On the surface, the tone of *Friday Foster* seems lighter than her previous works. The film does not revolve as much around outsiders and criminals and street hoods. Rather, it portrays a world full of black Americans, fashion designers, photographers, politicians and millionaires. Friday fits right in with this world, wearing some of her most stylish outfits, a far cry from the rough streets in *Coffy* or *Foxy Brown*. Nonetheless, sexism pervades, with Friday described as having 'more balls than brains', as being 'all woman', and told to 'get laid' and 'have a baby' at various points throughout the film. There are also several nude scenes to remind us of Grier's sex appeal. The underlying message of racial oppression is also just as dark as in her previous films. Friday discovers that there is a plan to assassinate black politicians who are working together to dismantle racial discrimination, possibly a reference to the violence targeted at so many leaders of the Civil Rights movement. The worst part, however, is that the person planning the assassination attempts is a black man.

The Later Years: Supporting Roles and *Jackie Brown*

Even though *Friday Foster* appears to have more mainstream appeal than Grier's previous works, and one might hope that Grier's career would, in turn, also have more mainstream appeal, this film would be her last lead role until Quentin Tarantino's *Jackie Brown* in 1997. Between *Friday Foster* and *Jackie Brown*, Grier could only be found in smaller supporting roles in films such as *Drum* (Steve Carver, 1976), an action film about a mulatto slave forced to fight other slaves for the entertainment of the white owners, and *Fort Apache, The Bronx* (Daniel Petrie, 1981), a crime drama about a tough cop (Paul Newman) who works in a tough neighbourhood in the Bronx. In *Drum*, Grier plays a sex slave; while in *Fort Apache*, Grier plays a drug-addicted prostitute who kills cops and johns, usually with a razor blade she hides in her mouth, reminiscent of her earlier blaxploitation roles.

An odd footnote to her career are two small roles. The first is in John Carpenter's sequel to *Escape from New York* (1981), *Escape from L.A.* (1996). Described by Roger Ebert as a 'go-for-broke action extravaganza', the film is set in a Los Angeles cut off from the rest of the mainland as a result of a substantial earthquake and 'converted into a prison camp for the nation's undesirables' (1996, para. 1). Here Grier plays a transsexual named Hershe Las Palmas (her original name is Jack 'Carjack' Malone and he/she was a former acquaintance of Snake Plissken (Kurt Russell) but ran out on him during a heist), one of the rulers of this dystopian wasteland. With her voice lowered in post-production, Grier's Hershe cuts an odd figure. She lives on a dry-docked oil tanker surrounded by her minions. Hershe's long, golden brown hair is in plaits. Her elaborate low-cut, high-slashed gold and leopard print brocaded outfit (worn when onboard ship) is countered by a black leather jacket, fishnet stockinged trousers and black boots as she soars through the air on a glider, in the hope of helping Snake's (and herself) flight to freedom. The character appears onscreen for approximately 10 minutes. On first meeting, Snake puts his hand between Hershe's legs, slowly moving up under the dress only to retrieve a small pistol. Snake says, 'Still packing, Carjack', to which Hershe replies that her name is Hershe. This bizarre encounter – where Snake tells her he can get her out of Los Angeles if she and her men help him – is certainly playing on the Grier-formula from past movies. She remains a terrific screen presence, but with her freakish settings, bizarre outfits, deep voice and the way that she is almost treated in a throwaway manner in the narrative (after shooting numerous villains, she climbs aboard a helicopter only for her and her compatriots – except Snake and Utopia, the president's daughter – to be burned alive) is made all the more odder by the fact that it is Grier in the role. Whether or not Carpenter and, to an extent, Grier are 'toying' with past associations of her screen persona is certainly open to debate. It is hard to know if we should be happy or sad for Grier that this is where she found herself in 1996. It could be argued that at least she is finally not playing a half-naked prostitute.

The second notable movie in this period is John Carpenter's *Ghosts of Mars* (2001), which sees Grier playing the tough, no-nonsense Commander Helena Braddock. Sent to Mars to investigate the disappearance of a settlement of miners (who have been taken over by the spirit of 'something' that has attacked their colony), Braddock's screen time is limited at best. Whilst Grier holds a commanding onscreen presence in a long black leather jacket, hard combat boots and carrying a massive rifle, her character has limited lines and screen time. Indeed, even her murder occurs offscreen, and her decapitated head is unceremoniously plonked onto a pole amongst many others. It feels as if Grier is there as a 'name' from the hazy past of Hollywood, rather than for any nuances that could have been brought out in what is, ostensibly, a bit-part role taken on by a powerful, talented actress. This is a real shame.

Other than a few small roles in movies such as *Something Wicked This Way Comes* (Jack Clayton, 1983), *Stand Alone* (Alan Beattie, 1985) and *On the Edge* (Rob Nilsson, 1985), not much else stands out until *Jackie Brown* (1997), based on Elmore Leonard's novel *Rum Punch*. Quentin Tarantino, who wrote the role with Grier in mind, finally gives Grier the spotlight she has long deserved, and she shines in a lead role where she does not play either a prostitute or a prisoner. Instead, Grier plays a flight attendant working for a low-budget airline. In order to supplement her meager income, she smuggles money from Mexico into the United States for Ordell (Samuel Jackson), an illegal gun dealer. After she is arrested, she concocts an elaborate scheme to keep herself out of jail while also stealing the rest of Ordell's money. Whilst the film's poster clearly references the posters for *Foxy Brown* and *Coffy*, with a larger-than-life Pam Grier towering over the other characters from the film, gun in hand, this particular poster has Grier fully clothed in her work uniform. In this regard, the film appears to be a refreshing step forward. However, within the narrative of the film itself, Jackie is unable to pull off her scheme by herself, requiring the assistance of Max Cherry (Robert Forster). At least in her earlier films, Grier's characters were able to accomplish their intended goals on their own.

The Sexist Trap: Lesbian Bars, Catfights and Messing Up Her Nails

Beyond the physical violence tucked within the plots of these movies is the element of constant sexism. Having little to do with the progress of the actual plots are scenes like a fight in a lesbian bar in *Foxy Brown* or an over-the-top cat fight in *Coffy* where a party full of prostitutes devolves as various prostitutes are jealous over who is getting the most attention (Coffy, of course) and they all start tearing at each other's clothes and rolling around on the floor. Coffy's boyfriend, Councilman Howard Brunswick, initially describes her to a colleague as a 'liberated woman' but then describes her as a 'lusty, young bitch' after having sex. Later in the movie he describes her as 'just some broad I fuck'. As Marquita R. Smith describes in her article on the struggles of the black militant woman, 'The power and honor he bestowed on her just hours before is stripped away as he reduces her to a mere sex object'. Smith points out how many times Grier's breasts are exposed in *Coffy*, and quotes director Hill stating that beautiful actresses are 'not afraid to show [their bodies]' and that Grier believed it was something she was 'expected and proud to do' (2009, para. 12).

To make matters worse, not only did Grier have to suffer through this sexism but she was even criticised for it. In her book *Women of Blaxploitation*, Yvonne D. Sims writes that, of all the actresses starring in blaxploitation films, Grier 'received the harshest criticism for her willingness as part of her character to remove her clothing when necessary and engage in violent acts when necessary' (2006, p. 26). With the tone-deafness that often accompanies criticism of people struggling to overcome systemic racism and misogyny, left out of the conversation was a discussion of the fact that maybe Grier had to go along with her directors' demands in order to get on screen at all. As Grier herself puts it, 'I took the parts no other Hollywood starlet would touch because they didn't want to be demeaned or mess up their nails. It was a risk but I didn't know any better and somehow I came out on top'. Grier continues to say that, if she had not taken these roles, if she had 'held out for those sweet, pretty, demure parts', she would still be waiting (quoted in Schubart, 2007, p. 61). There were no other roles available for black actresses at the time. The dismal decrease in roles for black actors following the demise of the blaxploitation era is all the proof you need to see how little choice Grier had (Schubart, 2007, pp. 167–169). While there were 45 starring roles for black actors in 1973, by 1987 there were only seven (Matza, par.10, 1988). While the roles might have been sexist and stereotyped, vulgar, and violent, they were still the only roles out there – and because she took these roles, Grier became one of the few bankable actresses of the 1970s, along with Barbra Streisand and Liza Minnelli.

Conclusion

In her book *Femme Fatales: Feminism, Film Theory, Psychoanalysis*, Mary Ann Doane writes about women in action films. She points out that it is significant that 'we can speak of a woman using her sex or using her body for particular gains'. In contrast, 'it is not that a man cannot use his body in this way but that he doesn't have to' (1991, p. 26). Along the same lines, Jacinda Read writes, 'the avenging woman is frequently eroticized rather than masculinized' (2000, p. 35). The unfortunate truth laid bare by Grier's career is how right Doane and Read are. A woman's body is so often her weapon, a tool used either to vanquish villains or seduce audience members, and in Grier's case, her body did both. At the same time, however objectified she may have been, Grier still 'kicked the door open' for actresses like Theron and Hamilton, and even blazed a trail for black women like Halle Berry to take lead roles in films like the *X-Men* franchise, *Die Another Day* (Lee Tamahori, 2002) and *Catwoman* (Pitof, 2004), all roles which give women more agency and more tools than Grier ever got.

References

Big Rental Films of 1973. (1974, January 9). *Variety.*
Cook, P. (1993). Border crossings: Women and film in context. In P. Cook & P. Dodd (Eds.), *Women and film: A sight and sound reader* (pp. ix–xxiii). Philadelphia, PA: Temple University Press.
Doane, M. A. (1991). *Femme fatales: Feminism, film theory, psychoanalysis.* New York, NY: Routledge.
Dunn, S. (2003). Foxy Brown on my mind: The racialized gendered politics of representation. In S. Inness (Ed.), *Disco Divas: Women, gender, and popular culture in the 1970s* (pp. 71–86). Philadelphia, PA: University of Pennsylvania Press.
Dunn, S. (2008). *'Baad bitches' and sassy supermamas: Black power action films.* Chicago, IL: University of Chicago Press.
Ebert, R. (1996, August 9). Escape from L.A. Retrieved from https://www.rogerebert.com/reviews/escape-from-la-1996
Gross, L. (1975, March 28). Pam Grier in Sheba, baby. *Los Angeles Times.*
Guerrero, E. (1993). *Framing blackness.* Philadelphia, PA: Temple University Press.
Jacobson, M. (1975). Foxy lady: Honoring Pam Grier. *New York Times Magazine.* Retrieved from https://pleasekillme.com/pam-grier/
Johnson, L. D. (2012). *Iconic: Decoding images of the revolutionary black woman.* Waco, TX: Baylor University Press.
Matza, M. (1988). She's still b-a-a-a-d. *Chicago Tribune.* Retrieved from https://www.chicagotribune.com/news/ct-xpm-1988-09-11-8801290443-story.html
Read, J. (2000). *The new avengers: Feminism, femininity and the rape-revenge cycle.* Manchester: Manchester University Press.
Rosenthal, L., & Lobel, M. (2016). Stereotypes of black American women related to sexuality and motherhood. *Psychology of Women Quarterly, 40*(3). Retrieved from https://www.ncbi.nlm.nih.gov/pmc/articles/PMC5096656/
Schubart, R. (2007). *Super bitches and action babes: The female hero in popular cinema, 1970–2006.* Jefferson, NC: McFarland & Company, Inc., Publishers.
Sims, Y. (2006). *Women of blaxploitation: How the black action film heroine changed American popular culture.* Jefferson, NC: McFarland & Company, Inc., Publishers.
Smith, M. R. (2008–2009). Afro thunder!: Sexual politics & gender inequity in the liberation struggles of the black militant woman. *Michigan Feminist Studies, 22*(1). Retrieved from http://hdl.handle.net/2027/spo.ark5583.0022.104

Chapter 11

Playing With Type? Dwayne 'The Rock' Johnson, Rivalry, and Race in *Hobbs and Shaw*

Renée Middlemost

Abstract

Dwayne 'The Rock' Johnson is one of the most bankable stars in Hollywood, in addition to his broad popular appeal. Since his transition from a successful pro-wrestling career to a full-time actor, his onscreen persona has transitioned from one dimensional action hero to more balanced star 'type' (Dyer, 1991), alternating action films with more family-friendly fare. Johnson's starring role in the *Fast and the Furious* franchise has been central to the growth of his career, yet as I will argue, this success is fuelled by his apparent rivalry with other action stars onscreen (Jason Statham) and offscreen (Vin Diesel). As I will show, these rivalries are rooted in the star 'types' formulated by Richard Dyer (1991), and this tension is central to the ongoing fan interest in the series.

Johnson's expanding profile has also led to the establishment of his own production company, Seven Bucks, and transition into television series *Ballers* (2015–2019) and *Young Rock* (2021–), both of which allowed him to explore autobiographical elements of his early life. As I will demonstrate via a case study of *Hobbs and Shaw* (2019), Johnson's success as a transnational action star and creative control allowed by Seven Bucks has allowed more explicit on-screen engagement with his Sāmoan heritage. The production history of *Hobbs and Shaw* illustrates both the successful co-existence of rivalry between action stars as a successful marketing strategy for action franchises, and the evolving action genre which allows a more personal exploration of race and masculine identity.

Keywords: Dwayne 'The Rock' Johnson; *Hobbs and Shaw*; star image; rivalry; feuds; masculinity

Since his transition from a successful pro-wrestling career to full-time acting, Dwayne 'The Rock' Johnson has become one of the most bankable stars in Hollywood, in addition to his broad popular appeal. Beginning his acting career while still wrestling in WWE, he featured in guest roles on *That 70s Show*, and *Star Trek: Voyager*, leading to his breakthrough role of The Scorpion King in *The Mummy Returns* (2001). This role was so well received that a spinoff film *The Scorpion King* (2002) was developed for him, and he received the highest ever fee ($5.5 million USD) for a debut lead role (IMDB, 2022). After several roles in smaller productions such as *The Rundown* (2003) and *Walking Tall* (2004), he appeared in the role of Luke Hobbs in *Fast Five* (2011), widely considered to be his break out mainstream role. In 2013, he was credited with 'reinvigorating' the *GI Joe* franchise, and was described as 'kicking ass, and saving franchises' (Pomerantz, 2012), and 'franchise viagra' (Mendelson, 2015). As his career has evolved, so his onscreen persona transitioned from one dimensional action hero to a more balanced star 'type' (Dyer, 1991), alternating action films with more family-friendly fare. Johnson's starring role in the *Fast and the Furious* franchise has been central to the growth of his career, yet as I will argue, this success is fuelled by his apparent rivalry with other action stars onscreen (Jason Statham) and offscreen (Vin Diesel). These rivalries are rooted in the star 'types' formulated by Richard Dyer (1991), and this tension is central to the ongoing fan interest in the series (Outlaw, 2021, n.p.)

Johnson's expanding profile has also led to the establishment of his own production company, Seven Bucks, and transition into independent film such as *Fighting With My Family* (2019), and television series *Ballers* (2015–2019) and *Young Rock* (2021–), all of which allow him to explore autobiographical elements of his early life. As will be demonstrated via a case study of *Hobbs and Shaw* (2019), Johnson's success as a transnational action star and creative control through Seven Bucks has enabled for more explicit on-screen engagement with his Sāmoan heritage. The production history of *Hobbs and Shaw* illustrates the co-existence of rivalry between action stars as a successful marketing strategy for action franchises, in addition to the evolving action genre which allows a more personal exploration of race and masculine identity.

From the Rock to Dwayne Johnson – Shaping the Star Image

In many ways, it was Dwayne 'The Rock' Johnson's destiny to combine athletic prowess and charisma to first pursue a successful wrestling career, before moving into acting. Born into a family legacy of wrestling, his father, Canadian Rocky 'Soul Man' Johnson, was well known on the American regional wrestling circuit, and his maternal grandfather, Sāmoan Peter 'High Chief' Maivia, also wrestled professionally in the 1960s and 1970s. His grandmother, Lia Maivia, was the first female pro-wrestling promoter, running Polynesian Pacific Pro Wrestling from 1982 to 1988. While at high school, Johnson excelled at gridiron football, and played for the University of Miami, before being signed in the Canadian football league; however, injury cut his football career short. He then decided to chase a professional wrestling debut, making his debut as Rocky Maivia in 1996, his name a tribute to his wrestling lineage. WWF promoters played on his family legacy, and he was initially billed as a 'face'. Professional wrestling has long centred on the conflict between the good guys ('baby-face') and the bad guys (heel). 'Typically, heels have always been portrayed as either arrogant, cowardly, monstrous or any combination of the three, and they often cheat to win. Faces have typically been portrayed as brave, wholesome, friendly guys who pander to the crowd and stand up to the heels' (Singh, 2011, n.p.). As Singh (2011, n.p) has observed, citing Stone Cold Steve Austin and CM Punk, it is now more common for wrestlers to inhabit both roles, or acting as a 'tweener': 'someone who acts like a heel, but is treated by the majority of fans as a face'. After winning the WWF Intercontinental title, Johnson rejected his 'Rocky Maivia' name, turning heel and taking up his iconic character of 'The Rock'. Johnson's turn to inhabiting The Rock role instantly increased his popularity, and was, significantly, built on the back of feuds with other key figures in the WWF such as Steve Austin and John Cena.

Beginning his acting career while still wrestling in WWE, he featured in guest roles on *That 70s Show*, and *Star Trek: Voyager*, leading to his breakthrough role of The Scorpion King in *The Mummy Returns* (2001). This role was so well received, that a spinoff film, *The Scorpion King* (2002) was developed for him, and he received the highest ever fee for a debut lead role (IMDB, 2022). Many wrestling fans began to turn against The Rock because of his shift into acting, and he took a sabbatical from the circuit in 2002. He appeared in the WWF sporadically between 2003 and 2004 before announcing his (first) retirement from wrestling and moving into full time acting. After several roles in smaller productions such as *The Rundown* (2003) and *Walking Tall* (2004), he appeared in the role of Luke Hobbs in *Fast Five* (2011), widely considered to be his breakthrough mainstream role.

As Ward (2019, p. 481) highlights, Johnson's subsequent success as a bona fide 'movie star' is the result of:

> ...the distinctive modes of character performance and audience interaction inherent in professional wrestling have significantly informed the development of Dwayne Johnson's star brand. Unlike his cartoonish predecessors such as Hulk Hogan, who struggled to translate the over-the-top histrionics of his wrestling persona into lasting crossover success in Hollywood, Johnson has cultivated an appeal that owes as much to affability, humour and easy charm as to his bulging biceps. While his hulking frame has undoubtedly informed his formidable presence as a mainstay of contemporary Hollywood action franchises, his 'easy geniality' and 'Buddha-like calm' have also made him a popular fixture on the talk show and *SNL* circuit, as well as allowing him to command an equally eager audience in family-friendly and comic roles. Johnson has curated this hugely successful and highly adaptable star persona not through pivoting away from

his wrestling background, but rather through utilising the grounding it has given him – particularly in the unique performative practice of kayfabe. This can be seen particularly through his use of social media.

As highlighted by Ward above, Johnson's success is closely linked to 'likeability', which can be traced back to his early wrestling career. Although in the WWF he moved from 'face' to 'heel', he remained one of the most popular figures in the league. In his films, he successfully moves between action film, and more 'family-friendly' fare, in line with his evolving personal life as a husband and father. This is echoed on-screen, with Johnson frequently taking on the 'cool dad' persona – strong yet caring; tough yet fair. Playing the 'family man' is also central to Johnson's appeal, and 'family first' is the central theme running through both the *Fast and Furious* franchise, of which *Hobbs and Shaw* is a spin off, and the on/off screen feuds which fuel interest in the series – most notably between Johnson and Jason Statham on-screen, and with Vin Diesel off-screen.

Rivals on Screen: Johnson and Statham in *Hobbs and Shaw*

Following their pairing in *Furious 7* (2015) and *The Fate of the Furious* (*Fast and the Furious 8*, 2017), it was announced that Johnson and Jason Statham would reprise their characters Luke Hobbs and Deckard Shaw for a spin-off film originally titled *Fast and Furious Presents: Hobbs and Shaw* (2019). In interviews, Johnson confirmed the on-screen chemistry with Statham had evolved from their improvisation during the filming of *The Fate of the Furious*:

> ...we had such a good time. And it was after that movie that Universal said they [played the] movie back, audience tested it and loved our characters together and loved what we were doing. And that was the creative inroad we needed that made sense for the spin off. And then we made *Hobbs and Shaw*. ... There's a lot of trust between us, and the chemistry just explodes onscreen.
> (Johnson, in Deckelmeier, 2019, n.p.)

Hobbs and Shaw is notable for being the first film in the franchise not involving Vin Diesel; it was also produced by Johnson's Seven Bucks, rather than Diesel's company, One Race films. As the next section shows, there is speculation that *Hobbs and Shaw*, as a spinoff from the main franchise, and outside of Diesel's control, increased tensions between Johnson and Diesel.

The success of *Hobbs and Shaw* is dependent on Johnson and Statham embodying distinctive star types – Johnson as 'the good Joe', and Statham as 'the tough guy'. As I have argued elsewhere of Statham (Middlemost, 2019, p. 29), his popularity can be attributed to the leveraging of '...his laconic "real life" personality as an untrained actor, but skilled man of action, into an authentic star persona'. The same could be said for Johnson, although he inhabits a different star type to Statham. As Richard Dyer (1998) contends, one of the key features of stars is their tendency to inhabit a particular star 'type' (or persona), using the three main types identified by Klapp (1962): the Good Joe; the Tough Guy; and The Pin Up. Dyer acknowledges the flaws in Klapp's typology, particularly the use of stereotyping, and the exclusion of many: '...women only fit uneasily, whilst blacks, gays and even the working class hardly fit at all' (Dyer, 1998, p. 47). Despite these limitations, these star types continue to remain a useful starting point for the analysis of star persona.

If Statham is the quintessential tough guy, Johnson can be read as a modern performance of the Good Joe type:

> He is 'friendly and easy going; he fits in and likes people; he never sets himself above others but goes along with the majority; he is a good sport – but also a he-man who won't let anyone push him around where basic rights are concerned'. He is characterised by a 'dislike of bullies, snobs, authoritarians and stuffed shirts; sympathy for the underdog; and liking for the good Joe or regular fellow who, for all his rough-and-ready air wouldn't try and dominate anybody, not even his wife'. And is to be distinguished from squares, sissies and eggheads.
> (Klapp, 1962, in Dyer, 1998, p. 48)

While on the surface Johnson is a typical Good Joe, his Sāmoan/African/Canadian heritage sets him apart from typically white renderings of the type. The good Joe is often characterised in contrast to other men 'who don't fit' (Dyer, 1998, p. 48), and yet, it is often Johnson's characters that don't fit – either literally, or figuratively – a point highlighted throughout *Hobbs and Shaw*. Shaw frequently taunts Hobbs throughout the film about his inability to successfully blend in as a spy, due to his large frame, and distinctive appearance: 'This job requires stealth. Look at you'.

If we think of the Good Joe and the Tough Guy as opposite types, we can see Johnson and Statham's on-screen chemistry and competitive 'buddy banter' (Raphael & Lam, 2016) offscreen, as key to their success as a pairing. For Raphael and Lam, 'buddy banter' illustrates: '... the presentation of close celebrity friendships... as a marketing device', and how these displays '... generate online discussion, audience hype and reward loyalty, and the significance of perceived authenticity on the reception of the bonds portrayed' (2016, p. 159). Promotional interviews for *Hobbs and Shaw* with Johnson and Statham (often together) reinforced the perception of an authentic off-screen friendship rooted in competition. Rather than being pitted against one another, they must join forces to fight Brixton (Idris Elba), a genetically modified mercenary intent on destroying the world by unleashing a deadly virus.

The film opens with an M16 unit conducting a raid to intercept a chemical weapon known as 'Snowflake' from the Eteon group of cyber terrorists. Snowflake is a programmable disease that can target any DNA sequence within 72 hours, resulting in 100% mortality. The raid is quickly intercepted by Brixton,

Eteon's cybernetically enhanced, lead operative. Brixton and his associates kill the entire unit, but Hattie Shaw (Vanessa Kirby) a MI6 agent, and Deckard's estranged sister, manages to escape having injected the Snowflake virus into her hand. Brixton and Eteon frame Hattie for the murder of her team, releasing her image to the media and forcing her to go on the run. A series of sequences contrasting the lifestyle of Hobbs in Los Angeles, with Shaw in London, setting up the rivalry/odd couple scenario of their pairing follows. These early sequences, like the rest of the *Fast and the Furious* franchise, establish family as a central preoccupation and motivation for the adventures that will ensue. Over breakfast in L.A., Hobbs is asked about Sāmoa, and why he doesn't see his brother Jonah by his daughter Samantha (Eliana Su'a); Shaw visits his mother Magdalene 'Queenie' Shaw (Helen Mirren) in prison, who asks him why he doesn't speak to his sister Hattie, given their close relationship as children. In flashback, we see one of their childhood grifts – 'The Keith Moon' (named after The Who's famous drummer) – setting the scene for plans we will later see in action.

Hobbs and Shaw are separately recruited to help locate Hattie. CIA agent Locke (Ryan Reynolds) briefs Hobbs on Hattie as a 'rogue agent' accused of stealing Snowflake; meanwhile the CIA stop Shaw following his visit to Queenie. Shaw is convinced to work on the case in exchange for immunity for Hattie. The recruiting CIA agents assume that Hobbs and Shaw will be able to put aside their previous rivalries to work as a team. After their initial meeting at CIA headquarters in London, this seems unlikely; they exchange verbal barbs, and quickly part ways to attempt to locate Hattie. Hobbs locates Hattie first, subduing her in a physical confrontation, and returning to the CIA black site to question her. Hattie manages to escape her cuffs; Shaw arrives to find Hattie's legs around Hobbs's neck. A three-way standoff is interrupted by Shaw's revelation that Hattie is his sister, and the arrival of Brixton and his team who blow the building apart and escape with Hattie. Hobbs and Shaw follow and confront Brixton on the street below. Brixton acknowledges Shaw and their history; Shaw shot Brixton in the head when they were in the armed forces after Brixton turned traitor, believing him dead. Brixton was saved by Eteon, while Shaw refused to join. Hobbs, Shaw and Hattie escape, chased through the streets of London by Brixton and his motorcycle pursuit team. The trio manage to lose Brixton, who vows revenge. Brixton returns to Eteon, where his faceless master threatens him with harm if he does not bring Hobbs and Shaw into 'the cause'. Eteon leaks false information to the media, framing the three heroes for terrorism, and their faces are plastered all over the news and digital signage.

Meanwhile, Hattie becomes exasperated with the constant 'alpha male shit' between Hobbs and Shaw when they are no closer to removing Snowflake from her body. They agree to a truce, and to seek out Professor Andreiko (Eddie Marsan), the Russian scientist who invented the extraction machine. Professor Andreiko explains that he developed Snowflake to efficiently deliver life-saving vaccines worldwide, believing that Eteon shared his goal of 'saving the world through science'. He also notes that they will need to break into Eteon headquarters in Chernobyl to retrieve the only extraction device, telling Hattie that her risk of death is 'high'. The trio return to Shaw's workshop where he distributes new identities and disguises. Hattie questions his motives, still believing that he has avoided the rest of the Shaw family after betraying his M16 team – an accusation Shaw doesn't deny. Although Shaw tries to have Hobbs detained by airport security care of the innuendo'd alias 'Mike Oxmaul', Hobbs nonetheless manages to board the plane to Moscow with Shaw and Hattie. While Hattie sleeps, Hobbs and Shaw argue. Shaw has noticed the chemistry between Hobbs and Hattie, and tells him to stay away from his sister. Hobbs' retort in this scene references Johnson's ethnicity for the first time: 'If she chooses to look the way of this big, brown, well-endowed, tattooed, mountain of a man, then guess what? I'm going to let her climb this mountain, over, and over, and over again'. This both infuriates Shaw, and sets the scene for the third act, where the trio return to Sāmoa. Meanwhile, Professor Andreiko is kidnapped by Brixton, and taken to the Chernobyl headquarters – Eteon want the virus reprogrammed.

The trio arrive in Moscow, where they meet Madame M/Margarita (Eiza González), Shaw's former lover and associate who has the resources they need to enter Eteon headquarters. M lures Brixton to her location. Hattie suggests that once inside they pull the 'Mick Jagger' – where she showboats, drawing attention, allowing Hobbs and Shaw to break in. Brixton arrives to claim Hattie, threatening Madame M with harm should this be a set up. Both men parachute into the facility, indulging in some further rivalry as they dispatch an array of minor operatives. As they emerge into the heart of the facility, they are surrounded and captured by Brixton and his team, chained to metal chairs and rigged to electrodes for some 'old school interrogation'. Elsewhere in the facility, Hattie has already escaped with the extraction machine and Professor Andreiko in tow. Brixton works on convincing Hobbs and Shaw they should join Eteon, reliving the night that Shaw came to kill him after learning Brixton had betrayed their team. Hattie overhears that Shaw was framed for killing his own team. After Brixton electro shocks Hobbs and Shaw several times, Hattie seizes her chance and begins 'The Mick Jagger', which allows Hobbs and Shaw to escape their bonds. Andreiko is killed by Brixton during the commotion, but Hattie manages to jump aboard a truck with Hobbs and Shaw, and the extraction device in tow. Hobbs and Shaw fight Brixton on the back of a flat bed truck, where Brixton is knocked off by falling debris, as the Eteon headquarters explodes around them. The extraction machine is damaged during their escape, which Hattie believes is a death sentence. For the first time, Shaw invokes the traditional *Fast and the Furious* attitude regarding the bonds of family, as he cajoles Hattie: 'We're the Shaw family – we never, never, never give up'. Hobbs realises they need to get off the grid to regroup and save Hattie, invoking his own family history by proposing they go to 'the last place on Earth I want to go. Home'.

The climax of the film reinforces the central preoccupation with family and returning home, shared by the rest of *The Fast and the Furious* franchise. However, it is distinct for featuring Johnson's Sāmoan heritage. Following their escape from Chernobyl, the trio travel to Sāmoa to ask Hobbs' brother Jonah to repair the extraction machine. Upon their arrival at the family home, Jonah punches Hobbs in the face, telling him: 'You are not welcome here! After 25 years, bringing your problems here to this house! You betray our family and bring shame on this house, bring shame on our blood!' Their mother Sefina (Lori Pelenise Tuisano) quickly steps in to defuse the tension between the brothers and pledge the support of the family: 'This is your home. We are Sāmoans, we can handle troubles'. On their way to Jonah's workshop, Hobbs explains the source of tension to Hattie; Hobbs' father was a thief, who convinced his brothers to work with him, risking their lives in the process. Hobbs reported his father to the police to save his brothers, left Sāmoa and never looked back. Since then, the brothers have dedicated themselves to a legitimate, successful custom car workshop, and have expelled all guns from the site and their workers. For their final battle against Brixton, they will need to rely on traditional Sāmoan weapons. Attention turns to preparing the island for Brixton's ambush, which they expect at dawn the following day. Hattie and Hobbs share a quiet moment at sunset, reflecting on family, and what they will do differently if they survive. As dawn approaches, Jonah completes his repairs, and begins the extraction process on Hattie. Hobbs apologises to Jonah in Sāmoan, while Hattie tells Shaw she knows the true reason he stayed away was to protect the Shaw family.

As dawn comes to the island, Brixton's team arrives. Here we see the most overt representation on Sāmoan culture, as the Hobbs family and their allies emerge wearing lavalava (sarongs) and carrying traditional weapons. They begin to perform the Siva Tua (a traditional Sāmoan war dance). Standing side by side with his family and the Shaws, Hobbs begins to speak in Sāmoan:

> Brothers of Sāmoa! We call upon our Gods and ancestors to ask for strength – for now is the time for war! Rise! Look into my eyes – they will be the last thing you see before you die. TO WAR!

As the battle begins, Hattie remains hidden as the extraction process continues. She impedes the progress of Brixton's team by hacking into the software that controls their weapons, shutting them down for several minutes to allow Hobbs, Shaw and their allies to gain the upper hand. Brixton's team are surrounded by a ring of fire and forced to retreat, as he calls in their helicopters. Brixton captures Hattie, and they escape in a helicopter, followed closely by a convoy of custom-built Hobbs cars which connect in a chain to pull Brixton's helicopter down over a cliff. Hobbs and Shaw finally realise that to hurt Brixton, they need to work together; for the first time, Hobbs calls Shaw his 'uso' (brother). As they begin to gain the upper hand over Brixton, Hattie lies in the ruins of the wrecked helicopter, defeating an Eteon assailant just as the extraction process is complete. Hobbs gives a final speech to Brixton, summarising the key themes of the film: 'You may believe in machines, but we believe in people. You may have all the technology in the world, but we have heart, and no machine will ever beat that'. Just as Brixton looks to be defeated, Eteon suddenly decommission him, and his lifeless body falls into the ocean. The threatening voice of the Eteon organisation emerges from the helicopter, threatening Hobbs and Shaw with revenge, setting the stage for the promised sequel (see Malhotra, 2021). Despite Hobbs and Shaw's best efforts at traditionally vanquishing the villain, their opportunity is snatched from their grasp at the last minute. This clearly signals a sense of loss in masculinity for the two men: they both remain unfulfilled in their violence, and Brixton becomes representative of the shift in narrative tone.

With the immediate threat passed, a mid-credits sequence drives home the centrality of family to both the characters, and the franchise as a whole. First, we see Hattie and Shaw visit Queenie in prison together, presenting her with a birthday cake filled with explosives, implying an impeding family reunion on the outside. Second, Hobbs returns to Sāmoa with his daughter Sam, where she is enveloped with love from grandmother Sefina and the extended family. The end credits establish a possible narrative for *Hobbs and Shaw 2*, as Locke reveals another virus worse than Snowflake has been discovered; and Hobbs sends the police to arrest Shaw in revenge for the Mike Oxmaul prank, telling them his name is 'Hugh Janus'.

Although many of the film's reviews were critical of the 'nonsensical' storyline (Debruge, 2019), and leaning 'comically' into the family theme of *Fast and Furious* in the final act (Tallerico, 2019, n.p.), most (Campbell, 2019; Hans, 2019; Loughrey, 2019) commented positively on the chemistry between the two leads. Tallerico suggests: 'Johnson and Statham became the most entertaining things about this franchise years ago, and they know how to lean into their on-screen personas perfectly. In a sense, it's an old-fashioned 1980s buddy comedy, but with modern technology and sensibilities' (2019, n.p.). While the buddy comedy elements of *Hobbs and Shaw* are notable, the onscreen rivalry of Johnson and Statham creates both the tension and 'buddy banter' that drives the narrative forward. Thus, star types and onscreen rivalry, balanced with themes concerning the centrality of family, make these elements of the *Fast and the Furious* franchise work, whilst helping to continue the series as a profitable franchise at the global box office. While the onscreen rivalry has seemingly borne a healthy offscreen friendship in the case of Johnson and Statham, the following section shows that fictional feuds can easily translate into real-world rivalry.

Rivals off Screen: Johnson and Diesel, and Other Action Feuds

Rivalries between action stars have been a staple of the genre since the 1970s – from Bruce Lee to Chuck Norris, through to the rivalry between Stallone and Schwarzenegger (Burwick, 2019). While Hollywood feuds may once have been insider knowledge, they are increasingly played out on social media, as can be seen in the off-screen tension between Johnson and 'head' of the *Fast and Furious* franchise, Vin Diesel. Chow and Laine (2019, p. 218) contend: 'The trope of feuding women is often characterised by a slippage between the representational and non-representational worlds, between character and performer'. Although they write about a female coupling, much of their argument is applicable to the feud between Johnson and Diesel that has played out on social media, where neither wishes to lose 'face' when their alpha-masculine persona is threatened.

Diesel embodies the tough guy type, making him an onscreen rival; but unlike Statham with whom Johnson appears to share an offscreen rapport, Johnson and Diesel have had a notoriously tense working relationship. The tension can be traced back to a 2016 Instagram post from Johnson during the final weeks of shooting *The Fate of the Furious* (*Fast and Furious 8*). In the since-removed post, Johnson praises the film studio (Universal), his female co-stars and most of his male co-stars. Although he does not refer to any co-star by name, he remarks that:

> ... My male co-stars however are a different story. Some conduct themselves as stand-up men and true professionals, while others don't. The ones that don't are too chicken shit to do anything about it anyway. Candy asses. When you watch this movie next April and it seems like I'm not acting in some of these scenes and my blood is legit boiling – you're right. Bottom line is it'll play great for the movie and fits this Hobbs character that's embedded in my DNA extremely well. The producer in me is happy about this part? Final week on FAST 8 and I'll finish strong. #IcemanCometh #F8 #ZeroToleranceForCandyAsses.
>
> (Leadbeater, 2017, n.p.)

Despite not using his name, this post was read by fans as targeting Diesel, who has earned a reputation for turning up late to the set. A follow up post a few days later appeared to indicate that the issue had been resolved, with Johnson posting that: 'Family is gonna have differences of opinion and fundamental core beliefs'; but at the conclusion of the film shoot, another Johnson post thanked the entire cast except for Diesel. At the time, there was speculation that the feud was manufactured to promote the upcoming Wrestlemania 33 event, at which The Rock and Vin Diesel were rumoured to appear (Leadbeater, 2017, n.p.). As Ward notes (2019, p. 484), there is a further temptation to read the feud with Diesel as manufactured, as Johnson has previously used social media to instigate tension with John Cena, in preparation for their championship match (2011–2012). Ironically, Cena has since moved into acting, most recently appearing as Dom Toretto's (Vin Diesel's) brother, Jakob in *Fast and Furious 9* (*F9*, 2021).

Universal were apparently unhappy with the feud detracting from the upcoming release, despite Johnson and Diesel elaborating on the cause of their ruction to various media sources. Johnson reframed his initial statement as 'different professional philosophies' at work, claiming the feud ultimately increased interest in the forthcoming film. Diesel tried to downplay the issue, claiming: 'It's not always easy being an alpha, and it's two alphas', but he always wants the best for Johnson (Clute, 2021). While there were further comments made, the feud seemed to de-escalate following the release of *The Fate of The Furious* and their joint appearance at the premiere in 2017. However, when it was revealed that the release of *Fast and Furious 9* was to be delayed, co-star Tyrese Gibson responded angrily in an Instagram post, blaming Johnson amid accusations of making the franchise 'all about him'. The delay of *F9* was partially attributed to the release of *Hobbs and Shaw*, but Diesel defended Johnson, noting that the delay was no one person's fault (Clute, 2021).

Following the successful release of *Hobbs and Shaw* in August 2019, Johnson thanked Diesel for his support, calling him 'brother', seemingly indicating a thawing of tensions. Meanwhile press sources began reporting on the set dynamics between Johnson, Diesel and Statham, where various metrics were established to ensure no individual's alpha male reputation was diminished (Bakare, 2019; Schwartzel, 2019). According to former *Fast and Furious* producer Michael Fottrell, Johnson, Diesel and Statham have contract provisions to 'limit the amount of punishment their characters take in fights'. In response, Diesel developed 'a complicated rating system tallying how many times each actor was kicked, punched or headbutted to ensure violence was being doled out equally' (Bakare, 2019, n.p.). Although none of the actors confirmed these claims, it is common for stars to list their demands during any production. In this specific instance, Universal issued the following statement: 'The fights ensure every character has their moment, and that all are seen as formidable opponents. Each Fast character is a hero to someone watching, and we never forget that' (Schwartzel, 2019, n.p.). This sense of equality is apparent in *Hobbs and Shaw*, where Johnson and Statham primarily team up, rather than oppose each other; and in most fights, they easily dispatch with their opponents. As Campbell (2019, n.p.) observes, in *Hobbs and Shaw*: '…Leitch gives each fight flair and clarity, playing to the different physicality of each performer'.

Following the stand-alone success of *Hobbs and Shaw*, speculation began to build about Johnson's future in the main franchise, which was in doubt following Vin Diesel's interview with *Men's Health* in June 2021. Diesel again attributed their tension to being two 'alphas', and claimed that as a director, he had inflicted some 'tough love' on Johnson in his early appearances (*Fast Five*, 2011) to achieve the best onscreen performance (D'agostino, 2021, n.p.). Diesel followed up in late 2021, by appealing to Johnson via Instagram to return for the final two instalments of the main franchise, activating the discourse of family, and memory of Paul Walker. Walker played Brian O'Conner in the *Fast and the Furious* franchise before a fatal single vehicle collision in 2013. Diesel was known to be very close to Walker, and has repeatedly referred to his desire to finish the franchise in a way that would honour Walker's memory (David, 2022). In a subsequent *Vanity Fair* article, Johnson flatly rejected Diesel's 'tough love' remarks, refusing to '…dignify that bullshit with an answer' (Heath, 2021, n.p.); he has since widely stated there is 'no chance' of him returning to the main franchise (Holmes, 2021; Jones, 2021). Johnson has instead been spruiking the sequel for *Hobbs and Shaw*, which he has openly described as the 'antithesis of *The Fast and the Furious*' (Malhotra, 2021, n.p.), a claim which could well further inflame tensions with Diesel.

Reshaping Type? Dwayne Johnson as Transnational Action Star

Johnson and Diesel's feud can be read as the culmination of Johnson's stratospheric rise to global fame, which has certainly appeared to eclipse Diesel's own popularity. In 2017, Diesel claimed: 'I'm the first multicultural megastar in

Hollywood. They didn't exist. To see another multicultural star come up is something I am very proud of. I'm always rooting Dwayne on' (Evans, 2017, n.p.). While this feud continues, it is impossible to deny Johnson's status as a transformative, transnational star, whose status allows for increasingly authentic performances of Sāmoan identity on screen. The 'Good Joe' type described by Dyer (1998) is overtly linked with (white) American masculinity; thus Johnson's star image depends on reshaping this type, by including elements central to his cultural identity. As Ward observes (2019, p. 485), '... the wrestling character of The Rock and the star persona of Dwayne Johnson have evolved in a fluid synergy through a range of performative platforms. ... Johnson sees the development of this persona as an active, collaborative process'. While films such as *Skyscraper* (2018) used Johnson's transnational appeal to target the lucrative Chinese market, both *Moana* (2016) and *Hobbs and Shaw* are distinguished by their focus on Johnson's evolving star persona that centres his Sāmoan heritage.

While *Moana* was broadly praised for its central focus on Indigenous Sāmoa, and the inclusion of a strong female lead, commentators such as Herman (2016, n.p.) criticised the 'Disney-fication' of indigenous culture and mythology. Both Herman and Ito (2016, n.p.) single out Johnson's character Maui for critique. Johnson's Maui is not true to traditional renderings (Maui is typically depicted as a lithe teenager on the verge of manhood); and Maui's considerable size has been read as perpetuating stereotypes suggesting Sāmoans are obese. Overall, as Sloss (2020) observes, *Moana* generated mixed feelings from those with Sāmoan heritage: on the one hand there was pride in representation, but there was also a need and desire for greater accuracy when it came to cultural specificity.

In contrast, the third act of *Hobbs and Shaw* has been described as Johnson's 'greatest love letter to [Sāmoa] so far' (Desta, 2019, n.p.). As the first film of the *Fast and Furious* franchise to be produced by Johnson's Seven Bucks company, his increased creative control allowed for the integration of authentic elements of Johnson's culture, while retaining the focus on the *Fast and Furious* family-ethic. This authenticity included the use of Sāmoan language, cultural consultants advising on content and the inclusion of supporting Polynesian and Sāmoan actors, most notably Johnson's cousin, and WWE star Joe Anoa'i (Roman Reigns). Although the sequences were filmed in Hawaii, Sāmoan culture is at the forefront of the narrative, which sees Hobbs, Shaw and Hattie arrive in need of refuge and assistance from Hobbs' family. With the realisation that they will soon be ambushed by the firepower of Brixton's Eteon team, the Hobbs's knowledge of the island and their use of traditional weapons becomes their secret assets. *Hobbs and Shaw* writer Chris Morgan deliberately set about creating a connection between the Hobbs character, written specifically for Johnson from his earliest appearance in the franchise, *Fast Five*. In conversations with Morgan, Johnson recounted various instances from his personal history, some of which appeared in *Hobbs and Shaw* virtually verbatim: this included the use of traditional weapons and the 'heart' for battle: 'It was important to him [Johnson] because for the first time he's really able to, in a blockbuster film, embrace his cultural heritage' (Desta, 2019, n.p.). Indeed, *Hobbs and Shaw* is the first blockbuster film, and one of the few films of any kind to showcase Sāmoan culture. As Johnson states:

This movie was an opportunity for us to, No.1, send the audience home happy. No. 2, if we can, in our small way, showcase inclusivity, showcase culture and love others – and again, in our small way show that there is power in putting your differences aside, and there is power in lateral thinking and remaining big picture and accepting of all cultures – I think there is something important in that.

(Yamato, 2019, n.p.)

In addition to bringing focus to traditional Sāmoan culture, the film may also be indicative of the slowly evolving action genre. The modern action film not only allows for the resurgent careers of 'geri-action' stars (Donnar, 2016), but, as in *Hobbs and Shaw*, incorporates crowd-pleasing elements of traditional masculinity, whilst also offering up discussions of contemporary masculine identity *and* authentic portrayals of culture in relation to family, however brief these considerations may be in the actual narrative. Faced with the prospect of professional redundancy as a consequence of aging, the evolution of action star personas in franchises is clearly important in initiating a shift towards a modern masculinity that holds space for diverse and authentic storytelling. In sum, the production of content that reflects on Johnson's cultural heritage acts as a further insulation against the professional redundancy faced by action stars, while simultaneously broadening the appeal of his star persona.

Conclusion

Dwayne Johnson's rise to fame as a transnational, transmedia star can be read through a series of strategic career moves that have raised his global profile. As he progressed from WWE wrestling to acting, so too has his onscreen persona transitioned from one dimensional action hero to more balanced star 'type' (Dyer, 1991). As the 'Good Joe', Johnson has infused the likeability of the type with his own distinctive toughness, cultivating: '…an appeal that owes as much to affability, humour and easy charm as to his bulging biceps' (Ward, 2019, p. 481). Johnson's 'Good Joe' type has been contextualised in terms of his onscreen and offscreen rivalries with Statham and Diesel, both of whom inhabit the 'Tough Guy' role. These rivalries are particularly well placed to serve as a promotional tool for the ongoing *Fast and Furious* franchise, and its subsequent spin offs. While scholars such as Donnar (2016) have pointed to action franchises as insulating stars either tagged with, or approaching 'geri-action star' status, these rivalries, whether authentic or constructed for social media consumption, ensure ongoing audience interest in both the stars and franchises under analysis in this chapter.

Finally, the transition to producing more-authentic (and personal) content through Seven Bucks has allowed Johnson to develop beyond the 'Good Joe' type, to a distinctive, transnational star persona of his own. In particular, the greater creative control exerted by Johnson via his production company has allowed for more explicit on-screen engagement with his Sāmoan heritage. The case study of *Hobbs and Shaw* demonstrates that Johnson's successful, transnational star persona has allowed space for an authentic engagement with cultural diversity. Just as importantly, it also hints at the possible evolution of contemporary masculine identity in relation to family bonds (regardless of age) within the action genre.

References

Bakare, L. (2019). Jason Statham and the Rock "refuse to lose fights against one another". *The Guardian*, August 2. Retrieved from https://www.theguardian.com/film/2019/aug/02/fast-furious-stars-contract-demand-not-lose-fights-jason-statham-dwayne-johnson. Accessed on March 7, 2022.

Burwick, K. (2019). Schwarzenegger & Stallone hilariously reignite their '80s action star feud. *MovieWeb*. Retrieved from https://movieweb.com/arnold-schwarzenegger-sylvester-stallone-80s-feud-revisited/. Accessed on January 11, 2022.

Campbell, K. (2019). Fast & furious: Hobbs & Shaw. *Empire*. Retrieved from https://www.empireonline.com/movies/reviews/fast-furious-hobbs-shaw/. Accessed on April 12, 2022.

Chow, B., & Laine, E. (2019). Between antagonism and eros: The feud as couple form and Netflix's GLOW. *Women and Performance: A Journal of Feminist Theory*, 29(3), 218–234.

Clute, E. (2021). The Rock & Vin Diesel's feud – Complete timeline explained. *ScreenRant*. Retrieved from https://screenrant.com/fast-furious-rock-vin-diesel-feud-timeline-explained/. Accessed on January 11, 2022.

D'agostino, R. (2021). Vin Diesel is 53 and still shifting up. *Men's Health*. Retrieved from https://www.menshealth.com/entertainment/a36663682/vin-diesel-f9-interview/. Accessed on April 14, 2022.

David, J. (2022). Ahead of Fast and Furious 10, director Justin Lin recalls his conversations with Paul Walker about the franchise capper. *CINEMABLEND*. Retrieved from https://www.cinemablend.com/movies/ahead-of-fast-and-furious-10-director-justin-lin-recalls-his-conversations-with-paul-walker-about-the-franchise-capper. Accessed on April 17, 2022.

Debruge, P. (2019). Film review: "Fast & furious presents: Hobbs & Shaw". *Variety*, July 31. Retrieved from https://variety.com/2019/film/reviews/fast-and-furious-presents-hobbs-and-shaw-review-1203286293/. Accessed on April 12, 2022.

Deckelmeier, J. (2019). Dwayne Johnson Interview: Hobbs and Shaw. *ScreenRant*. Retrieved from https://screenrant.com/dwayne-johnson-interview-hobbs-shaw/. Accessed on March 7, 2022.

Desta, Y. (2019). Hobbs & Shaw: How Samoa became the fast & furious spin-off's star. *Vanity Fair*. Retrieved from https://www.vanityfair.com/hollywood/2019/08/fast-and-furious-hobbs-and-shaw-samoa-dwayne-johnson. Accessed on April 17, 2022.

Donnar, G. (2016). Narratives of cultural and professional redundancy: Ageing action stardom and the "geri – action" film. *Communication, Politics and Culture*, 49(1), 1–18.

Dyer, R. (1991). *Stars*. London: BFI.

Dyer, R. (1998). *Stars.* London: British Film Institute.
Evans, G. (2017). The Rock and Vin Diesel finally address their feud. *Men's Health.* Retrieved from https://www.menshealth.com/trending-news/a19545246/the-rock-addresses-feud-with-vin-diesel/. Accessed on April 17, 2022.
Hans, S. (2019). Fast and Furious: Hobbs & Shaw review – Silly spin-off. *The Guardian,* August 4. Retrieved from https://www.theguardian.com/film/2019/aug/04/fast-and-furious-hobbs-and-shaw-review. Accessed on April 12, 2022.
Heath, C. (2021). Dwayne Johnson lets down his guard. *Vanity Fair.* Retrieved from https://www.vanityfair.com/hollywood/2021/10/dwayne-johnson-speaks-his-truth. Accessed on January 11, 2022.
Herman, D. (2016). How the story of 'Moana' and Maui holds up against cultural truths. *Smithsonian Magazine.* Retrieved from https://www.smithsonianmag.com/smithsonian-institution/how-story-moana-and-maui-holds-against-cultural-truths-180961258/. Accessed on February 17, 2022.
Holmes, A. (2021). Hobbs and Shaw producer reacts to Vin Diesel asking the Rock to return for final Fast and Furious movies. *CINEMABLEND.* Retrieved from https://www.cinemablend.com/movies/hobbs-and-shaw-producer-reacts-to-vin-diesel-asking-the-rock-to-return-for-final-fast-and-furious-movies. Accessed January 11, 2022.
IMDB. (2022). *The Scorpion King.* Retrieved from https://www.imdb.com/title/tt0277296/trivia/. Accessed January 15, 2022.
Ito, R. (2016). How (and why) Maui got so big in 'Moana'. *The New York Times.* Retrieved from https://www.nytimes.com/2016/11/20/movies/moana-and-how-maui-got-so-big.html. Accessed on February 17, 2022.
Jones, D. (2021). Dwayne Johnson says there's 'no chance' he will return to 'Fast & Furious'. *NME.* Retrieved from https://www.nme.com/en_au/news/film/dwayne-johnson-confirms-theres-no-chance-of-him-returning-for-fast-furious-10-3127754. Accessed on April 17, 2022.
Klapp, O. E. (1962, December). Heroes, villains and fools: The changing American Character. *Social Forces, 41*(2), 215–216. doi:10.2307/2573621
Leadbeater, A. (2017). Why did the Rock & Vin Diesel feud on fate of the furious? *ScreenRant.* Retrieved from https://screenrant.com/vin-diesel-rock-fast-furious-argument-explained/. Accessed on April 13, 2022.
Loughrey, C. (2019). Fast & Furious: Hobbs & Shaw review: Complete nonsense but disarmingly pleasurable. *The Independent.* Retrieved from https://www.independent.co.uk/arts-entertainment/films/reviews/fast-furious-hobbs-shaw-review-cast-dwayne-johnson-jason-statham-a9030776.html. Accessed on April 12, 2022.
Malhotra, R. (2021). Hobbs & Shaw 2: Dwayne Johnson wants the antithesis of fast & furious. *Collider.* Retrieved from https://collider.com/hobbs-shaw-2-dwayne-johnson-antithesis-fast-furious/. Accessed on March 7, 2022.
Mendelson, S. (2015). The Rock isn't just franchise Viagra, he is red Bull for cinematic universes. *Forbes.* Retrieved from https://www.forbes.com/sites/scottmendelson/2015/06/02/the-rock-isnt-just-franchise-viagra-he-is-red-bull-for-cinematic-universes/. Accessed on January 15, 2022.
Middlemost, R. (2019). "I'm certainly not Tom Cruise or Brad Pitt": Jason Statham, fandom, and a new type of (anti) hero. In S. Gerrard & R. Shail (Eds.), *Crank it up:*

Jason Statham – Star! (pp. 29–43). Manchester: Manchester University Press. doi: 10.7765/9781526142788.00010

Outlaw, K. (2021). Fast & furious fans debate the Rock and Vin Diesel feud. *Comicbook.com*. Retrieved from https://comicbook.com/movies/news/dwayne-rock-johnson-vin-diesel-fast-furious-10-feud-fan-reactions/#3. Accessed on April 20, 2022.

Pomerantz, D. (2012). The Rock is kicking ass and saving franchises. *Forbes*. Retrieved from https://www.forbes.com/sites/dorothypomerantz/2012/05/16/the-rock-is-kicking-ass-and-saving-franchises/. Accessed on January 15, 2022.

Raphael, J., & Lam, C. (2016). Marvel media convergence: Cult following and buddy banter. *Northern Lights: Film & Media Studies Yearbook*, *14*(1), 159–178. doi:10.1386/nl.14.1.159_1

Schwartzel, E. (2019). "Fast & furious" stars' complicated demand—I never want to lose a fight; franchise leads Vin Diesel, Jason Statham and Dwayne Johnson wrestle for more "muscle" time, forcing fight choreographers to get creative. *The Wall Street Journal*, August 1. Retrieved from https://www.wsj.com/articles/fast-furious-stars-complicated-demandi-never-want-to-lose-a-fight-11564673490. Accessed on March 7, 2022.

Singh, P. S. (2011). *WWE: Have the words 'face' and 'heel' become meaningless?* Bleacher report. Retrieved from https://bleacherreport.com/articles/808170-wwe-have-the-words-face-and-heel-become-meaningless. Accessed on February 14, 2022.

Sloss, M. (2020). Here's what Pacific Islanders really think of 'Moana'. *BuzzFeed*. Retrieved from https://www.buzzfeed.com/morgansloss1/heres-what-pacific-islanders-really-think-of-moana. Accessed on April 18, 2022.

Tallerico, B. (2019) Fast & Furious presents: Hobbs & Shaw movie review (2019). *Roger Ebert, RogerEbert.com*. Retrieved from https://www.rogerebert.com/reviews/fast-and-furious-presents-hobbs-and-shaw-2019. Accessed on April 12, 2022.

The Scorpion King. (2002). IMDb (2022). Retrieved from https://www.imdb.com/title/tt0277296/trivia/. Accessed on January 15, 2022.

Ward, D. (2019). "Know your role": Dwayne Johnson & the performance of contemporary stardom. *Celebrity Studies*, *10*(4), 479–488. doi:10.1080/19392397.2019.1672998

Yamato. (2019). Dwayne Johnson brings Samoan heritage to 'Fast and Furious' spinoff 'Hobbs and Shaw'. *Los Angeles Times*. Retrieved from https://www.latimes.com/entertainment-arts/movies/story/2019-07-25/dwayne-johnson-speaks-samoan-fast-and-furious-hobbs-and-shaw. Accessed on April 18, 2022.

Conclusion

Steven Gerrard and Renée Middlemost

This volume has highlighted some of the shifts in action films during the 2000s. As stated in the Introduction, while the thematic concerns of the genre have remained relatively stable since its inception, the four thematic themes of this volume (star bodies; transmedia action; intergenerational action; and politics and race) are intended as a starting point for further insights and interventions; particularly where race, gender and sexuality, and interdisciplinary exchange are concerned. If we observe some of the changes that have occurred in the genre during the 2000s, one must consider the growth in franchises, remakes and reboots during this period as one of the most significant movements, mimicking broader cinematic trends towards seriality. As Gaughan (2020, n.p.) has suggested of this period, audiences are perhaps more likely to gravitate towards action films because of their connection to characters such as Spider-Man or Ethan Hunt, rather than the big names of the 1980s like Schwarzenegger and Stallone.

The increasing prominence of leading female action stars has also been highlighted during this period, and in this volume. While these chapters have dealt with relatively established stars such as Charlize Theron and Michelle Rodriguez, there is potential to further reflect on the interventions being made by younger stars such as Zendaya, Florence Pugh and Imam Vellani. Part 4 on Politics and Race also highlights the underacknowledged contributions of African American action stars such as Wesley Snipes and Pam Grier, and a need for further research into diversity within action cinema as a whole.

Contemporary research on action cinema has highlighted the resurgence and emergence of geri-action stars – a term defined by Donnar (2016, p. 2) as '...a less-than-kind combination of geriatric and action' – and one of the thematic concerns of Book 3 in this series. Book 3 rounds out this series, and offers an insight into current trends, and future directions for the action genre. Opening with a section on aging action stars, before reflecting on the evolution of the genre, and rounding out with insights into narrative transformation, and possible futures for action cinema, we encourage you to take a look.

References

Donnar, G. (2016). Narrative of cultural and professional redundancy: Ageing action stardom and the "geri-action" film. *Communication, Politics, and Culture*, *49*(1), 1–18.

Gaughan, L. (2020). The 20 best action movies of the 2000s. *Taste of Cinema*. Retrieved from http://www.tasteofcinema.com/2020/the-20-best-action-movies-of-the-2000s/. Accessed on April 25, 2022.

Selected References

Select Bibliography

Abbas, A. (1997). *Hong Kong: Culture and the politics of disappearance*. Hong Kong: Hong Kong University Press.

Andris, S., & Frederick, U. (Eds.). (2007). *Women willing to fight: The fighting woman in film*. Newcastle: Cambridge Scholars Publishing.

Baker, B. (2015). *Contemporary masculinities in fiction, film and television*. London: Bloomsbury.

Benshoff, H. M., & Griffin, S. (2006). *Queer images: A history of gay and lesbian film in America*. Oxford and Lanham, MD: Rowman and Littlefield Publishers, Inc.

Berry, C., & Farquhar, M. (2006). *China on screen: Cinema and nation*. Hong Kong: Hong Kong University Press.

Beynon, J. (2001). *Masculinities and culture*. Buckingham: Open University Press.

Bordwell, D. (2000). *Planet Hong Kong: Popular cinema and the art of entertainment*. Cambridge, MA: Harvard University Press.

Bourdieu, P. (2001). *Masculine domination*. Cambridge: Polity Press.

Broderick, M., & Ellis, K. (2019). *Trauma and disability in Mad Max: Beyond the road warrior's fury*. Cham: Springer Nature.

Brown, J. A. (2011). *Dangerous curves: Action heroines, gender, fetishism, and popular culture*. Jackson, MS: University Press of Mississippi.

Brown, J. A. (2015). *Beyond bombshells: The new action heroine in popular culture*. Jackson, MS: University Press of Mississippi.

Bruzzi, S. (2013). *Men's cinema: Masculinity and mise-en-scene in Hollywood*. Edinburgh: Edinburgh University Press.

Butler, J. (1990). *Gender trouble: Feminism and the subversion of identity*. London: Routledge.

Butter, M., Keller, P., & Wendt, S. (Eds.). (2001). *Arnold Schwarzenegger – Interdisciplinary perspectives on body and image*. Heidelberg: Universitätsverlag Winter.

Clover, C. J. (1992). *Men, women and chainsaws*. Princeton, NJ and Oxford: Princeton University Press.

Cohan, S., & Hark, I. R. (Eds.). (1993). *Screening the male: Exploring masculinities in Hollywood cinema*. London: Routledge.

Connell, R. W. (1995). *Masculinities*. Berkeley, CA: University of California Press.

Creed, B. (1993). *The Monstrous-Feminine: Film, feminism, psychoanalysis*. London and New York, NY: Routledge.

Dissanayake, W. (2003). *Wong Kar-wai's ashes of time*. Hong Kong: Hong Kong University Press.

Donnar, G. (2016). Narratives of cultural and professional redundancy : Ageing action stardom and the " geri – action " film. *Communication, Politics and Culture*, *49*(1), 1–18.

Selected References

Ewing, J., & Decker, K. (Eds.). (2017). *Alien and philosophy*. London: Wiley & Sons.

Fu, P., & Desser, D. (Eds.). (2000). *The cinema of Hong Kong: History, arts, identity*. Cambridge: Cambridge University Press.

Gallardo, C. X., & Smith, J. (2004). *Alien woman: The making of Lt. Ellen Ripley*. New York, NY, NY: Continuum.

Gerrard, S. (Ed.). (2020). *From Blofeld to Moneypenny: Gender in James Bond*. Bingley: Emerald Publishing Limited.

Grosz, E., & Probyn, E. (Eds.). (1995). *Sexy bodies: The strange carnalities of feminism* (1st ed.). London: Routledge.

Hooks, B. (2003). *We real cool: Black men and masculinity*. New York, NY: Taylor & Francis.

Hopkins, S. (2002). *Girl heroes: The new force in popular culture*. Sydney, NSW: Pluto Press.

Inness, S. A. (1999). *Tough girls: Women warriors and wonder women in popular culture*. Philadelphia, PA: University of Pennsylvania Press.

Inness, S. A. (Ed.). (2004). *Action chicks: New images of tough women in popular culture*. New York, NY: Palgrave Macmillan.

Jeffords, S. (1994). *Hard bodies: Hollywood masculinity in the Reagan era*. New Brunswick, NJ: Rutgers University Press.

Kendrick, J. (Ed.). (2019). *A companion to the action film*. London: Wiley – Blackwell.

King, N. (1999). *Heroes in hard times: Cop action movies in the U.S.* Philadelphia, PA: Temple University Press.

King, G. (2000). *Spectacular narratives: Hollywood in the age of the blockbuster*. London: I.B Tauris.

Lane, C. (2000). *Feminist Hollywood from born in flames to point break*. Detroit, MI: Wayne State University Press.

Lichtenfeld, E. (2007). *Action speaks louder: Violence, spectacle, and the American action movie* (Revised and Expanded ed.). Middletown, NY: Wesleyan University Press.

Lumby, C. (1997). *Bad girls: Media, sex and feminism in the 90s*. St. Leonards, NSW: Allen & Unwin.

McCaughey, M., & King, N. (2001). *Reel knockouts: Violent women in the movies*. Austin, TX: University of Texas Press.

Murphy, B. (2020). *Flame and crimson: A history of sword-and-sorcery*. Pismo Beach, CA: Pulp Hero Press.

Newton, J. (2021). *The Mad Max effect. Road warriors in international exploitation cinema*. London: Bloomsbury.

O'Brien, H. (2012). *Action movies: The cinema of striking back*. New York, NY: Columbia University Press.

Pang, L.-k., & Wong, D. (Eds.). (2005). *Masculinities and Hong Kong cinema*. Hong Kong: Hong Kong University Press.

Purse, L. (2011). *Contemporary action cinema*. Edinburgh: Edinburgh University Press.

Robinson, S. (2000). *Marked men: White masculinity in crisis*. New York, NY: Colombia University Press.

Schubart, R. (2007). *Super bitches and action babes: The female hero in popular cinema 1970–2006*. Jefferson, MO: McFarland.

Street, S. (2001). *Costume and cinema: Dress codes in popular film*. London: Wallflower.
Tasker, Y. (1993). *Spectacular bodies: Gender, genre and the action cinema*. London: Routledge.
Tasker, Y. (1998). *Working girls: Gender and sexuality in popular cinema*. London: Routledge.
Tasker, Y. (Ed.). (2004). *Action and adventure cinema*. London: Routledge.
Thorndyke, P. J. (2020). *Barbarians at the gates of hollywood: Sword and sorcery movies of the 1980s*. Wordpress.com/Amazon/Independent Publisher.
Yarrow, A. (2018). *90s bitch: Media, culture and the failed promise of gender equality*. New York, NY: Harper Perennial.

Selected Journals and Other Printed or Online Sources

Barbour, D. H. (1999). Heroism and redemption in the *Mad Max* trilogy. *Journal of Popular Film and Television, 27*(3), 28–34. doi:10.1080/01956059909602806
Bordun, T. M. (2021). 'We live in the past with Kari': Memory, fandom and online porn histories. *Celebrity Studies, 12*(1), 132–147.
Boyle, E., & Brayton, S. (2012). Ageing masculinities and 'muscle work' in Hollywood action film: An analysis of the expendables. *Men and Masculinities, 15*(5), 468–485.
Briggs, L., & Kelber-Kaye, J. I. (2000). There is no unauthorized breeding in Jurassic Park: Gender and the uses of genetics. *NWSA Journal, 12*(3), 92–113.
Brown, J. A. (1993). Gender and the action heroine: Hardbodies and the point of no return. *Cinema Journal, 35*(3), 52–72.
Caldwell, T. (2010). Aliens: Mothers, monsters and marines. *Screen Education, 59*, 125–130.
Connell, R. W., & Messerschmidt, J. (2005). Hegemonic masculinity: Rethinking the concept. *Gender & Society, 19*(6), 829–859.
Creed, B. (1987). From here to modernity feminism and postmodernism. *Screen, 28*(2), 47–68.
Dyer, R. (2015). Jurassic world and procreation anxiety. *Film Quarterly, 69*(2), 19–24.
Engelbrecht, J. (2020). Ellen Ripley, Sarah Connor, and Kathryn Janeway: The subversive politics of action heroines in 1980s and 1990s film and television. *Image & Text, 34*, 1–19. doi:10.17159/2617-3255/2020/n34a6
Faithful, G. (2016). Survivor, warrior, mother, saviour: The evolution of the female hero in apocalyptic science fiction film of the late Cold War. *Implicit Religion, 19*(3), 347–370.
Falicov, T. L. (2005). US-Argentine co-productions, 1982–1990: Roger Corman, Aries Productions, "Schlockbuster" movies, and the international market. *Film & History: An Interdisciplinary Journal of Film and Television Studies, 34*(1), 31–38. (2004). doi:10.1353/flm.2004.0015
Gates, P. (2004). Always a partner in crime: Black masculinity in the Hollywood detective film. *Journal of Popular Film and Television, 32*(1), 20–29.
Gill, R. (2003). From sexual objectification to sexual subjectification: The resexualisation of women's bodies in the media. *Feminist Media Studies, 3*(1), 100–106.
Guyot, N. (2017). Knowing the land: Women in James Cameron's science fiction movies. *British Fantasy Society (BFS) Journal, 17*, 99–107.

Hampshire, K. (2017). "Who killed the world?": Monstrous masculinity and Mad Max. *Digital Literature Review, 4*, 177–190. Retrieved from https://openjournals.bsu.edu/dlr/article/view/2715. Accessed on September 23, 2021.

Hills, E. (1999). From 'figurative males' to action heroines: Further thoughts on active women in the cinema. *Screen, 40*(1), 38–50.

Hopkins, S. (2017). Girl power-dressing: Fashion, feminism and neoliberalism with Beckham, Beyonce and Trump. *Celebrity Studies, 9*, 99–104. Retrieved from https://www.jstor.org/stable/10.1525/fq.2015.69.2.19

Johinke, R. (2001). Manifestations of masculinities: *Mad Max* and the lure of the forbidden zone. *Journal of Australian Studies, 67*, 118–125.

King, N. (2008). Generic womanhood: Gendered depictions in cop action cinema. *Gender & Society, 22*(2), 238–260.

Kirby, R. (2019). 'Toxic masculinity': The problem with men. *Trends in Urology & Men's Health, 10*(5), 4.

Lei, C.-P. (2021). 'Indecent' women and gendered memory: Reflective Nostalgia in Hong Kong cinema. *Asian Journal of Communication, 31*(3), 163–178.

Magoulick, M. (2006). Frustrating female heroism: Mixed messages in Xena, Nikita and Buffy. *Journal of Popular Culture, 35*(5), 729–755.

Mulvey, L. (1975). Visual pleasure and narrative cinema. *Screen, 16*(3), 16–18. Autumn 1975.

Nelson, T. (2004). Even an android can cry. *Journal of Gender Studies, 13*(3), 251–257.

Nulman, E. (2014). Representation of women in the age of globalized film. *Journal of Research in Gender Studies, 4*(2), 898–918.

Ortíz, C. M. (1991). Violencia política de los Ochenta: Elementos para una Reflexión Histórica. *Anuario Colombiano de Historia Social y de la Cultura, 18–19*, 245–280.

Payne, D. (2017). Shifting gears and paradigms at the movies: Masculinity, automobility, and the rhetorical dimensions of *Mad Max: Fury road*. *Studies in Popular Culture, 40*(1), 102–135.

Schuckmann, P. (1998). Masculinity, the male spectator and the homoerotic gaze. *Amerikastudien/American Studies, 43*(4). Engendering Manhood (1998). Universitätsverlag WINTER GmbH.

Sharrett, C. (1985). The hero as pastiche: Myth, male fantasy, and simulacra in Mad Max and the road warrior. *Journal of Popular Film and Television, 13*(2), 80–91.

Sutherland, J., & Feltey, K. M. (2016). "Here's looking at her:" An intersectional analysis of women, power and feminism in film. *Journal of Gender Studies, 26*(6), 618–631.

Temelli, Y. (2017). Vivir el Momento y Morir al Instante: el Sicario Como Figura Efímera en la Narrativa Colombiana. *Romance Notes, 57*, 245–254.

Wright, A. (2012, December). A sheep in wolf's clothing? The problematic representation of women and the female body in 1980s sword and sorcery cinema. *Journal of Gender Studies, 21*(4), 401–411.

Select Filmography

Æon Flux (Karyn Kusama, 2005).
Armed Response (John Stockwell, 2017).
Atomic Blonde (David Leitch, 2017).
Black Mama, White Mama (E. Romero, 1973).

Black Panther (Ryan Coogler, 2018).
Blade (Stephen Norrington, 1998).
Blade II (Guillermo Del Toro, 2002).
Boiling Point (James B. Harris, 1993).
Bombshell (Jay Roach, 2019)
Brooklyn's Finest (Antoine Fuqua, 2009).
Casino Royale (Martin Campbell, 2006).
Catwoman (Pitof, 2004).
Charlie's Angels: Full Throttle (Joseph McGinty Nicol, 2003).
China O'Brien (Robert Clouse, 1988).
Cleopatra Jones (J. Starrett, 1973).
Coffy (J Hill, 1973).
Coming 2 America (Craig Brewer, 2021).
Deadpool (Tim Miller, 2016).
Demolition Man (Marco Brambilla, 1993).
Die Another Day (Lee Tamahori, 2002).
Die Hard (John McTiernan, 1988).
Dolemite Is My Name (Craig Brewer, 2019).
Drop Zone (John Badham, 1994).
Drum (S. Carver, 1976).
Escape from L.A. (J. Carpenter, 1996).
Escape from New York (J. Carpenter, 1981).
Fort Apache, the Bronx (D. Petrie, 1981).
Foxy Brown (J. Hill, 1974).
Friday Foster (A. Marks, 1975).
Gallowwalkers (Andrew Goth, 2012).
Game of Death (Georgio Serafini, 2010).
Ghosts of Mars (J. Carpenter, 2001).
G.I. Jane (R. Scott, 1997).
Hancock (Peter Berg, 2008).
Haywire (Steven Soderbergh, 2011).
Jackie Brown (Q. Tarantino, 1997).
Jason Bourne (Paul Greengrass, 2016).
Jungle Fever (Spike Lee, 1991).
Kill Bill Volumes One and Two (Quentin Tarantino, 2003/2004).
Kings of New York (Abel Ferrara, 1990).
Lone Star (John Sayles, 1996).
Long Shot (Jonathan Levine, 2019).
Mad Max: Fury Road (George Miller, 2015).
Minority Report (Steven Spielberg, 2002).
Mo Better Blues (Spike Lee, 1990).
Money Train (Joseph Ruben, 1995).
Monster (Patty Jenkins, 2003).
Murder at 1600 (Dwight H. Little, 1997).
New Jack City (Mario Van Peebles, 1991).
On the Edge (R. Nilsson, 1985).
One Night Stand (Mike Figgis, 1997).
Passenger 57 (Kevin Hooks, 1992).

Quantum of Solace (Marc Foster, 2008).
Rising Sun (Philip Kaufman, 1993).
Shaft (Gordon Parks, 1971).
Sheba, Baby (W. Girdler, 1975).
Skyfall (Sam Mendes, 2012).
Something Wicked This Way Comes (J. Clayton, 1983).
Spectre (Sam Mendes, 2015).
Stand Alone (A. Beattie, 1985)
Star Trek: First Contact (Jonathan Frakes, 1996).
Super Fly (G. Parks Jr., 1972).
Sweet Sweetback's Baadasssss Song (M. Van Peebles, 1971).
Terminator 2: Judgment Day (James Cameron, 1992).
The Big Bird Cage (J. Hill, 1972).
The Big Doll House (J. Hill, 1971).
The Bourne Identity (Doug Liman, 2002).
The Bourne Legacy (Tony Gilroy, 2012).
The Bourne Supremacy (Paul Greengrass, 2004).
The Bourne Ultimatum (Paul Greengrass, 2007).
The Expendables 3 (Patrick Hughes, 2014).
The Fast and the Furious 6 (Justin Lin, 2013).
The Matrix (Lana and Lilly Wachowski, 1999).
The Old Guard (Gina Prince-Bythewood, 2020).
The Recall (Mauro Borrelli, 2017).
The Terminator (J. Cameron, 1984).
The Waterdance (Neil Jimenez and Michael Sternberg, 1992).
To Wong Foo, Thanks for Everything! Julie Newmar (Beeban Kidron, 1995).
Tully (Jason Reitman, 2018).
The Fast and the Furious 7 (James Wan, 2015).
U.S. Marshalls (Stuart Baird, 1998).
White Men Can't Jump (Ron Shelton, 1992).
Wildcats (Michael Richie, 1986).
Women in Cages (G. De Leon, 1971).

Index

Acceptable femininity, 35–36
Acting, 8
Action, 22, 92, 133–134
   cinema, 1–2, 22, 159
   films, 1, 8, 34–35, 119–120, 159
   genre, 1, 23, 159
   heroines, 15–16
   stars, 1–2, 9
'Action babe' cinema, 37–38, 40
Action heroes, 61–62
   all access action, 70–71
   cyberpathy in action, 62–66
   new media, 70
   wireless action, 66–69
Actor, 120–121
Actresses, 22–23
Advertising, 35–36
Æon Flux (2005), 9–11
Aesthetics, 60
Agency, 49–50
Aggression, 8, 37
Alias, Nikita (2010–2013), 48–49
Alien (1986), 23–24, 49
'All access action heroes', 62, 70–71
Alphas and *Heroes*, 1–2, 60–62
American International Pictures (AIP), 136
Anaconda (1997), 22
Angel (1999–2004), 47–48
Armed Response (2017), 130–131
Athletic female body, 35–36
Atomic Blonde (2017), 1, 8, 13, 16
   image, persona and embodiment, 8–9
Audiences, 159
Authenticity, 1–2, 8
Avatar (2009), 26

Baad Bitches' and Sassy Supermamas: Black Power Action Films, 134–135
Baguazhang, 104, 108, 111
Ballers (2015–2019), 144
Battle Los Angeles (2011), 26, 30
Betrayal, 90
Big Bang Theory, The, 65
Big Bird Cage, The, 136
Big Doll House, The (1971), 136
Black, 133–134
   actresses, 135
   star, 119–120
Black Panther (2018), 126
Black Panther: Wakanda Forever, 1
Blade, 126–129
Blade II (2002), 129
Blaxploitation, 134–135
Bloodrayne (2004), 26
Blue Crush (2002), 26
Boiling Point (1993), 126
Bombshell (2019), 8
Bourne Identity, The (2002), 92–93, 95
Bourne Supremacy, The (2004), 95–97
Bourne Ultimatum, The (2007), 97–98
Brooklyn's Finest (2009), 130–131
Buck Rogers in the 25th Century (1979), 30
Buffy and *Alias* (2001–2006), 48–49
Buffy the Vampire Slayer (1997–2003), 47–48

Carano, Gina, 35
   complicating, 41
Casual revolution, 79–80
Characterisation of Gong Ruomei, 107, 110, 112
Charlie's Angels (1976–1981), 50–51
Charlie's Angels (2000, 2003), 1

Charlie's Angels: Full Throttle (2003), 39
Chicago Tribune, 134
China O'Brien (1988), 39
Chinese action films, gender subjectivity and women in, 106–107
Cleopatra Jones, 136
Coffy, 136, 140–141
Coldest City, The, 13
Coming 2 America (2021), 120
Con Air (1997), 23
Confucianism, 106
Contemporary Superhero, The, 63
Corman, Roger, 136
Crisis (2021), 26
Crouching Tiger, Hidden Dragon, 108–110, 112–113
Culture wars, 79–80
Cyberpathy, 60–61
  in action, 62–66
Cyborg heroes, heroines and villains, 62–63

Demolition Man, 123, 125–126
Die Another Day (2002), 39, 92–93
Die Hard series (1988–2013), 92–93
Digital Natives, 63–65
Doctor Who (BBC, 1963), 62–63
Dolemite Is My Name (2019), 120
Dollhouse (television series), 1–2, 47–48, 51, 55
  final girls, warrior women and avenging angels, 49–51
Driving under the influence (DUI), 25
Drop Zone (1994), 126
Dwayne 'The Rock' Johnson, 144, 146, 153, 155

Ebony, 134
Echo, 52, 54
Embodiment, 1–2
Empowerment, 49
Enlightenment, 106
Escape from L. A. (1996), 139–140
Escape from New York (1981), 139–140

Eureka (2006–2012), 60–61
Expendables 3, The (2014), 120, 130

Falling Down (1990), 23
Fast and Furious 6 (2013) and 7 (2015), 39
Fast and Furious 9, 152
Fast and the Furious, The (2001–2023), 28–29, 146, 151–152
Fast Five (2011), 144–145
Faster Pussycat, Kill! Kill (1966), 23
Father hunger, 90–92
Fathers, 90–93
Female action hero, 51
Female action stars, 1–2, 23
Female muscularity, 36
Female subjectivity, 110–112
Female violence, 8
Femininity, 28
Feuds, 151–153
Fifth Element, The (1997), 49, 52
Fighting With My Family (2019), 144
Film stars, 24
Films, 35–36, 120
Firefly (2002–2003), 47–48
Foxy Brown, 136–139
Framing Blackness, 134
Franchises, 90
Friday Foster, 137, 139
Furious 7 (2015), 146

G. I. Jane, 133–134
Gallowwalkers (2012), 130–131
Game of Death (2010), 130–131
GamerGate, 79–80
Games, 74
Gaze, 9
Gender, 1, 22, 90, 129
  dynamics, 39–40
  subjectivity and women in Chinese action films, 106–107
Genre, 47–48
Geri-action stars, 159
Ghosts of Mars, 140
Girlfight (2000), 26, 30
Good Joe, The, 24

Grandmaster, The (2013), 104–105
   characterisation of Gong Ruomei, 107–110
   daughterhood with female subjectivity, 110–112
   gender subjectivity and women in Chinese action films, 106–107
   woman's romance in, 112–114
Grier, Pam, 134
   blaxploitation, 134–135
   career, 136
   Foxy Brown, 136–139
   sexist trap, 140–141
   Sheba, Baby, 136–139
   supporting roles and *Jackie Brown*, 139–140

Hancock (2008), 11–12, 16–17
Hardbody, 78, 122
Hardcore gamers, 83
Haywire (2011), 35
   'Action Babe' Trope, 38–40
   hotel fight scene, 40–41
   musculinity, 37–38
   women and sport, 35–36
Hegemony of play, 80
Heroes, 60–61
Heroes, Villains and Fools, 24
Heroes 360 Experience, 63–65
Heroes Reborn, 70
Heroine, 59
Heroine-hood, 105
High Noon (Ramirez), 22–23
Hill, Jack, 136
Hobbs and Shaw (2019), 2, 144, 146, 151, 153, 155
Hollywood, 134
   action film, 22
Homicide: Life on the Street, 93
House of Flying Daggers, 109–110

iBoy (2017), 60, 69
Ideation, 104
iNAPPROPRIATE COMEDY (2013), 26

Independent Woman, 24
Internet of things, 70
Internet/wireless, 66–67
Iron Man (2008), 1, 62–63
Italian Job, The (2003), 9

Jackie Brown (1997), 2, 139–140
Jason Bourne film, 90, 98, 101
   Bourne Identity, The (2002), 93–95
   Bourne Supremacy, The (2004), 95–97
   Bourne Ultimatum, The (2007), 97–98
   father and son in cinema, 90–93
John Wick: Chapter 2 (2017), 16
Jungle Fever (1991), 120–121

Kill Bill: Volume One and *Two* (2003/2004), 34
Kings of New York (1990), 120–121
Kung fu, 107–108

Lara Croft, 78–79
Last Airbender: The Legend of Korra, The (2005–2008), 34
Last of Us Part II, The, 74–75
   authenticating hard virtual body through motion capture, 81–84
   female hard and soft (ware) bodies in action games, 78–81
   murder of Joel Miller and symbolic death of male gamer, 75–77
Latin American actresses, 22–23
Latina performers/performances, 22–23
Latinas, 22
Long Kiss Goodnight (1996), 48–51
Long Shot (2019), 16–17
Lost (2005), 26–27

Machete Kills Again (2010 and 2014), 30
Machete Kills Again–In Space, 30
Mad Max: Beyond Thunderdome (1985), 12–13

Mad Max: Fury Road (2015), 8, 34, 133–134
  dramatic roles, 11–16
  image, persona and embodiment, 8–9
Magazines, 35–36
Male gaze, 1–2, 9
Marvel Cinematic Universe (MCU), 1
Masculinity, 92, 150–151
Mass media, 35–36
Matrix, The (1999), 1, 10, 126
Media studies, 60
Media technologies, 1–2
Men's Health, 153
#MeToo, 1
Miami Vice (2006), 1, 120–121
'Mind wiping' technology, 48
Mo Better Blues (1990), 120–121
Moana (2016), 153–154
Money Train (1995), 126
Monster (2003), 9
Motion capture, 81–84
Mummy Returns, The (2001), 144–145
Murder at 1600 (1997), 126
Muscularity, 36
Musculinity, 34, 37–38
Music videos, 35–36
My Darling Clementine (1946), 22–23

National Black Feminist Organisation, 135
New Jack City (1991), 120–121
'New media superheroes', 62, 70
Non-actional ideation, 104

Old Guard, The (2020), 17–18
On the Edge (Rob Nilsson, 1985), 140
One Night Stand (1997), 126
#Oscarssowhite, 1
Out of Sight (1998), 22

Passenger 57 (1992), 121
Personal Digital Assistant (PDA), 70
Phoenix, 123–125
Physicality of Theron, 16–18
Pin Up, The, 24

Point-Of-View effect (POV effect), 60
Predator (1986), 22
Predator 2 (1990), 22
Predator films, 23
Psychology, 60

Race, 1
Ready Player Two, 79–80
Rebel, 24
Recall, The, 130–131
Red Sonja (1985), 39
Reindeer Games (2000), 9
Resident Evil (2002–2016), 27–28
Resident Evil: Retribution (2012), 27
Rising Sun (1993), 121–122, 126
Rivalries, 151
Rodriguez, Michelle, 22
  acting career, 25–27
  body of work, 22–23
  Fast and the Furious, The (2001–2023), 28–29
  prison, 25
  recognising, 29–31
  Resident Evil (2002–2016), 27–28
  types and, 24–29
Rundown, The (2003), 144–145

S. W. A. T (2003), 26
Scorpion, 63–65
Second Sex, The, 106
Sexism, 137–139
Sexuality, 1
Shaft, 134–135
She Dies Tomorrow (2020), 26
Sheba, Baby, 136–139
Sky High, 61
Smurfs: The Lost Village, 26
Something Wicked This Way Comes (Jack Clayton, 1983), 140
Spectacular Bodies, 74
Sports, 34
Spy Kids films, 22
Spyglass, 15–16
Stand Alone (Alan Beattie, 1985), 140
Star Bodies, 1–2
Star image, 8, 144, 146

Star personas, 8
Star Trek: First Contact (1996), 62–63
Star Trek: The Next Generation, 62–63
Star Trek: Voyager, 144–145
Star Wars (1977), 30
Star-reception, 25
Stars (2002), 24
Stars, 25
'Streaming superheroes', 62
Subjectivity, 106
Super Fly, 134–135
Sweet Sweetback's Baadasssss Song, 134–135

Tarantino, Quentin, 139
Technokinesis, 60
Technokinetics, 62–63
Technology, 60
Television, 35–36
Terminator, The, 133–134
Terminator 2: Judgement Day (1991), 34, 48–51
Terminator: The Sarah Conner Chronicles (2008–2009), 48–49
That 70s Show, 144–145
The Sarah Conner Chronicles (*TSCC*), 49
Theron, Charlize, 8–9
    physicality of, 16–18
Thor: Love and Thunder, 1
3AM (2001), 26
TLOU2, 74–77, 82
To Wong Foo, Thanks for Everything! Julie Newmar (1995), 126
Tomb Raider, 80
Tomboy, 30

Total Film magazine, 120
Total Recall (1990), 23
Tough Guy, The, 24
Trauma, 49–50
'Treadstone' assassination programme, 93
Trópico de Sangre (2010), 30
Tully (2018), 16–18
2001: A Space Odyssey, 124–125

US Marshalls (1998), 126

Violence, 49–50, 137, 139
Violent female action character, 18

Walking Tall (2004), 144–145
Warehouse 13 (2009–2014), 60–61
Waterdance, The, 121
Wesley Snipes, 119–120
West Side Story (1961), 23
White Men Can't Jump, 121
Widows (2018), 26
Wildcats (1986), 120–121
Woman (1975–1979), 50–51
Women, 49–50
Women in Cages, 136
Wuxia, 107–108

X-Men Origins: Wolverine, 62–63
Xena: Warrior Princess (1995–2001), 48–49

Yards, The (2000), 9
Young Rock (2021), 144

Zhang Ziyi, 104–107

Printed in the United States
by Baker & Taylor Publisher Services

WHAT THE RABBIS KNOW

THAT I NEVER LEARNED IN CHURCH